C000265345

ZULMA REYO

UPDATED AND REVISED EDITION

INNER ALCHEMY

THE PATH OF MASTERY

For Chris, and the Spirit he embodies

*To one degree or another, negatively charged personality traits are the
burden we each carry as members of humanity. These commonplace and
often fleeting thoughts and feelings lower our vibrational frequency
and bring out the villain in spite of good intentions, while polluting
our atmosphere.*

*Having understood that our ecological programme begins with ourselves, a
human being who has been touched by the grace of Light decides to embrace
all of life in order to grow and bloom into a fully-fledged soul-connected
individual who can change this world simply by his or her presence.*

– Zulma Reyo, Part Four, page 179

First published in 2021 by Zulma Reyo
in partnership with LightEn Publishing
https://light-en.org/
Copyright © Zulma Reyo, 2021

The author asserts her moral right to be identified as the author of this work. All rights reserved. No part of this publication may be reproduced, stored in a retrieval system or transmitted in any form or by any means, electronic, mechanical, photocopying, recording or otherwise, without prior written permission of the authors. While every effort has been made to trace the owners of copyright material reproduced herein, the author and publisher would like to apologise for any omissions and will be pleased to incorporate missing acknowledgements in any future editions.

ISBN 978-1-83846-960-3
eBook ISBN 978-1-83846-961-0
Audio ISBN 978-1-83846-962-7

Cover design by Dominic Forbes
Interior page design and layout by Karen Lilje, Hybrid Creative
Project editor: Lisa Dyer
All illustrations by Cameron Gray, except the following:
Courtesy © Rainer Galea: page 107; Glen Wilkins: pages 82, 85, 87, 91, 93;
Patricia Bedin: pages 49, 50, 51, 52, 53, 54, 55, 84, 233, 275.

Printed and bound in Great Britain by Bell and Bain Ltd, Glasgow

CONTENTS

LIST OF MEDITATIONS, VISUALISATIONS AND EXERCISES

For animated and recorded meditations please visit:

www.zulmareyoschoolofconsciousness.com

LIST OF ILLUSTRATIONS AND TABLES

PREFACE TO REVISED EDITION

When the first edition of this book, *Mastery: The Path of Inner Alchemy,* came out in 1989, it was a mere curiosity. In 2021, amid a global pandemic, economic instability and worldwide anti-racism demonstrations, among other things, it has become necessary for survival. Understanding ourselves, one another, and what is happening in the world is difficult, as too many elements influence and greatly distort our perception. The mixture of personal, physical and spiritual priorities adds to the general confusion. Updating the book has become a matter of urgency. With this edition, now renamed *Inner Alchemy: The Path of Mastery*, I seek to provide something that is lacking in the world today: an inner anchor enabling conscious management of the self and understanding of what you are, what your role is and what the world is actually made of.

Inner Alchemy offers much more than personal training; it lays bare the dynamics involved in the management of self and world, opening the door to an 'alchemical' and global transformation of and through the individual.

The terms 'to think out of the box' and 'think tank' have become very popular. The Inner Alchemy system does not teach you to think 'out of the box' because it recognises that *there is no box*. This illusory box is a construction that has lasted as long as human interest remains at the personal level. It is dissolvable, and when this happens, perception expands to gigantic proportions.

Higher laws that have been encrypted in complex and ancient treaties are for the first time explained and applied concretely. The focus of perception developed alters the entire body-mind network. Based in ancient practices of energy management, this system increases the proportion of Light-consciousness in a human being, opening transcendental awareness in ways that are useful. The ensuing shift restructures old patterns and beliefs to reveal new tangible possibilities. To view the world differently implies finding solutions that escape the ordinary mindset. Here you learn to see the world differently, not just

—

Inner Alchemy offers much more than personal training; it lays bare the dynamics involved in the management of self and world, opening the door to an 'alchemical' and global transformation of and through the individual.

—

from another angle or because it is suggested, but because inner reality demands it.

Inner Alchemy is first and foremost training in the correct and immediate use of the higher, non-linear Mind. Combined with dynamic energy-altering practices involving body circuitry and circulation, and the development of special sensibilities, it produces a flexibility that allows you to tap unlimitedly into universal Mind and substance.

Inner Alchemy addresses those who want to see change happen and know that this begins with themselves. It appeals to those eager for total transformation without violence or imposition – emerging from within – leading to the rebuilding of a more humane society.

The first and most obvious application is to human *health*, both physical and mental, restructuring relationships of all sorts, and contributing significantly to the gradual effacing of self-importance and world illusion. Inner Alchemy is a path to inner peace, meaning, purpose, joy and wisdom.

A wholly new way of 'seeing' shifts attention from quantity to quality, from the particular to the global, without losing perspective of particular needs and dynamics. The implications of this system in *business and commerce* open options capable of benefitting everyone in the present and in the future by revealing real priorities. It calls for a re-evaluation of elements that separate rather than unite, bringing a tangible sense of justice to the foreground.

The application of this system to *economy* calls for a revision of values, privilege, leadership and control, issues that are no longer appropriate. It does this through understanding and the application of higher intelligence and sensibility. In this light, money stands revealed for what it is: energy employed as power. Those who manage money may do so knowing the correct use of both personal and global energy, which implies tremendous awareness and responsibilities rather than superiority and privilege.

Perhaps the most important and most difficult application of the Inner Alchemy system is in *government*, calling forth a redefinition of humanistic priorities that are always based on personal example by world leaders. Under this category are included concerns that affect the entire planet, such as *ecology* and *human resources*, *education* and all forms of *creative expression*, namely art and music.

A wholly new way of
'seeing' shifts attention
from quantity to quality,
from the particular to the
global, without losing
perspective of particular
needs and dynamics.

How much better the world would be if leaders could understand and apply the dynamics behind appearances that move and shape our world!

The reader should bear in mind that the sequential presentation of this book is different to the practice we follow in our School of Consciousness. In our School, energy dynamics and theory are taught through multifaceted, multi-levelled experiences that gradually grow in complexity, making the material practical and personal. It is hoped you will be able to digest this text with innermost intimacy, making it as personal as it needs to be, and to find your own way of understanding and implementing its content.

This edition contains issues, concepts and definitions that did not seem to me to be relevant in the past. The careful revision of the text and the addition of new chapters provide more clarity concerning our innermost needs and queries.

Furthermore, to reflect how both the school of Inner Alchemy and the book, *Inner Alchemy*, have blossomed out of what was once my own, personal labour of love into truly collective endeavours, I often refer to the group of teachings as 'our' School. For the same reason, you, the reader, may see the voice of this edition alternate between the first person singular 'I' and the plural (collective) 'we'.

A suggestion on the manner of reading this book: mostly, its concepts deal with mystery and revelation, rather than dwelling on literal comprehension. Read without worrying too much about the exact sense of the words; allow yourself to sink into the text and be taken over. Once you have read the book in this way, set it aside. When you feel ready, go back to it again and you will find that it makes sense in a wholly different way. Over time, phrases might re-surface in your consciousness with a clarity that is in coherence with your own inner voice.

—

How much better
the world would
be if leaders could
understand and apply
the dynamics behind
appearances that move
and shape our world!

—

ACKNOWLEDGEMENTS

The purity of heart and hunger for authentic spiritual knowledge shown by Chris Hohn and Kylie Richardson, combined with the fervent desire to bring coherent practicality into spirituality, led me to reformulate the teaching of Inner Alchemy into this new revised edition. The humanitarian purpose behind the initiative is to make this book freely available, reaching people in every walk of life capable of truly changing this world. The subjacent recognition is that it is time for Inner Alchemy, time to enable a radical change from the density of lead into the brilliance of gold.

Kylie's painstaking effort, coupled with love throughout the countless months of revisions, was the patient, steady presence that held us all in the spirit of peace, possibility and practicality. Her research assistant, Daisy Gibbons, cannot go unmentioned. Without these two formidable ladies, I could not have handled the rewriting, additions and revisions that a text of this magnitude and purpose requires.

An unequalled spirit of genuine service, loyal companionship and multifaceted engineering describe the participation of Dolores Mihanovich through the innumerable scribbles that speckled every edit. After thirty years of caretaking, she is, truly, the direct heir to the legacy that has been years in the making.

Special thanks to the 'team': Kristine Rumjanceva, Alianna Morris, Vanessa Jeffery, Claire Smith and Fraser Wilkinson. I am also so grateful to Elizabeth Sheinkman and Mark Gober for feedback, and the illustrator team: Cameron Gray, Patricia Bedin, Glen Wilkins and Lilia Rodrigues. I especially thank Lilia for her careful, loving and professional supervision on some of the illustrations in this book. A final thanks also to the team at whitefox.

Behind all this work and for the last three decades stand my faithful students, the children of my heart, spread throughout South America and Europe, whose experience and application of the teaching prove that living the Light in the world and inducing change through adherence to the Law of the One can and does bring miracles.

The good news is that, with this book, a plan was formulated to create the physical space for the teaching. This culminated in a not-for-profit School of Consciousness in Mallorca; a training retreat centre that welcomes all whose desire, like ours, is to teach and spread truth in all its forms, preparing leaders that they may bring Light into all corners, aspects and functions of this world.

Finally, I am forever thankful for the forces of Light that lead the way and are always with me. It is a privilege to be inspired, led and cared for by the Love that today brings kindred souls together for the construction of a better world.

GLOSSARY OF KEY TERMS

Akashic Records

The Akashic records are the repository of all memory (past, present and possible future) in the Universe. They are located as impressions in a dimensional space outside our third-dimensional perception.

Alchemical Alignment

An energy circuit formed by linking the Earth and the heavens, shifting perception from ordinary, denser awareness (of lower physical, emotional and mental energies) to the elevated perspective of the Spirit-self (see 'Spirit' below). Its practice affects the body's physical cellular structure by recalibrating it in patterns of Light-substance. It is also known as the Alchemical Circuit and the Master Practice.

Alchemical Circuit

The terms 'Alchemical Alignment' and 'Alchemical Circuit' point to the same practice, although the use of 'Circuit' is more often used to denote visual imagery that the practitioner invokes when performing the Master Practice.

Alchemy

The science of the transmutation of matter in all its forms, elevating it into a higher frequency or state.

Ascended Masters

These are teacher-guides who have completed the incarnational cycle of human experience. They have attained full mastery over the human energetic anatomy and use of human powers and faculties. This grants them access to a higher evolutionary cycle in the planetary scheme of service to humanity, and they may choose to act as assistants and servers to humanity.

Astral

The term 'astral', meaning 'star-like', refers to the illusory quality of human thoughts and desires formed in third-dimensional reality.

Astral Realm

The astral realm is a multifaceted phenomenon. The lower astral dimension mirrors the third dimension, and is an energy field of vibrationally-lower thoughtforms that magnify self-centred, unconscious behaviour. The upper astral realm reflects benign, higher-frequency thoughtforms. The astral realm includes astral entities, 'shells' of human beings bound to physical existence.

Aura

The energy field surrounding a human body that reflects the nature and quality of the energy fields or bodies (see 'Body' below) generating it.

Being

'Being' or 'Being state' refers to the primary, formless experience of Spirit as manifest Consciousness. This is one step down vibrationally from unmanifest Spirit. Being is very close to soul. It is a generic name for individualised Spirit. Being expresses itself dimensionally as various 'states' of Being. The 'Human Model' or 'Human Being' is one sort of Being, ours, the only one with individualised Self-consciousness. This evolutionary strain can be understood through the multidimensional chart in Part Five (see pages 200–1). Here you see how the human body and personality is a final creation, a thoughtform serving Consciousness and constructed out of planetary matter.

Body

The human body is a dynamic composite of seven energy fields, also referred to as 'bodies'. The original spark of Spirit becomes coated in each of these energy fields in its descent into embodiment. Each body is a step-down transformer of the Spirit-self, a further condensation of its Light. After various stages of lowering its frequency, the inherent spark merges with the field of the Earth and acquires a physical form.

Consciousness

The first and primary expression of Spirit or Source.

consciousness

When written in lower case, 'consciousness' denotes the activity of awareness in an embodied human being.

Dimensions

The dimensions are stages of adaptation of the Spirit-self that become progressively denser as it journeys into physical embodiment. Each stage defines a capacity of Intelligence to handle elements that range from vast cosmic consciousness to the minutest detail in matter.

Ego

Not to be confused with 'egoism', which is the self-centred personality, the ego is the Self's necessary and unique personal perspective in incarnation. The personality is built around its ego structure.

Feeling vs emotion

Pure Feeling is Love, the cohesive force of the Universe. 'Feeling' is a capacity, the energy of love, which may be qualified as higher or lower. Denser forms of love manifest as human emotion. When related to the belief in separation and linked to matter, love produces emotions such as fear (which is the absence of Love). 'Feeling' is a capacity, whereas 'feelings' are emotions.

Higher Self

The Higher Self, as distinguished from the lower self, is elevated human awareness in a higher frequency 'body'. When the personality (see 'personality' overleaf) has integrated its lower bodies of experience in matter, it aligns with its state of Being as soul, becoming a fully conscious personality. The Higher Self is a frequency of holistic intelligence, which then allows the personality to function interdimensionally. The human evolutionary purpose is to reach and sustain this vibrationally higher form of self and become soul-infused.

Incarnational Cycle

The completion of the life cycles, the purpose of which is the full integration of body-mind with soul, perfecting human powers and faculties in mastery. The final purpose is the construction of an 'immortal' body of Light.

Inner Alchemy

Inner Alchemy is both structural and qualitative. It defines the process of transmuting the lower self's personality through the inherent power of Spirit to become soul-infused. In this process, surrounding reality is refined, including the body and its faculties. The addition of 'Inner' to 'Alchemy' refers to the subtle, innermost reality that comes alive with the transmutation (transformation) of the personality.

Intelligence

The cognitive aspect emitted by Spirit-consciousness.

intelligence

When written in lower case, 'intelligence' denotes the usual definition as the capacity for reason, learning, knowing and understanding.

Karma

The Sanskrit term for the feedback circle of energy created by an individual through their interaction with others and with life. It is commonly referred to as the 'law of cause and effect'. There is 'positive' and also 'negative' karma.

Law of Matter

The Law of Matter or the Natural Law, involves nature, physical instincts and the body. This law relates to the constitution of the material world and determines the basis of perception and management in the third-dimensional world. This is the perspective of separate distinctions and measurement, i.e. duality or polarity.

Law of the One

The Law of the One refers to the non-existence of separation or duality. When the mind takes on the all-embracing qualities of Light, and thinking is raised beyond the polar perspective of matter, thinking is raised to the level of Higher Mind, which operates in accordance with the Law of the One. The individual then perceives the world differently: they begin to understand the workings of the whole and their responsibility within the whole. Mind and emotions take on a new expression, becoming more refined and compassionate. Also known as the Law of Light or the Law of Love.

Light

The emission of Spirit or Source; the core of matter and also its transmuting agent.

light

When written in lower case, 'light' denotes the usual definition of it as electromagnetic radiation, rather than spiritual 'Light'. Light and light function similarly to reveal the essence of reality.

Master Practice

The procedure performed to invoke the Alchemical Alignment.

Mind

The faculty of Intelligence in the worlds of manifestation. The power that invokes and precipitates energy into form through thought. There are two levels to Mind: lower mind (linear thought), applied to personal need; and Higher Mind (holistic comprehension), employed in the understanding and application of soul-level frequencies.

Multidimensionality/Interdimensionality

The concept of multidimensionality recognises the simultaneous existence and interrelationship of what are defined here as twelve dimensions or levels of Consciousness. The experience of interdimensionality is an inner phenomenon: it is access to the human being's complete array of dimensional faculties, while also performing in third-dimensional time and space. Through interdimensionality we draw valuable information and refined faculties required to administer life, thus enhancing perception.

Personality

Personality is a constructed, temporary identity, which acts as an instrument for the soul to relate directly to third-dimensional experience in matter. It is made up of a conglomeration of thoughtforms, acquired through environmental conditioning, alongside individual preferences carried through from previous incarnations.

Ray

The seven basic emanations (variations of energy) of Source responsible for the existence of all life on the planet. The building blocks of the Universe.

Sensibility

Human perceptive capacity through the senses, both in their ordinary as well as subtle faculties. In Light-work, sensibility denotes a holistic and flexible perception that transcends sensory perception.

Soul

A state of Being vibrationally midway between Spirit and body, soul is a vehicle for Spirit, and harbours the stock of experiences and integrated lessons achieved through many incarnational cycles. Both container and content, the soul is the intermediary between the lower self (manifested human being) and Spirit. Soul exists throughout all dimensions and is an energy field (although not a 'body' in the seven-body system presented in this book).

Spirit or Source

The unmanifest principle of Oneness behind all Creation.

Sublimation

The alchemical practice that ennobles a form by raising its frequency into a higher state.

Thoughtform

Formed when an image (a thought), constructed by human beings, is imbued with human vitality (emotion). This gives it personal meaning and form.

Transmutation

All healing and recalibration that involves an energy leap from lower into higher expression corresponding to the increase of light content at the core of matter, often involving molecular shifts.

Vibrations

That which vibrates in 'things' is Consciousness itself, i.e. Consciousness is the essence of the elements it creates. Consciousness can be perceived through attuning to the core of creations and their energy fields. Crucially, Consciousness is what generates forms to begin with (and is not a 'field of energy' generated by the forms themselves).

AUTHOR'S PREFACE

It often seems to me as if I am constantly dying and being reborn. Sometimes I cannot relate to the person I was last year, or even last month – and yet something of whom I was then, as if it were fifty years ago, filters through and connects all the people I have been. Each one brings an experience, a depth, an energy. I have learned to grow with and use these lessons to my advantage, even in the most trying situations, to this day.

I have lived life on the fringe; it seemed to me that was where life was. I grew up in the Sixties, a time of alternative lifestyles. As a child I travelled with my parents from country to country without time to establish any roots or continuity. I was fully bilingual and multinational at a very early age.

After completing my university degrees, I dabbled here and there teaching, exploring new horizons, marrying and having a child before I became a psychotherapist. After a few years of my own practice and undergoing some training in alternative therapies, I felt a call to go to India. This was a major turning point in my life. I left everything behind. There I remained for twelve years, imbibing the spirit of the spiritual path, studying ancient traditions and partaking of the mystery of my Self.

Without knowing it yet, I was training in the management and control of the different expressions of the psyche, as I delved into discovering the inner dynamics of being human. Surprisingly, I found these resembled how Creation works as a whole: the human being is merely a microcosm of the macrocosm. My experiences led me still further into deeper studies of the Self.

I cannot answer the question of who or what I am in conventional terms. I know I have a state of knowing that has spanned my entire lifetime. My aim has been to make some sense out of my life, the energies and elements within it and its moods, which extend way beyond the reaches of psychology. I sought to bridge inner and outer reality, the rational and nonrational, mind and no-mind, form and formlessness, to reach the state of Being behind all form and culture.

—

It often seems to me as if I am constantly dying and being reborn.

—

—

Without knowing it yet, I was training in the management and control of the different expressions of the psyche, as I delved into discovering the inner dynamics of being human.

—

Nobody taught me the kind of devotion I have for divine Light: this sense of religiousness was always private, personal, even irreverent. I loved and wanted to be Jewish. I loved and wanted to be a Muslim. I never considered, however, that I could be an atheist. My inner drive to know God led me to travel to different countries, to meet different teachers and to learn from many traditions. In my journey, insight followed insight; occasionally, I remembered other lives, other times. I connected directly with a source that gave access to information that blew my mind. Alchemy was not only a method; it was a perspective opening dimensional doorways through time and space within me. I realised that this was what I have come to share. I had so embodied the process that I could not see it at first. The key to this alchemy and its method was within me, in the awareness of my state of Being. Alchemy was that state of Being. I teach what I have lived, not what I have learned intellectually.

I have now spent four decades of my life dedicated to teaching, writing, trainings, workshops and conferences. Thanks to so many students, I have learned about myself and the magic of becoming. My life, and whatever I can offer you, is a tribute to all those whose love and trust constantly remind me what a privilege it is to teach and learn. The purpose of all of this has always been to advocate for personal transformation as a way of securing social and world change, while training others in Inner Alchemy, the path of mastery.

Zulma Reyo
London 2021

In my journey, insight followed insight; occasionally, I remembered other lives, other times. I connected directly with a source that gave access to information that blew my mind.

A DIFFERENT KIND OF BIBLIOGRAPHY

Although bibliographies traditionally go at the back of a book, this is not a traditional sort of book. Neither is this a traditional bibliography. People ask me where I get my information. Explaining how I came to know what I teach is a lot more complicated than reeling off a list of books. The sources that have gone into producing *Inner Alchemy* are too numerous and subtle to be listed, and they arise not so much from books as from my own direct experience.

I am naturally mediumistic, with access to information at levels beyond the physical or astral realms. I 'see' beyond ordinary, third-dimensional perception into the structure of things – and people – as well as the Universe. This is something I invoke at will. It may be best described as the effect of sustaining the Alchemical Alignment and accessing the dimensional stages I present here in this book. I find that the system I use is best suited to our contemporary, more mental turn of mind, which also harbours an innermost hunger for humane sensitivity. That is why I teach this system here as the means of accessing perception and knowing.

This is how it works for me: once I ask a question or evoke a condition, the whole picture comes together through a telepathic affinity with my own Spirit-self that reveals dynamics, purpose, causes and implications through my own train of thoughts and, often, images. I piece everything together at the integration stations (as you will read in the chapter on the dimensions). Through the years I have learned to distinguish which are my own thoughts from those of my Spirit-self in a sort of 'conversation' or intimate dialogue with my Self. This, too, is how I 'know' and how many things are revealed through me, while I maintain the linear alignment (the Alchemical Alignment) with my own Self positioned in various dimensions simultaneously.

Rather than seeking sources of information, direct observation is backed by information gathered from many texts and from people who taught me, largely through non-verbal transmission. The main people who have influenced my life's journey and work, beside my equally

> —
> I am naturally mediumistic, with access to information at levels beyond the physical or astral realms. I 'see' beyond ordinary, third-dimensional perception into the structure of things – and people – as well as the Universe.
> —

mediumistic family and friends, include Arthur Janov, the originator of Primal Therapy, author of *The Primal Scream*. He trained me carefully and closely in deep psychological perception.

Next is Bhagwan Shri Rajneesh (who later became Osho), an erudite, at times severe, but generous teacher, who in those early days in the Indian ashram allowed me all the room I needed for exploration and experimentation, as well as access to his personal library, which was a gift beyond price. Occasional attendance at Jiddu Krishnamurti's talks conveyed thought-provoking inquiries that served to contrast with Osho's, allowing me to enrich the newly acquired knowledge with a more rational approach.

My research and temporary position as interviewer for a local cable TV station would later take me to interact personally with contemporary well-known teachers.

My research and temporary position as interviewer for a local cable TV station would later take me to interact personally with contemporary well-known teachers. Among others, this included Barbara Brennan, who inspired the model of the seven bodies of this book with her then-manuscript *Hands of Light*. Finally, when I had already established the first School of Consciousness in Brazil, I set out to Cyprus to understand the workings of the shadows and how they can deter the working of the Light. My direct acquaintance with Stylianos Atteshlis (also known as 'Daskalos'), author of *The Esoteric Teachings*, was a pivotal point in my work of decoding human creation. He planted me firmly in the esoteric Christian tradition with deep roots to my own stock of ancient knowledge. His teachings were imbibed in person at his school 'The Stoa' in Nicosia, Cyprus.

A former period of residency at the I AM Temple in Chicago shaped the content and form of the teachings of Inner Alchemy. Their 'I AM' teachings, comprising volumes of lectures of Ascended Master transmissions, decree books, classes, temple practice and rather severe discipline, brought contour and depth to my past discoveries and shed light on my future experience. Three books containing the 'I AM' teachings became my bedside companions: *Unveiled Mysteries*, *The Magic Presence* and the *I AM Discourses*, all published by the Saint Germain Foundation in Schaumburg, Illinois.

These are by no means the only texts that have influenced the book you are reading today. I came upon an anonymous pamphlet that referred to a multidimensional system comprised of twelve layers of reality or dimensions, and this became the platform upon which the dynamic of my teaching now rests. A manual by Petey Stevens that outlined the out-of-the-body chakras, and gave exercises to access them vibrationally, has also added theoretical understanding to my insights. Finally, Olive Pixley's manual, *Armour of Light*, contains meditations and exercises, some of which have been included in this book, that became of utmost value to me as personal transformational instruments.

As with many of my generation and inclination, my acquaintance with the work of Alice Bailey, especially her *Treatise on the Seven Rays*, has had a deep and extensive influence on my spiritual work, alongside the work of Helena Blavatsky, mother of modern esotericism. From the Theosophical Foundation, Annie Besant and Charles Leadbeater's research in *The Astral Plane* and *The Mental Plane* has been instrumental. Profoundly revealing, these texts helped me sort through my own perceptions. Their effects can be clearly glimpsed in this book. The Agni Yoga book series and Helena Roerich's diaries also brought heart-warming inspiration.

A sequel of books in Spanish called *Origenes de la Civilización Adámica* and *Arpas Eternas* by Josefa Rosalía Luque Alvarez (Hilarión de Monte Nebo) have given me access to other cosmologies and ancient practices, often confirming my own memory. Spanish influences also include *La Magia Planetaria* by Vicente Beltrán Anglada, and my personal contact with Argentine mystic Yaco Albala.

In my search for integration with the body and the physical plane, I have followed the physical disciplines of Kundalini Yoga, Zazen (Zen), Vipassana, Shugendo and Katsugen Kai into my daily practice over the years. These Eastern practices, alongside my physical application of Taoist thought and the *I Ching*, have become potent instruments of knowledge, as the postures and breathing techniques they offer have served to connect me with inner faculties that reveal the worlds of Light that form the tapestry for Inner Alchemy.

As you may see, Inner Alchemy processes are the result of experience and are original. Direct experience has verified the knowledge of spirit life and the human energetic anatomy in embodiment; yet personal contact and energy transmission from people, circumstances and sometimes books offered confirmation and a subtle transmission that mere words could never provide.

—

As you may see, Inner Alchemy processes are the result of experience and are original.

—

INTRODUCTION

If you have picked up this book on Inner Alchemy, it is likely that you are looking to deepen your understanding of life.

In reading this book, it is crucial to understand that what follows is a manual of study and application that takes time to understand and experience to incorporate. You may gain deep understanding from the information and practices contained within it, and this will invariably help you in your own quest. The greatest benefit from this teaching, however, is gained when it is explored in a group setting, where combined energies and individual differences offer ample scope to discover all aspects of life and of yourself that might be 'hidden in plain sight'.

    Inner Alchemy has been written with all readers in mind, for both beginner and advanced students and teachers. If you are a beginner, do not be disheartened if there are things within these pages that you cannot at first understand. To all my readers: I recommend you constantly remind yourselves that this is a manual to return to again and again. That which is first 'hidden' may later be revealed.

The layout of this book has been designed to enable the reader to understand and apply the knowledge presented in an individual setting as well as in the classroom format of my School of Consciousness. The first three parts and the fifth part of the book lay out the theoretical basis of the Inner Alchemy teachings. The book has a change of pace in parts Four and Six, which contain practical offerings for the reader to effect transformation in their own physical reality. Crucially, this should not be read as a 'feel-good' book to consume hastily from cover to cover – this will only lead to indigestion. Take care to return to sections you may have trouble with. Linger on those meditations, passages or exercises that you are drawn to and identify with. Greater insights will pour forth.

Most importantly, suspend your accustomed posture of rationality and feel if you can resonate with what you have read. *Inner Alchemy* has the power to change how one sees the world, but only with an open heart.

WHAT IS THE NATURE OF LIFE?

Inner Alchemy begins by exploring the very nature of life, helping us to understand who we are and the power and responsibility that lies within our reach. When we ask, 'What is Inner Alchemy?', and 'Why is it relevant to me?', we are also asking ourselves what *our* life is all about and what it means to lead a spiritual life. We then approach the journey of mastery.

'What is the nature of life?': this is the essence of the quest, whether conscious or not.

Mastery depends entirely on the quality and intensity of the quest. The seeker must allow themselves the experience of the burning questions: 'Why?' and 'What for?'. The answers invariably lead to revelation. Asking what the nature of life is leads to more existential and unanswerable questions, and, for many, marks the entry into the spiritual experience. There are many ways of answering.

Habitually, we try to solve everything through the rational mind, formulating theories and finding empirical, scientific evidence to support our search. But do these explanations satisfy the hunger that is being increasingly sensed by a growing proportion of humanity, which feels, knows and longs for what it cannot yet understand? The usual method

---

'What is the nature of life?': this is the essence of the quest, whether conscious or not.

of analysis and comparison of visible phenomena, while suitable for the material world, is ineffective when we try to grasp the sentient life within every phenomenon. The key lies in *feeling*.

Life is energy in endless motion and transformation. Matter, mind, our thoughts and everything in the Universe is energy. This energy is Light. Without Light there is no life. Light is life, life is Light: Light-life is the nature of Creation. All is alive, nourished and nourishing, Source and emanation, healing, transforming, elevating and creating space and form. Light is the core and transmuting agent of matter. In our world, Light-life is the source and the transmuting power of Love within all expressions of life, especially in our own. We, too, are composed of Light. The journey begins when we develop our own receptivity and sensitivity to the Light.

The effects of Light upon the human structure are numerous: from improving organic functioning, to awakening intuition and refining the intellect, to heightened discernment and a more conscious lifestyle. In the social order, this manifests as kindness, awareness, concern with group progress, and dynamic, caring involvement in all types of relationships, especially our relationship with the planet.

This Light need not be yet another abstract concept beyond our mortal reach. 'Switching on the Light' can be as experientially real as switching on an electric lightbulb. For many, once they understand that this Light is everywhere (even within them), they are able to link directly with it – from subtle awareness to full-body sensation, and more. For many, herein lies the key to the onset of an understanding and an experience of what might lie beyond.

—
We, too, are composed of Light. The journey begins when we develop our own receptivity and sensitivity to the Light.
—

WHO ARE WE? WHAT ARE WE? WHERE DID WE COME FROM?

Consciousness is an undifferentiated, high-frequency energy field: a fiery activity of as-yet uncreated life. Consciousness can be thought of as the primary source, as yet unmanifest primary expression of Spirit. Everything that exists originates from Consciousness.

The undifferentiated energy field of Consciousness is 'spark-like', ready to ignite into innumerable forms of life. This field of Consciousness is so vast that to know itself, it must fragment into multiple sparks of Light. In order to construct a vehicle of expression,

an instrument, these sparks must lower their frequency and go through a process of densification. The same impulse in the human being to know itself stems from the urge of Spirit, as Consciousness, to know itself. This is 'what' we are.

To become a human being, a spark from Consciousness acquires the form of a soul as it travels through a scintillating, gestating ocean of undifferentiated and unqualified energy, which then spirals through progressively slower frequencies until it acquires a dense human form and a corresponding state of intelligence in matter. It can now identify itself as a human 'I'. It has set the stage for a transitory identity, its personality – a 'who'. The spark is now differentiated from its original high frequency, the 'what' it is as Source, to manifest itself in a slower, more tangible vibrational rhythm.

In essence, the soul is the vehicle containing the 'spark' of Spirit manifested in the physical world within a human being. The human being is born into a world of cause and effect, of instinct and survival, with the appropriate mental, physical and emotional equipment to manage this environment. Some people may never leave this level of awareness. Some people never relate to the 'spark' at the core.

As an embodiment of Light (soul) in matter (body), the human being obeys two distinct laws: the Law of Light and the Law of Matter. The body and its world resonate to the polar Law of Matter; the soul to the Law of Light. Energy, and, as a consequence matter, responds to the human will, to thought and direction. Human beings have a unique role in creation as they have the power to manipulate life energies and to engage with both the Creator (Consciousness and Light) and created matter, i.e. the physical world. This happens through the unconscious or awakened ability to contact the power of Spirit at the core.

Physical embodiment represents a commitment to the planet Earth: the human being takes on its very substance, coats itself with it. But our essence is not material. The human being is like a visitor within

> In essence, the soul is the vehicle containing the 'spark' of Spirit manifested in the physical world within a human being.

The Descent of Consciousness into Matter

physicality, a Light of Consciousness with multidimensional potentiality that reaches beyond its emotional and mental expressions. Knowing this ignites a direct link with the Light of source Consciousness.

WHAT IS THE PURPOSE AND MEANING OF LIFE?

Matter evolves; Consciousness expands. This is the very purpose of life.

On the human level, the purpose of life is not only to grow, expand and return, amplified, to Source, but also to bless, transmit and create; or better still, to co-create with Self as the highest state of Being. Each person has come to do something unique, to experience the desire for greater life and perfection as individuality. When that expression is found, there is great joy and fulfilment, and our evolution, the rhythm of our life, seems to expand and accelerate.

The mission of human beings is self-mastery and dominion over the energy fields we possess (more on these fields in Part Two). This knowledge is imperative to achieve mastery, that is, profound self-transformation as soul-Spirit awareness.

As we evolve in matter, we expand in Consciousness and cease relating to life externally through the linear mind only. We start to commune with the core of our Being. Gradually, being at one with our source becomes more important than anything else. Transmutation of matter then occurs as a natural consequence of intimacy with Light. This is how matter evolves, becoming more 'Light' and resonating at higher frequencies.

For those who ask how to 'do' it, it must be understood that this is not a matter of effort but rather one of acceptance and surrender to our inner, natural sensibility (i.e. our perceptive capacity). Reconciling with our true nature cannot be forced upon those of us who still want to experience personal power and control over matter.

If you are reading these pages, chances are you are already crossing the boundary between the old 'business-as-usual' dynamic and a new, spontaneous expression of authenticity and coherence. When Being becomes more important than doing, we fall in tune with our Source, aligning with our true nature, purpose and meaning in life.

> The mission of human beings is self-mastery and dominion over the energy fields we possess. This knowledge is imperative to achieve mastery, that is, profound self-transformation as soul-Spirit awareness.

WHAT IS A SPIRITUAL LIFE?

Asking the most fundamental questions about the nature of life, reality and ourselves is part and parcel of the spiritual journey. Still, there is much superficiality, illusion and confusion regarding spiritual living. Ordinary preoccupation is too often restricted to the immediate self or environment, instead of the global issues spiritual values would embrace. Applied spirituality addresses living in the world, which involves every thought, feeling and act in the Now. Spirituality demands commitment and constant awareness, not just removing yourself from the ordinary world in meditation and talking spiritual language. A spiritual life entails something that nobody really likes: 'discipline' and a switch of perspective from the personal self to collective reality.

True spirituality permeates the personality in such a natural way that ideals such as charity, peace, sensibility and transparency emerge spontaneously from within, instead of being deliberate acts of 'doing'. A spiritual person is already in communion with their soul and with their own embodied spark of Consciousness, where source Consciousness flows into it naturally, rather than as a result of effort. Anyone who responds to the needs of others out of a sense of duty or obligation is not being spiritual: genuine spirituality is an overflow of inner awareness and unequivocally leads to service.

Inner Alchemy is dedicated to unlearning the patterns of usual communication and perception in order to implement the voice of inner Consciousness through the correct refined use of the senses and human faculties in ordinary life. The practices outlined in the book are to be applied and incorporated, not merely understood.

When Being becomes more important than doing, we fall in tune with our Source, aligning with our true nature, purpose and meaning in life.

PERSONAL TRANSFORMATION AND SELF-MASTERY

Adopting a spiritual life results in personal transformation as you work towards mastery of the Self. Work on the body and personality is fundamental to spiritual awakening in a healthy, grounded sense. This work helps individuals link to their true Self, awakening the voice of their soul and ultimately blending with it, while remaining wholly active and joyful on the physical plane.

Spiritual work is about raising energy at every stage, particularly at the body-personality level. The more receptive you are to spiritual Light,

Spiritual work is about raising energy at every stage, particularly at the body-personality level.

the more that physical and mental structures resist the loss of boundaries that define them. Changing the life-patterns of the personality is not easy. This is because in order to survive, we have developed stubborn habits of self-sufficiency and independence that are difficult to dissolve without loving and intelligent understanding within a supportive environment. Remember that matter and consciousness operate under two entirely different laws and that the human being's energy structure is composed of both. Physical and personal rather than spiritual priorities result in reactions such as bodily pain, fever, illness; or alterations of character, such as impatience, excessive irritation, fear or inability to control ourselves. They form part of learning self-mastery through the application of Consciousness in every detail of human life.

Even if the effect of the awakening of Light is understood, for mastery of the personality the process still remains to be embodied. For real transformation – which in alchemical terms is 'transmutation' – to take place it is essential to contain the outburst of energies, not by repression, but by conscious self-control and redirection. In the same way that the medieval alchemist separated the components of a formula in order to extract the elixir, the inner alchemist must separate thoughts from feelings and body sensation, grasping all of the energy erupting from within. At that precise moment and with the practice of the Alchemical Alignment (as outlined shortly), the power contained in the focus of Consciousness, now directed by our Spirit-self, is able to shift the energy from its narrow focus to reveal more refined possibilities of expression. In Alchemy, this process, which happens within the individual, is called 'sublimation'; it has nothing to do with its modern interpretation as substitution, but is a deliberate use of trained will. Mastery happens when you are able to transform the energy 'in situ'. Life itself is the laboratory.

The shift from focus on the lower self's personality to soul is suggested throughout these pages and consists in switching from the perspective of body-personality to that of soul-Spirit, induced by the Master Practice (discussed in Part One) and reinforced by the exercises and meditations provided in this book. Inner Alchemy redefines ordinary thinking, turning the mind into an instrument of feeling and sensibility. A person's mind evolves according to experience. Sooner or later, nicely or painfully, this experience leads to greater awareness. Eventually, a gradual shift occurs from an ordinary, personally focused mind to the holistic

> —
>
> Mastery happens when you are able to transform the energy 'in situ'. Life itself is the laboratory.
>
> —

cognition that defines the Higher Mind. At this point, mind responds to the finer voltages of Intelligence and Spirit Consciousness.

Understand that soul is not synonymous with Higher Mind, as some might suppose; soul is a state of Being that enfolds the experience of Consciousness, of Spirit in all its incarnations, and serves to link upper and lower dimensional experience. Higher Mind, on the other hand, is the quality of applied intelligence when contact with holistic and higher dimensional experience is made and sustained consciously. It embraces sensibility as heart intelligence. A soul-connected person is one whose whole personality, and Higher and lower (or ordinary) mind, vibrate in resonance with the soul. The table below clarifies some of the distinctions between ordinary (lower) mind, Higher Mind, and what it means to be soul-awakened (read from left to right):

——

Understand that soul is not synonymous with Higher Mind, as some might suppose; soul is a state of Being that enfolds the experience of Consciousness, of Spirit in all its incarnations, and serves to link upper and lower dimensional experience.

——

LEVELS OF MIND

Ordinary/lower mind	Higher Mind inspiration	Soul-awakened
individual concern	collective concern	universal concern
body-personality needs	whole-body responsiveness	perception from heart
linear thinking	empathy	insight
listening	tuning-in	heart integration
information	knowledge	wisdom
pleasure	joy	bliss
emotions	sensitivity	state of being love
calculation	understanding	knowing
sharing	partnership	group consciousness

As this table suggests, self-mastery entails self-aware alignment with group consciousness. The keys to mastery and spiritual development in general are in the quality and extent of personal transformation. This is the lens through which you perceive and deal with the world and the innumerable forms of reality.

WHAT GOOD IS IT TO 'KNOW THYSELF'?

I have often heard comments such as, 'What good is it to clutter your mind with such technical information about the bodies, rays, chakras? Wouldn't it be much simpler to just 'meditate' and be a good person? Ultimately, isn't silence enough?' The answer is no, not if you are to make a difference as an active and participating server in the world. In this case, a silent, loving Presence is lovely, but not always useful.

In these pages, I share facts that are not always stated in various systems lacking the integration and application sought here: those that address separate parts of yourself and rely heavily on mental understanding, sensory awareness, emotional control or spiritual attunement independently of others, the whole, society and the world we live in. Too many other systems simply do not call for integrated action. We do.

It is not enough to meditate without a sound physical structure, one that is flexible and receptive to the inflow of Light that triggers the awakening of Consciousness. Nor is it enough to tame your instincts and emotions or to discipline your mind. It must be a unified effort with an integrated result. Flexibility is needed at all levels, because the human structure, as outlined in the text, is both material and subtle, physical and spiritual.

I often dream of a better world, as I am sure you do. Such a world is not possible without personal transformation. Nobody speaks of correct perception, pointing to a drastic shift away from egoism. Our vision furnishes and gives rise to a sense of responsibility in the construction of our collective world.

If you were to abolish all forms of slavery of perception that limit and bind individuals to one another and to a system, you would realise that transformation cannot happen through superficial adjustments. It is not enough to supply mechanical support or wish to help just causes. As noble as these intentions and efforts may be, they do not reach the mindset of humanity that repeatedly reconstructs the very mechanisms we wish to change. The change begins with each one of us: we must be the change we want to see in our world.

A genuine alignment with Earth and cosmic forces is not complicated or fanciful. It is real and demands a concerted effort to sense and feel it. It marks a drastic change in self-perception in order to know what

—

I often dream of a better world, as I am sure you do. Such a world is not possible without personal transformation.

—

is happening, as well as observe how one responds and contributes to what is happening. The choice is clear: either continued abuse and destruction, or group consciousness and construction of a new, more 'personal' world premise.

Inner Alchemy is much more than a technical system of perception. It is the manifestation of a personal search. It becomes yours and will respond to your temperament and talents. This is why, in teaching this system, we insist on authenticity and personal expression. These pages will become an intimate treasure chest from which you will draw what you need as and when you need it.

In this book I provide maps of Consciousness that detail the dynamics of being human, focusing on managing faculties and powers with awareness and deliberation to help you cultivate discernment, which in turn will help you choose your own genuine priorities and shape your degree of involvement with life. I hope this serves you in your inner quest.

Mastery evokes Spirit in the flesh; a Self-conscious personality is dynamically active in the world. It is attuned to and collaborating with planetary and cosmic law, yet it is joyous, and enjoys the pleasure of embodiment and the affection resulting from love in all its aspects, physical, emotional, mental and spiritual.

I hope you, as the reader, can reap the benefit of my 77-year (as I write) search for Truth and unfold your own unique authenticity and power of leadership. The world awaits you to nourish the Earth and hungry humanity.

Everything points to you, dear reader, your innermost Consciousness as the only Power, the only Intelligence, the only substance acting in your world. Our world.

———

Inner Alchemy is much more than a technical system of perception. It is the manifestation of a personal search. It becomes yours and will respond to your temperament and talents.

———

QUESTIONS FOR SELF-OBSERVATION

Before you dive headfirst into the book and explore what it has to offer, ask yourself who and what you are, and what you can become. Check your expectations. Ask yourself what you are ready to perceive and learn. For proper assessment, it will be helpful for you to identify your positive traits and your areas of difficulty.

Here are some questions for self-exploration. You may want to review these every few days to identify and accelerate whatever learning process life is providing you with.

Who am I?
How do I feel and function physically, emotionally and mentally? What is my relationship to my body (awareness, weight management); to my mind (my ability to concentrate, focus, direct or empty the mind); and to my emotions (my identifications, attachments, loss of power)?

Who am I to myself?
Do I feel the different aspects of myself? Identify these and give them specific names.

What is my posture in relation to others?
Note your relationships: the types, duration and capacity for intimacy. Note karmic traces you share with others, if any.

How do others see me?
Look at yourself through the eyes of others.

Who am I in relation to God? To my soul?

How do I perceive reality?
Note how your subjective perception shifts from moment to moment, with fine variations within these shifts.

How intuitive am I – when it comes to knowing about people, events, myself?

What are my habits?
Become aware of patterns and changes of habit. How does such awareness of habitual action increase my capacity for spontaneity? Note obsessive behaviour in areas like sex, food, thoughts, etc.

What is my relationship to work?
Describe how you feel and function at work.

Where in my life am I out of control or finding it difficult to manage?

When and with whom am I out of control? What do I control in myself, in my environment or in others in my environment?

What do I fear? Be honest and go beyond your first answer. What is at stake?

What do I dislike in others?
Notice three characteristics you dislike in at least three people. See if these also appear in you or in someone close to you.

How may I improve myself?
Be specific. Find an activity or action to generate that improvement.

What steps have I already taken to improve myself? Notice your progress and allow yourself the feeling of satisfaction.

What are my ambitions, desires, plans for the immediate future? For the remote future? How well am I manifesting my desires?

How sensitive am I to others? How do they affect me? Go more deeply into your feeling.

Now formulate a clear plan with a picture of yourself as happy, healthy, creative and productive. Hold that picture. Walk into the picture, or let the picture descend and enfold you. Absorb it into your cellular structure. Create the feeling of already having it. Allow that feeling to surround you in its fullness.

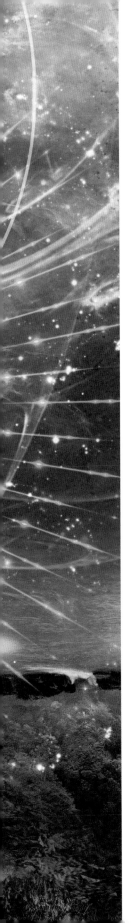

INNER ALCHEMY AND ITS BASIC CONCEPTS

Part One introduces the phenomenon of alchemy and its counterpart, 'Inner Alchemy', with the most important technique taught at the School: the Master Practice. This is accompanied by an explanation of the key points and concepts that lie behind the Inner Alchemy teachings.

WHAT IS ALCHEMY AND WHY 'INNER'?

Traditionally, the word 'alchemy' conjures up images of warlocks, spider-webs and cauldrons and an esoteric body of literature, with which most of us have never had any contact.

The alchemist is seen as an ageless, mysterious wizard like Merlin or a figure from popular fantasy fiction.

In reality, alchemy goes beyond the superstitions of the Middle Ages to the time when humans first came into embodiment. We were once aware of our energetic makeup and our role as an intermediary between physical and subtle realities. We understood that it is our state of consciousness itself that determines the laws of energy and matter – something eerily echoed now in the discoveries of modern science. Alchemical teachers, such as the legendary Hermes Trismegistus, and the Egyptian Thoth, right up to the medieval Paracelsus, taught this. This book, however, is not a guide to the history of alchemy; we are concerned with what we call 'Inner Alchemy', a practice that is highly personalised to the human being and in the knowledge that within them they hold the *paras*, or 'philosopher's stone', which, instead of transmuting lead into gold, transmutes matter into Light.

A stark contrast to today's superficial 'personal transformation' industry, Inner Alchemy is the science of applied consciousness to raise the vibration of the matter that comprises our physical and psychological self into finer states or frequencies. In essence, Alchemy is the transmutation from the lesser to the greater, and it embodies both structural and qualitative change. The addition of 'Inner' (i.e. Inner Alchemy) refers to the subtle, innermost reality that comes alive when the fully conscious personality blends with the guidance of the soul. Inner Alchemy is, in effect, inner mastery.

> In essence, Alchemy is the transmutation from the lesser to the greater, and it embodies both structural and qualitative change.

THE THREE BASIC HUMAN POWERS

The human being is a creator, an extension of divine Source, building surrounding reality in greater or lesser ways. Manifestation follows a formula that requires the use of three creative powers. In humans these powers are thought, feeling and the spoken word and they constitute the basic Alchemical Formula. Understanding one's power as a creator is so important for the study of Inner Alchemy that the process must be explained before continuing any further. This process will also be expanded upon in Part Three.

Power is managed by will. This may be higher Will aligned with Source, or personal willpower, an expression of self-centred wilfulness. Will is equivalent to attention and, together with trained focus of attention, in Alchemy, will is applied to visualisation. Visualisation, in turn, is applied to manifestation. Visualisation uses the subtle (i.e. non-physical) visual faculty we have, combined with imagination to create the image we intend.

THOUGHT

The power to manifest thought is understood as the capacity to create a mental blueprint for a concept. Thought constructs a form to be animated by vital human energy: this is the visualisation that constructs the moulds of creation.

FEELING

The power of feeling is understood as sensibility: the capacity for sense organ response and emotional response. This sensibility can denote a holistic and flexible perception, which can transcend bodily, physical perception, going beyond to the use of the subtle and inner senses.

Emotional response is very powerful. Emotions are often described as 'energy in motion'; waves of energy that add power and quality to an image conceived by the mind. Love is the primal state of emotion, the source of all emotions, and constitutes the greatest force in existence. As a concentration of the activity of Light, Love contains the maximum momentum of energy. It is the cohesive and sustaining force of the Universe. It is such a concentration of the feeling energy that wherever it is directed, it triggers manifestation or wish fulfilment.

Humanity no longer understands the core purity of Love, and has broken it up into lesser expressions, known as emotions; this, in turn, has created fear – after all, what is fear but the absence of Love?

THE SPOKEN WORD

The power of the spoken word creates the resonant field for materialisation of the image evoked by the mind and energised by the emotions. The spoken word is rarely recognised for the power that it holds and yet this, as sound, is responsible for the aligning of our worlds. Matter resonates to the spoken word and to the meanings transmitted. A thought, or blueprint, is like a photographic negative, energised by feeling: it is set into form by the word. The right tone and pitch, as well as the word into which sound is sealed, are important. The vibratory resonance of the spoken word acts as a fiat or decree. With this understanding the statement 'and the Word was made flesh' may be correctly understood.

Creation begins as intent and comes into manifestation through the use of these three powers. The threefold nature of the human being (body, mind and emotion), however, needs development, balance and integration.

As a concentration of the activity of Light, Love contains the maximum momentum of energy. It is the cohesive and sustaining force of the Universe.

Without a physical life force freely circulating through the body, the Higher Mind has no anchor through which to express itself in matter; it remains elusive and fragmentary, but physical life force without clear mental direction is open to excess and contamination. Once the threefold nature of the human being is harmoniously integrated, alignment with higher frequencies occurs. This process is not a linear progression, but rather a cyclical integration of more harmony into the bodies of the personality (the nature of the different bodies will be expanded upon in Part Two).

THE MASTER PRACTICE

This is the most important practice of those presented within this book, and it will be regularly referred to throughout. The Master Practice is the procedure that creates an alignment of the body with cosmic forces. With practice, we may live in an almost-permanent state of alignment, experiencing the world with the expanded perception that the identification with Source can offer.

The human structure is composed of both Earth-matter and Light. In order to function as an integrated personality with higher Consciousness, it is essential to acknowledge and understand our makeup.

We have three basic points of reference: the physical body, the soul and Spirit. Each offers a unique and different perspective. These three states are wholly available to you at all times. A conscious connection with your soul and with your Spirit can and does occur.

In the third dimension (our 'ordinary' reality), the body reflects a larger proportion of matter and a minimal proportion of Light in order to function appropriately in physical reality. This proportion rapidly shifts according to where our focus of attention lies. In meditative states, for instance, our body composition leans towards a greater proportion of Light.

Inner Alchemy works through visualised and/or sensed energy, using colour, breath and sometimes sound, to create Light forms, which act

———

The human structure is composed of both Earth-matter and Light. In order to function as an integrated personality with higher Consciousness, it is essential to acknowledge and understand our makeup.

———

The Master Practice

through the body or the environment, or the situation evoked. Visualisation is perhaps the most important sensory faculty for a student of Light.

Consider the illustration on page 20. The first thing that should strike you in this illustration is the orbs of colour. Each can be thought of as a type of sun, emitting a special frequency. From the middle of this multicoloured sun, Spirit emanates a current or ray of Light directly into the head of a human being. This current represents the lifestream. It flows down the spinal column to the base, spreading into the nervous system. This induces sentient life in matter.

Next, notice that the human figure is mirrored by an inverse figure below. This represents grounding of the Self, where this wholly luminous and transparent figure of Light is connected to the centre of the Earth. Nourishment is received now from two sources: from the Cosmos (Consciousness) and the Earth (and the vitality of frequency, her Light). In this way the body is, in reality, a passageway between the heavens and the Earth.

The white globe, midway between the physical body and the above Sun Presence, represents the soul. This globe shifts up and down the current of the lifestream, between greater and lesser light frequencies, depending on the degree of connection of the lower self with this Sun Presence. The Sun Presence above the globe is the same as the Sun Presence in the intimacy of the heart: the soul. It is the very essence of the human being.

Once the (inner) senses have been activated, the student then uses visualisation to invoke the Tube of Light, as seen in the illustration. This tube enfolds the body, including the mirrored Light body. It acts as protection, enabling the student to remain centred within the frequency of Light while engaged in everyday life. From this perspective, the human self is acknowledged and embraced.

 ## THE MASTER PRACTICE MEDITATION

Take care to perform the following Master Practice meditation slowly, and with intent. A suggestion for performing this, and the other practices suggested throughout the book, is to record them in the reader's own voice and set the meditation to music. The Master Practice may take as long or as little time as you like; a daily practice of 20 minutes is recommended.

> The Sun Presence above the globe is the same as the Sun Presence in the intimacy of the heart: the soul. It is the very essence of the human being.

Light-life follows attention.

Sense the body. This is very different from business-as-usual, when thoughts and emotions are allowed to wander freely.

Scan through different areas, activating visualisation of the body areas together with in-depth sensation. This is how frequencies are modulated, affecting health and physical wellbeing.

Feel every part of the body. Breathe consciously, until the body feels balanced and whole. Breathe with a stress on body stability, density and weight, producing a sense of solidity and safety.

Now direct your attention to the Earth below.

Evoke a subtle electric current from the figure of Light mirroring your physical form, absorbing its vitality on the inbreath and pulling the sensation upwards through the body slowly. This Light triggers an awakening at the centre of each atom, which responds in kind. Concentrate on each part of the illumination process.

On the outbreath, eject all excess thought, emotion and density through the feet into the figure of Light that absorbs this.

Feel how electricity and expansiveness suffuse the whole body, giving it a sense of physical lightness and extension into the surrounding space. Imagine and sense the powerful presence of Light above the head. Direct your full attention upwards to the Sun Presence, visualised above, as per the illustration on page 20. The higher you direct your attention, the greater frequencies of Light are reached. Sense this.

Focus on the feeling, as if you are in the middle of an ocean of Light without beginning or end. All is limitless space.

Rest. Allow the experience of fullness and impress this quality into your memory, so that you may evoke it at will.

From that sublimated stance, which is identified with Spirit, direct attention down to the physical self. Compassion flows inwardly into the lower (physical) self. Acknowledge the flow of energy into your cells and feeling. Feel how you are loved by Spirit.

Before returning, visualise and sense the Tube of Light descending over and around you, including the figure of Light, protecting and enabling high frequencies in the body.

Very gently and gradually come back to the initial stage in the body and modulate your frequency inversely towards greater weight and

—

Feel every part of the body. Breathe consciously, until the body feels balanced and whole. Breathe with a stress on body stability, density and weight, producing a sense of solidity and safety.

—

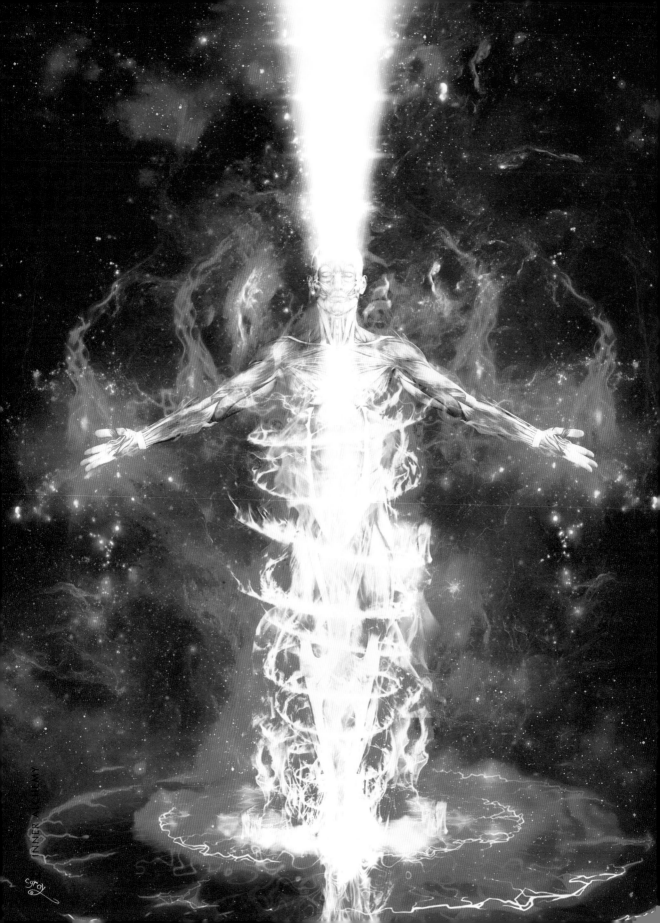

density. Know that you have the capacity to tune into other vibrations and states of being, and that no intermediaries are needed.

The path towards genuine independence and liberation has begun. Statements such as 'we perceive what (where) we place our attention on' (in other words where our interests are), and 'we create our own reality' begin to make sense.

THE VIOLET FLAME

Violet is a mid-stream frequency in our colour spectrum; it denotes the point where visible colour leaps into invisible and finer, more accelerated hues. It is in the perfect position to transmute matter, when used appropriately by a trained mind. It is the frequency used for healing, clearing and dissolving negativity. Together with gold, the violet fire has come to symbolise the alchemical process of transmutation, drawing cosmic Light into the deepest recesses of matter, absorbed by the breath and the spaces in your cells.

The next practice is an extension of the visualisation used in the Master Practice. Here, the violet fire is invited into and intensified in the body through vigorous shaking and breathing.

—

Violet is a mid-stream frequency in our colour spectrum; it denotes the point where visible colour leaps into invisible and finer, more accelerated hues.

—

 ## THE VIOLET FLAME ACTIVATION

Visualise the violet flame coming up from the centre of the Earth.

Imagine, and then sense, the violet flame coursing into and right through the pores of the body, affecting all your tissues and bones. Focus on how this fire enters through the soles of the feet, how it sweeps upwards, drawn by the breath and visualisation. Create the sensation of the flames spiralling around you and within you, just as they would around a log in a fireplace.

When ready, gently begin to shake.

———

The Violet Flame Activation

Keep your feet firmly planted on the ground. Shake your knees, with the movement spreading through the entire trunk of the body, loosening the muscles around your genital area and belly. Next, spread the shaking to your shoulders, arms and, ultimately, the head and face.

The shaking must be unified, responding to the knees and not initiated on command into separate parts of the body. Finally, the entire body is shaking like a rag doll, limp and yet held firmly, like on a string, by an aligned spinal column and firm foothold.

Simultaneously visualise the flames coursing through the body, responding as you intensify the breath.

If desired, the fire may be directed into especially troublesome areas of the body to dissolve impurities at the cellular and psychological levels, bringing forth a sense of lightness, greater vision and agility. The colour may vary from deeper and lighter tones to ultraviolet, pink and white.

To begin with, five minutes may suffice. As you become more familiar with the practice, extend it to ten. For people who have more difficulty connecting with the sensation of the body, it may take longer. For any results, you must do this daily for a minimum of two weeks.

When finished, sit or lie down to perceive the energies that have been set into motion as they sweep through the body. Feel the streams and eddies, the circles and bubbles that are spontaneously erupting inside you.

End by visualising a stream of golden Light flowing from above to down beneath your feet. Absorb this golden substance into the brain, the spine, the nerve endings and into every cell. Awaken subtle sensation as well.

Finally, ensure that you are firmly stabilised in your body, through the sense of weight and density, and that you have equal awareness of all parts of yourself. Then pull in the energies that have been mobilised now to surround the body. Sense the solidity of this compacted form by deliberately breathing into the belly. Move around freely, exploring sensation and the lightness perceived.

This return practice should be used after all the practices recommended in the book.

> The shaking must be unified, responding to the knees and not initiated on command into separate parts of the body.

DEFINITIONS AND TENETS

This section exists as an expanded reference for those who may encounter a term they do not understand later on in the book; or for those who feel they need a refreshment of concepts they have encountered before.

Countless volumes on mysticism, religion, philosophy and psychology have been written with the intent of providing a near-perfect and comprehensive definition of some of the following phenomena. I do not pretend to do so here. I cannot hope to give all-encompassing answers to such questions as 'What is the soul?' and 'Where is the soul?', yet here I provide some approximation, based on my years of learning and guidance.

SOURCE, SPIRIT, ONENESS

Source, Spirit, the Absolute Being, God, the Creator, Oneness, the I AM Presence, or just Presence: these are all terms often used interchangeably, but, in truth, transmit different qualities. All of them get to what is essentially the heart of the matter: they denote the unmanifest principle of Oneness behind all Creation. In this book, the word 'Source' is frequently used, as I think it denotes this principle best. I also frequently use the synonyms 'Spirit' or 'Oneness'.

A term such as 'Spirit-self' refers to the phenomenon of the blended frequencies of an individual when they reach the vibrational level of the spark of Source/Spirit that is within them.

CONSCIOUSNESS, INTELLIGENCE

The first and primary expression of Source is Consciousness. In this book I use upper case to denote Source or Spirit 'Consciousness' and the lower case to denote the activity of awareness ('consciousness') in an embodied human being. Consciousness, which I also call Intelligence, is the faculty manifest by this original state of Being: it can be understood as the *activity* of Source.

As Consciousness dives through progressively densifying strata of 'space' into its temporary abode in a body of matter, it gains awareness of itself. It acquires a point of reference as an 'I'. The deeper it goes into the third-dimensional state of polarity (our 'ordinary' reality), it becomes the thinking instrument we know as 'mind'. This is the concrete or linear mind, equipped to handle phenomena in a material world of apparent separation. This Intelligence, however, also operates in higher dimensional states of Being.

—

Source, Spirit, the Absolute Being, God, the Creator, Oneness, the I AM Presence, or just Presence: these are all terms often used interchangeably, but, in truth, transmit different qualities.

—

—

The first and primary expression of Source is Consciousness.

—

Consciousness merely *is*, it is not qualified in any way. Human beings experience its forms, but rarely experience its natural state as no-mind Presence, which is difficult for a normal person to sustain without losing coherence with physical identity and functions.

DIMENSIONS

As the Spirit-self journeys into physical embodiment, it drifts through different energy strata, from the finest to the densest, where physical life ultimately takes shape. At each stage, it stops to adapt its Consciousness–Intelligence and, in the process, acquires abilities to express itself within that particular dimension or plane. These powers, existing in different dimensions to our physical one, will later be available to the personality when it gains awareness of its Spirit-self.

In my Inner Alchemy system, I call these stages of adaptation 'dimensions'. Each dimension consists of progressive gradations of activity; they are grounds upon which the student moves through enquiry and general experience.

From our perspective at the physical level, the system of dimensions helps us to understand how the three main vehicles of the human being – our form (body), our emotions and our mental abilities – express themselves within different vibratory ranges. In other words, this system explains the dynamics of Consciousness itself, and how the person can and does access different ranges of vibrational frequency.

We access a higher dimension when we raise the frequency of these lower three vehicles (body, mind and emotional capacities). This may already happen spontaneously in dreams and in meditation, but I teach the student how to invoke higher dimensions consciously through guided practices under supervision. This is done through simultaneously applying intention, attention, sensibility and visualisation.

FORCE, ENERGY

For the purpose of my work, 'force' is directional and specific, whereas 'energy' is simply vibrational emission.

The Sun is a good example that illustrates the difference between energy and force. The Sun is an energy source that is used to feed the planetary system of this galaxy, but it is also emits certain qualities as a force that influence nature and humans in different constructive and also

These powers, existing in different dimensions to our physical one, will later be available to the personality when it gains awareness of its Spirit-self.

destructive ways. The Sun's force influences our vitality, affecting the energy patterns of the body and psyche – our physical and mental health, character and wellbeing.

The terms vibration, frequency, resonance, pulsation and oscillation refer to the activity of energy in matter. In this book, I use the term 'frequency' to distinguish vibration in the more subtle dimensions, whereas I limit 'pulsation' to the language of energy in matter. I hardly use the term 'oscillation' except as emission from sound and matter itself.

Importantly, that which vibrates in 'things' is Consciousness itself, i.e. Consciousness is the essence of the elements it creates. Consciousness can be perceived through attuning to the core of creations and their energy fields. It is perceived in various degrees or 'frequencies'.

SOUL

Some might ask if the soul even exists. For those who are constricted by living entirely through the bodily senses and who believe that life is only physical, of course it does not. For the more sensitive, it is the voice of conscience, a whispering certainty that can only be experienced within. For those trained in subtle perception, it may be defined as a scintillating quality of Light surrounding the aura, and this quality may be more luminous around some than others. In this book, I often refer to the soul as Being or a Being state.

Rather than an entity, the soul is both content and a container. As a container, it is the vehicle of Spirit into the incarnational cycle, the container for 'Being'.

The soul is an energy field; a projection of Spirit whose purpose is to serve as a living link with it throughout its life experiences in the third dimension (which indirectly includes all dimensions). Through incarnations, the soul gathers integrated life lessons; in other words, it acquires 'content'. This content, or wisdom, eventually fuses with the wisdom of other souls, to form the blanket of information and learning we tap into (known as the Akashic records, see glossary, xv), and thus the Universe 'expands'.

Eventually, the soul attains full integration back into Spirit. Its wisdom remains in the human field as a contribution to the evolution of the Human Model. It is this 'content' that 'talks to' and guides us when we have ears to hear. The soul serves as sentient memory, vehicle and guide

> The soul is an energy field; a projection of Spirit whose purpose is to serve as a living link with it throughout its life experiences in the third dimension.

for inner conscience during every incarnation or temporary personality, quietly insinuating what is right, just and beautiful. It is our individual voice of Spirit, but also of collective humanity, including Masters, teachers and guides.

Where and how is the soul 'found'?

There is no particular place in the body where the soul resides; nor is there a specific method to access it. At most, some people point to the heart as the seat of the soul, and this is not entirely incorrect. The awakened heart centre, as we shall see, corresponds to the vibrational frequency of higher-dimensional life, where the mind is inspired by the soul. The personality experiences the soul as inspiration and objective clarity.

PERSONALITY

Personality is a construction of the lower self to operate in this physical (third) dimension, developed gradually. It is composed of the physical, emotional and mental bodies, which are three of the seven energy fields (more on these in Part Two). Personality is the subjective identity that responds to the social need for individuality, for being separate and special. It is always changing, reacting to physical life as a composite of emotion and belief. It forms a transitory and yet somewhat coherent whole – coherent to the human self that insistently and automatically identifies with it, until this self can gain insight into the soul experience.

Personality revolves around physical spacetime reality, responding to the needs and demands of ordinary third-dimensional life. It responds instinctively to people and surroundings and depends upon them for evaluating itself and its environment. Depending as such on external reality, it survives in separation. Without the influence of a higher, more subtle contact, such as the soul, it cannot be stimulated into expanding its boundaries and relinquishing its ego-centric position. It is only in flashes, such as in dreams or insights, which it might interpret as angelic, divine or beyond itself, that it may feel soul connection.

Personal Focus of Consciousness (PFC) and Personal Energy Bodies (PEBs)

When working with the personality, I use the term 'Personal Focus of Consciousness' (PFC), which designates a mobile and subjective centre

---

Personality revolves around physical spacetime reality, responding to the needs and demands of ordinary third-dimensional life.

of attention that encompasses our personal priorities. The PFC may be directed either by the unconscious or automatic personality or by the conscious personality, which I call the Higher Self. The PFC reveals the degree of Consciousness employed by a person. The PFC may be centred anywhere in the body, or at any level of chakra activity, but tends to deal mostly with the Personal Energy Bodies.

The Personal Energy Bodies (PEBs) are entire energy fields, or 'bodies', to do with physical, emotional or mental activity. They relate to the lower-dimensional needs of the personality and have little to do with Spirit-self. More on these bodies will be dealt with in Part Three, the chapter on the human faculties.

Whenever I talk about a perceptual shift, it is a shift of the PFC, i.e. the viewpoint held by the individual with all their contrasting mundane and spiritual perspectives. When accompanied by the deliberate transference of the Personal Focus of Consciousness from the physical self to Spirit-self, the shift from body-personality to Source causes a radical rearrangement in all of the personality bodies. Rather than seeing and feeling from the ground floor, perception is elevated to the top of the mountain every time, promoting an in-depth understanding of human conditions and an ability to reach dimensional realities that offer tangible solutions. This is the posture that leads to the natural impulse towards service and the construction of a better world.

How may the personality be infused by the soul?

We do not usually take into account that personality is not an accident, or indeed that it is a conscious creation reflecting circumstances. It is, in fact, the result of choice. Spirit takes tremendous care in selecting and moulding its incarnational setting, and if you are reading this book, chances are that you have awakened to the fact that yours was perfect for who you have become and all that you have learned. Personality gives the human being the tools we will require to attain mastery and soul connection. Life circumstances serve as our laboratory for experience and ensuing service.

Without personality, the soul would not be able to express and communicate. Only when the personality is brought under the Will of Spirit, through its inner voice as the soul, is it useful as an instrument of service. No technique or person outside the individual can connect the personality to the soul. The soul functions as a channel of Spirit. The

—
We do not usually take into account that personality is not an accident, or indeed that it is a conscious creation reflecting circumstances.
—

key is to connect to Will, rather than willpower, its lower personality counterpart. This connection may only happen when intention and attention issue from the innermost Self.

Once under the influence of the soul, the personality is a unique window replete with peculiarities that make it fun, truly unique, spontaneous and natural. It is through these distinctions that the soul manifests best. Without this higher soul influence, the life of an individual is circumscribed to a life of limited time and space, to physical sensation and material goals.

Service is the goal of all incarnated life, and soul connection is the goal of personality experience. To serve the purpose of uplifting life everywhere, however, the soul must be able to express itself joyfully and authentically through personality, without mental inhibition.

CHARACTER, EGO

Character pertains to the personality. It reflects the quality of the personality developed through conscious choice and reflection. It is a construction qualified by thought and feeling in its current embodiment. It is what is normally called 'identity', which has both its strengths and flaws. The aim of the spiritual journey is to inject Consciousness into character, not to lose our uniqueness.

The word 'ego' is often taught as the self-centred personality, and many spiritual traditions teach that we must transcend it, even if it means transcending our identity. However, there is little sense in becoming totally ego-less, for the ego is used as a tool in this dimension. Instead, there is a focus on refining what we call the 'egoism', or self-centredness, in the personality. The ego is a necessary and unique personal perspective through which we may decode our perceptions in all dimensions of experience. Refining the personality is how the human being may refine the ego and use it optimally as the necessary tool that it is.

> The ego is a necessary and unique personal perspective through which we may decode our perceptions in all dimensions of experience.

MIND

There is a separate section later in the book about the mental activity that defines the thinking and evaluating process in a human being. Before this, however, mind must be explained as the phenomenon of Intelligence that manifests as a faculty.

Mind is a faculty of Intelligence, the cognitive aspect emitted by Spirit-consciousness. Mind is also a power, granting the ability to create, shape and relate to form through thought. Its quality and power define sensation and emotion in physical reality. In the elevated realms of soul and Spirit, the Mind can envision new life patterns that affect all of creation.

What are lower mind and Higher Mind?

Recall the distinctions between lower mind and Higher Mind, as presented on page xviii in the glossary and on page 9.

ORDINARY VS HIGHER MIND

Ordinary/lower mind	*Higher Mind inspiration*
individual concern	collective concern
body-personality needs	whole-body responsiveness
linear thinking	empathy
listening	tuning-in
information	knowledge
pleasure	joy
emotions	sensitivity
calculation	understanding
sharing	partnership

When restricted to material needs, the mind vibrates at a level appropriate to concrete reality. Here it is called the 'lower' or 'concrete' mind. The lower mind functions using logic, rationality; the concrete, lower or thinking mind: these are all names for the insatiable urge of the ordinary person to label, control, foresee and possess all phenomena (including invisible phenomena), yet this same person is unable to access the serene knowingness of true inner discernment. The lower mind's thinking processes are adapted to handling concepts related to weight and density; it is too heavy and constrained to understand or access soul frequencies.

For this, a different kind of thinking is needed, one that employs more feeling and sensitivity than words and concepts; one that knows and discerns what is right and true through an integrated and whole personality. This is the Higher Mind, which flexibly employs lower mind in order to handle concepts and ideas impersonally, but humanely. With this mental flexibility, a new vision and vocabulary emerges in which images and intuition play a great role. Disbelief is suspended. Inner sight is born.

The Higher Mind is an essential tool in our development as human beings and for our eventual expression as Spirit-selves in concrete reality. Lower mind evolves according to the quality of its experiences and the level of attention of an individual, shifting into the cognition of Higher Mind as it progressively connects to higher frequencies of Consciousness. When contact with higher dimensional experience is made, Higher Mind understands and discerns holistically. But in and of itself Higher Mind is useless in the physical dimension; its awareness needs to be translated into concrete reality through the lower mind.

THE SENSES

Sensory awareness is fundamental to the practice of Inner Alchemy, particularly sensation and vision. Besides the known physical senses of sight, hearing, smell, touch and taste, the human being also possesses subtle and inner senses.

One of the favourite complaints of students who believe they cannot visualise is that they do not see the visualised images in the same way they perceive outer objects. It is then that I stress that the vision involved in alchemical work involves all the senses. Alchemical work entails exercises to awaken alternate ways of communicating, intuiting and perceiving.

There are different sorts of intelligence and many ways of 'seeing' and perceiving. A kinaesthetic person will see through their predominant sense, which in this case is tactile. A more intellectual person will see through their mental evocation of things.

In subtle perception, the senses often cross over: one sees through hearing, senses through colour, tastes emotions and smells danger. It is then a question of instilling confidence and awareness in the manner in which each person perceives. Every sense, in a way, has its own kind of seeing. It is up to the student to be guided into validating how it works for them.

There is another depth to sensory capacity which relates to the perception of inner phenomena, involving what I call the 'inner senses'. These are linked to intuition directly and involve feeling, both in its sensory as well as its emotional connotations. An example of this is the activity in dreamlife and meditation, where perception reveals other

There are different sorts of intelligence and many ways of 'seeing' and perceiving. A kinaesthetic person will see through their predominant sense, which in this case is tactile. A more intellectual person will see through their mental evocation of things.

forms of reality that are happening simultaneously to the experience of the physical environment.

AWARENESS, 'BEING CONSCIOUS'

These terms are very closely related. I make a distinction only when I am pointing out the mental process of perception as an understanding 'awareness' and distinguishing it from the whole-body-soul phenomenon of 'being Conscious'.

INTUITION

The term, 'intuition' is used almost synonymously with the terms 'insight' and 'premonition'. Many see it as a form of emotional psychic ability at the lower astral level (please refer to pages 204–6 should you have questions about the astral realm). It might manifest, for instance, as a knot or flutter in the belly, and relates to daily physical phenomena, bringing forth some form of answer, guidance or solution. But this is not the form of intuition I speak of in this book.

Intuition is the voice of higher conscience, as well as the stirrings of Consciousness. It is experienced by the student of Truth at the level of the heart and transmits its language, often going against the reasoning of the mind. Closely allied with the Higher Mind and the soul, intuition is a basic form of 'knowing without knowing'. It may come in flashes and depends largely on the sensitivity and evolution of the individual for their interpretation of the knowing it provides. In its pure form it is not emotional, nor is it a magical or an accidental gift of the select. It, and the certainty that it brings, are the result of spiritual stirrings and sensitive awareness. With sufficient training it becomes the kind of 'knowing' that is typical of higher chakra perception.

Intuition is the voice of higher conscience, as well as the stirrings of Consciousness.

SPIRITUALITY, ESOTERICISM, OCCULTISM

Spirituality is often considered to be a state of Being elevated above the egoistic, self-centred personality. In reality, it is a little more subtle than that: spirituality is a process of gradual refinement of the personality unit, including the body, and it is not separate from ordinary life.

Some esoteric and occult teachings would fall under today's umbrella term of spirituality, but these teachings are only a fraction of what is really encompassed beneath the umbrella, as will become clear throughout this book. Esotericism and occultism are often confused with one another. In this book, esotericism refers to all processes that involve working on the subtle aspects of the self and the world. Occultism, on the other hand, refers to more secret or hidden organisations, methods, rituals and formulae reserved for the limited few. It is 'reserved' for the simple reason that it cannot be understood and, much less, practised by those whose interest is personal power and control. The 'secrets' of the occult have been kept under lock and seal for many centuries. Some of these secrets were revealed at the end of the nineteenth century, which, in turn, provided the catalyst that gave birth to the 'New Age'.

Both terms can cause a visceral reaction among people who confuse the terms with the darker practices. In the case of occultism, there is an association of the occult with 'dark', rather than 'hidden', which is unfortunate. Darker practices stimulate a personal image based on bodily senses and the supremacy of the thinking mind, artfully manipulating the individual to believe they should seek self-gratification and self-worth as the ultimate good.

In the world of matter, Natural Law functions in terms of polarity and duality: higher and lower, white and black, true or false.

THE LAW OF MATTER AND THE LAW OF THE ONE
I refer repeatedly to the activity of these two laws throughout this book.

In the human being, the Law of Matter (Natural Law) rules over physical instincts, the body and nature. It relates to the constitution of the physical world and becomes the foundation of perception and management in the third-dimensional world. When the person perceiving is identified with matter, their world is seen as one of objects and conditions, each composing a separate reality. Humanity collectively considers itself to be apart from Source and innermost Self, whereas great emphasis is placed on personal identity and difference. The principles of the Law of Matter are projected onto everything, even onto Spirit, something that appeals to the agnostic and the doubting Thomas.

In the world of matter, Natural Law functions in terms of polarity and duality: higher and lower, white and black, true or false. Taoism paints a very good picture of this dynamic: Taoism defines life as composed of *yin* and *yang*. *Yin* is the receptive modality and *yang* is the expressive force. Where there is one, the other is present, although not always manifested. This applies to light and dark, and the so-called positive and negative poles. When this duality is understood and managed intelligently, it leads to an equilibrium and balance of forces. One cannot exist without the other.

When thinking is raised beyond the usual polar perspective of separate distinctions and measurement, such as good–bad, better–worse, male–female, more–less, the mind takes on the all-embracing qualities of Light and functions in attunement with the Law of the One. Note that the terms 'Law of the One' and 'Law of Light' (as referred to in Part One) are synonymous and will be used as such throughout the book.

Examples of this way of thinking are thoughts relating to unity and highest ideals such as beauty, service, peace and so on. Everything functions in wholeness and synchronicity, like a great symphony. When the individual is sufficiently sensitive to innermost Self, they begin to perceive the world differently: instead of taking sides, they start to understand the workings of the whole and their responsibility within the whole. Mind and emotions take on a new expression, becoming more refined and compassionate.

Normally, the Law of the One rules the highest level of thought (Higher Mind) and is capable of functioning on multiple levels of conception and imagination. Your thoughts, even the most insignificant, have a tremendous effect upon your physical body and world (more of this will be covered later in the section on the human faculties).

—

Your thoughts, even the most insignificant, have a tremendous effect upon your physical body and world.

—

ALONENESS AND WHOLENESS

Aloneness is not loneliness. To experience aloneness is to experience wholeness. In true aloneness, in the company of yourself, you uncover the mechanisms that create a habit. A habit engenders unconsciousness and mechanical behaviour; it takes the energy away from the awareness of the present moment. In conscious awareness there is constant and total freedom of choice and with that freedom comes a growing responsibility. You are responsible for what you absorb and what you emit. At higher levels you are aware of affecting others and influencing the world.

A person who has experienced the totality of themselves will not look outwardly for gratification, for meaning, for direction. Seeking outside oneself for the answers to life is childish: a demand for energy from the environment in one way or another. Maturity comes with the courage to be alone, and in that aloneness comes fullness, the power, the overflow, the blessing. Usually, this power is given away to parents, partners, bosses and things. You empower others and conditions you think possess an ability you believe you lack. To regain power and the vision of yourself as you truly are, you need to stand alone and, in that aloneness, rediscover the all-potentiality that you are. No one and nothing can do it for you.

LIGHT AND DARK: A CHOICE

The outcomes of the alchemical process, that is, the dissolution of density into Light and the transformation of unconsciousness into discernment, creates a vacuum. This vacuum allows you to attract Light, but also that which is not Light. From the outset, you must know that opening to the Light is also opening to darkness.

It is important to understand the nature of darkness. There are two distinct kinds of darkness: the darkness that contains the Light, and the darkness that shuts the Light out. The first is a phenomenon of a cosmic nature, the second is man-made. Lies, secrecy, trickery and manipulation belong to the second kind. This is negativity, which is not a polarity to the Light, but a negation of it. Most people are confused in the belief that this type of darkness is an essential part of life. Some uphold that it is necessary training; others that it can be easily replaced by rightful thinking. Darkness in the form of negativity is not a necessary part of life; it is a distorted or wrong creation of the personal self, animated and augmented by thousands of years of spiritual and psychological ignorance. It must be embraced by the Light, not ignored or re-formed by the self.

Recognise that Source is the only Presence, the only Intelligence, the only energy and substance acting everywhere. Ultimately Light and Dark are mere energy. Both are of Source. It is the human being that gives them shape and meaning.

The greatest practice that ensures adherence to the Light is the practice of gratitude and the acknowledgement of divine partnership. All practices of Inner Alchemy should end with a benediction, an expression of thankfulness to life, Love and Light.

TRANSMUTATION: EXPANSION AND EVOLUTION

The human essence emerges from the realm of Light and again returns to it after embodiment. Establishing the circuit between matter and Light is the first step towards becoming an integrated whole again. By accessing the Light source that lies at the core of matter, you tap into the power of

> It is important to understand the nature of darkness. There are two distinct kinds of darkness: the darkness that contains the Light, and the darkness that shuts the Light out.

transmutation. As the human being evolves in matter and Consciousness expands, the Light-vacuum created attracts the finest frequencies of Light, catalysing what has been called the alchemical marriage of fire and water: the fire of Spirit, the water of life.

The Master Practice outlined on pages 21–5 (i.e. the Alchemical Alignment) is the basic tool for accessing Light and transmuting matter. It enables transformation, which invites a shift of focus from the ordinary sensory state to a holistic frequency that invokes sublimation. Energy is refined; instead of provoking a 'doing', a higher state of 'being' is induced. The anchor for the body-personality is transferred from the bodily senses to the intelligence of the heart.

The forces of Light illuminate the way towards inner truths that are irrefutable and irreversible once experienced. Only personal experience reveals that there is but one energy, one substance, one source – Spirit-self (God) within. Inner Alchemy is thus a process that leads to the very source of All That Is.

The forces of Light illuminate the way towards inner truths that are irrefutable and irreversible once experienced.

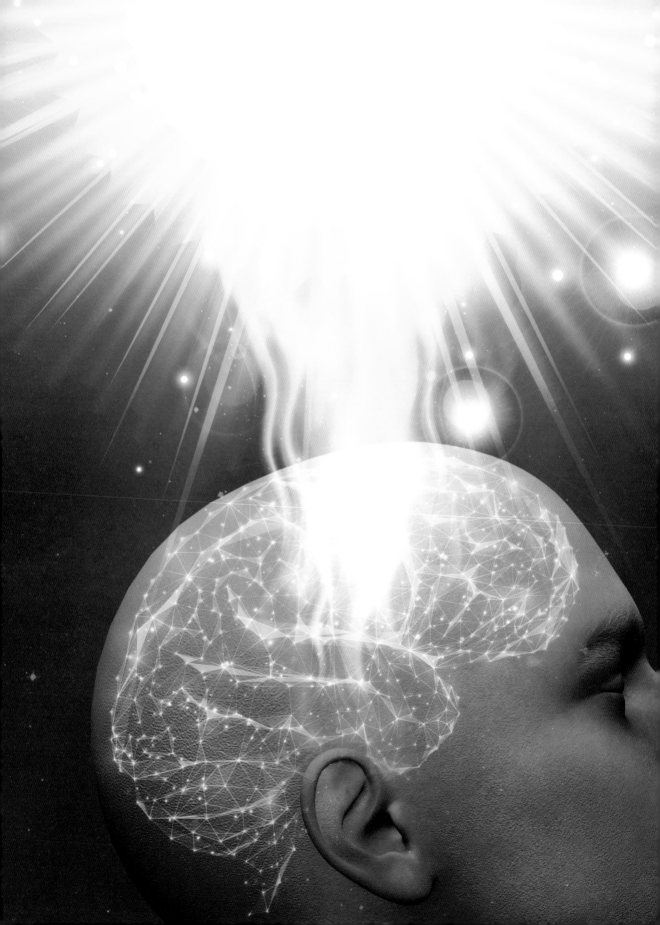

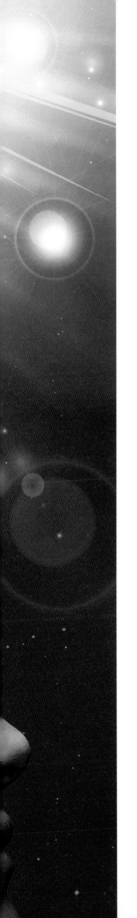

PART TWO

THE HUMAN ENERGETIC ANATOMY

Part Two lays out the theoretical foundation of the Human Energetic Anatomy: the points of Light, the seven bodies, the seven rays and the seven chakras. This is accompanied by an outline of human energetic techniques, meditations and exercises, which teach the reader how to use energy for grounding, protection and healing.

THE HUMAN
ENERGY FIELDS

The human body is a dynamic composite
of different energy fields. What are they?
How do they interrelate, and what directs
them? What happens when we interact
with others? How do we affect or influence
life through them?

The fact is that we lose, dissipate, enhance, disturb or alter our own
energies and that of everything around us. Can we learn to manage our
energy fields appropriately? How may we find and link directly with the
master power that reformulates and directs them?

In this second part of the book, you will learn about human energy fields and how you may direct them ethically and effectively in your world.

Finding answers to basic questions about human energy fields, or 'bodies' as we see them, begins with you in the present moment, in alignment with who and what you really are. Our approach teaches the management of energy and reveals how conscious control entails mastery of the personality. We unfold essential knowledge about transformation, such as the transformation of ordinary human states like fear and anger into more creative and useful states of Being that enhance both self and humanity.

Besides the physical anatomy, the human being possesses a very complex and subtle energetic anatomy that regulates the mind, emotions and the psychic and spiritual faculties. This anatomy responds to the way attention and intention are handled; in other words, to the degree of consciousness (as conscious intelligence) that a person applies in the third dimension. The human energetic network is wholly programmable. If we understand this, we will be able to manifest our creations constructively, since the immediate world is a creation of our own making.

The state of mind of the alchemist must express harmonious control and management of the three lower energy fields or bodies: the physical, the mental and the emotional bodies. Mastery involves, above all, the requalification of emotional energy; nothing is impossible when the individual understands and tempers the emotional body. Control of energy fields requires mental ecology or resourcefulness. This suggests disassociation first, and then requalification of the emotional energy that powers thoughts. In addition, all mastery implies care of and attention to the physical body, with focus on harmony throughout the whole organism. This harmony comes from the recognition that it is the consciousness of the inner self that commands energy into form.

Science, especially medical science, does not understand what makes a human being 'tick' physically, psychologically and spiritually, focusing solely on the physical body. As we see it, our body exerts a powerful influence over life forces everywhere on the planet, while also being subject to all sorts of emissions. This is because the planet is composed of the individual bodies that inhabit it, each with their own emotional and mental fields, as well as being an intelligence beyond the sum total of

> Mastery involves, above all, the requalification of emotional energy; nothing is impossible when the individual understands and tempers the emotional body.

humanity's mindset and emotional constitution. The planet is us and also our potential.

In order for the substance of our bodies, just like planetary matter, to hold together, there needs to be both negative and positive polarity. The electromagnetic charge – the positive and negative poles – of subatomic particles holds atoms and molecules, and therefore matter, together. What we perceive as solid substance is overwhelmingly empty space. It is the charge, the push-and-pull of positive and negative, that creates the physical world. Duality rules matter. This duality, be it light or dark, positive or negative, determines the actions and reactions of humanity and our home, the planet.

At the level of higher consciousness, there is no polarity. When our intelligence attains higher states of awareness, our energy fields are no longer subject to the tension and battle of the positive and negative polarities that rule instinct in the lower bodies.

The way to mastery of the personality, which precedes spiritual mastery, lies in understanding the dualities operating within every human being. The moment you try to force permanence in one polarity (one we might call 'positive'), say joy, love or harmony, without taking into consideration (i.e. ignoring) the other polarity, you create imbalance. Rather than repressing the opposite energy, the intelligent solution is to requalify it. For instance, rather than denying the experience of an emotion, it is integrated within your totality, dissipating its initial charge. The energy of anger, for example, may be transformed into creative initiative, persistence or drive. The energy of fear may be transformed into heightened awareness of surroundings or finer sensibility. Instead of shutting out energy – of any sort – it is possible to alter its quality; this is 'alchemy', which in turn increases one's tolerance level for higher voltages of energy in every way.

Your world is a reflection of your mastery or lack thereof. If you have problems and believe they are someone else's fault, clearly something about you is attracting this experience. Mastery is not attained by thinking lofty thoughts or performing beautiful acts of charity alone. Mastery is reached through your own physical and mental expressions managed consciously, down to the tiniest detail.

Helplessness stems from believing that you are matter alone. It also stems from the belief that you cannot transcend duality. The only way out

—
Your world is a reflection of your mastery or lack thereof. If you have problems and believe they are someone else's fault, clearly something about you is attracting this experience.
—

of this dilemma is to step aside from the personality and identify with a greater state of Being instead.

Understanding your energetic makeup is the first step towards knowing who and what you are. Discovering that we are composed of Light, and not restricted by the polar dynamics of matter, helps us to gain awareness of our true nature.

POINTS OF LIGHT

The first thing to understand about the human energetic anatomy is that within each atom of physical matter is a point of Light that contains the original spark of Light. These points of Light reflect Spirit and constitute your body of Light. Inner Alchemy deliberately trains you to expand them within the centre of your cellular structure under controlled conditions. This expansion of Light within the body at the core is a cellular calibration, a word used to describe the alteration of its vibratory frequency. As we grow in awareness and Consciousness, we become lighter and more vibrant – in every sense.

The purpose of life is to bring down Light and raise (or bless) matter. In this way, matter evolves and Consciousness expands. We do this through integrating the energy from each act, each emotion and each thought. As the process of illumination progresses, it affects all of our bodies, and constructs what is referred to as the rainbow bridge or *antahkarana*: this is the passageway for conscious forces circulating through the entire human energetic anatomy along the spine via the chakra system and is an energetic bridge between the personality and soul (this will be explained in more detail on page 88).

Now I shall move on to a discussion of the three main expressions of the human energetic anatomy – the seven bodies, rays and chakras. In this detailed discussion, however, the basic premise is that every single atom of the body is made up of Light, and it is the expansion of this very Light that we work towards when we explore and refine our energetic anatomy.

The purpose of life is to bring down Light and raise (or bless) matter. In this way, matter evolves and Consciousness expands.

THE SEVEN BODIES

In this book, I use the traditional energetic system of seven fields of subtle energy surrounding a life form. These fields are typically referred to as energy 'bodies'. They are, in 'descending' order:

- Electronic body
- Causal body
- Higher Mental body
- Etheric body
- Lower mental body
- Emotional/astral body
- Physical body

The following illustration is an interpretation of how these seven bodies encase an individual. Not everyone is able (at least without training) to perceive these subtle energy fields visually. Those who are indeed able may also find that their perception differs to this chart. The chart, therefore, merely acts as an approximate guide for the reader and reflects the way we teach the seven bodies.

The Seventh Body: Electronic body

The Sixth Body: Causal body

The Fifth Body: Higher Mental body

The Fourth Body: Etheric body

The Third Body: Lower mental body

The Second Body: Emotional/astral body

The First Body: Physical body

Chart of the Seven Bodies

As discussed previously, when the original spark of Spirit – the Spirit-self – descends into embodiment, it becomes coated in each of these energy fields or bodies. It is important to note that Source, as the original spark, remains active in the uppermost vibrational scale through the higher bodies, providing power and a source of nourishment for all aspects of its lower self. Each body is a kind of step-down transformer, a further condensation of the original Light, until the inherent Spirit-self, after various stages of lowering its frequency, merges with the field of the Earth and acquires a physical form.

Each energy field acts as a protective shield for the next. Each one harbours sentience and faculties appropriate to its frequency. The last body to form is the physical, which acts as a precious container for all the faculties and powers of the previous bodies. The physical body is, in truth, a conglomerate of all the other bodies, but is coated by physical and planetary collective matter and memory. It is subject to the laws of polarity and tension, which together respond to the Law of Matter, or Nature. At this point of embodiment, Consciousness, now wholly immersed in the density of matter, does not recognise the treasures that lie within the body until it begins to awaken and initiate the return journey inward, linking with the faculties and powers of each energy field to return home.

The full array of bodies function unconsciously in the physical world. The upper three bodies are spiritual in nature, serving as interdimensional and cosmic receptors and transmitters for the lower three bodies in their quest for beauty, truth, love and perfection. The upper three bodies interact mainly within higher, spiritual dimensions. The lower three bodies compose of what I refer to as the Personal Energy Bodies (PEBs), and are the known physical, emotional and mental bodies of the physical self and its personality. The frequencies of these lower three bodies are slower. They interact within our physical third dimension and intermediate levels (up to the so-called seventh dimension, which will be clarified in Part Five). The etheric body, which contains the matrix of the lower bodies, serves as a bridge between the lower and higher dimensions.

During the experience of ordinary life, in the search of perfection, some more sensitive human beings have access to a mid-station along the trajectory of Spirit into matter. We may call this mid-station the

---

The full array of bodies function unconsciously in the physical world. The upper three bodies are spiritual in nature, serving as interdimensional and cosmic receptors and transmitters for the lower three bodies in their quest for beauty, truth, love and perfection.

Intelligence of the heart. This is a space in Consciousness that is not part of our rational mind, but is more 'intuitive', neutral and holistic. It is an inner state of knowing. This midway station is the junction between the upper and lower bodies of Consciousness: a mobile positioning that links with dimensional awareness such as the Akashic records, by accessing registers of human experience. It acts as a portal to the soul.

The higher bodies obey the Law of the One. As explained in Part One, this is the law where separation, or duality, does not exist. Their Light-nature makes them appear invisible to the physical senses, but not to the subtle or inner senses. Recall that our senses function at different levels. In the normal range of activities, the physical senses, together with the brain, perceive and evaluate the material world. At the same time, the human being is gifted both with subtle senses that perceive in nonlinear ways and with spiritual (inner) senses that capture invisible forces at work in different dimensions.

Light is the master key to all dimensions of Being. This is why divine or 'Inner' Alchemy functions through formulas and evocation of Light as the means to dimensional access, transformation and, ultimately, transmutation: the recalibration of the lower into the vibrationally higher. Inner Alchemy focuses on the awakening and the integration of the Light body – the Consciousness of Light in matter – with all aspects of living.

Notice that when I refer to the bodies, I am referring to levels of Consciousness, the stages of manifestation of the original spark in its journey into matter.

In the next pages I review the seven bodies and their attributes in 'descending' order. The illustrations resemble Barbara Brennan's models and depict the general characteristics of each of the seven bodies, in order of their creation.

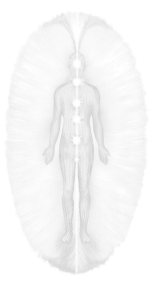

The Seventh Body:
The Electronic Body

THE SEVENTH BODY: THE ELECTRONIC BODY

The electronic body is cylindrically shaped and contains all the other bodies. The substance of the electronic body permeates all the sheaths right into the cellular structure, but is found in its purest spiritual form here. This body is of the finest grade of Light-substance, which appears as threads of silvery-golden Light.

In our dreaming or meditative states, when we feel expanded and uplifted, we are often in touch with the formless purity of the electronic body. It is a cosmic presence with little relation to physicality.

If we could talk about sense-perception from the seventh body's viewpoint, we would say this body is attuned to infinity. The experience is one of huge space, Light, diaphanous substance and vast Light forms.

Aurally, sound here is sensed as white noise or a deep throbbing or humming. Sensorially, there is tremendous peace and stillness, inexplicable and without content. From this level, one has a direct grasp of power, akin to being a sun of majestic proportions with commensurate luminosity.

When an individual is able to maintain awareness at this level, this typically happens, for instance, in meditation in environments that are removed from external – in particular, urban – stimulation, or in extraordinary circumstances, such as during near-death experiences. The experience is what Eastern traditions have called 'seedless-*samadhi*' ('seedless' because there is no perspective from which to observe reality; there is pure 'Being-ness').

Buddhas and enlightened ones who still watch over this planet, as well as our own Spirit-self, reside at this level. In order to reach them and understand their teachings, we must raise our own vibrational frequency. As we rise, they typically descend to blend with us to enable communication at an intermediary level.

The Sixth Body:
The Causal Body

THE SIXTH BODY: THE CAUSAL BODY

The shape of the causal body is egglike, and it occupies a slightly reduced sphere within the container of the seventh body. It has been perceived as a form made up of rays of iridescent pastel Light around the aura. This body is associated with activities at the seventh and higher dimensional levels.

Whereas the electronic body defines the electronic form corresponding to Source, the causal body is the individualised expression of pure Essence. It is the perfect Self; what Christians call the 'Son' in relation to the 'Father'. In the East, consciousness in this body is known as the experience of '*samadhi*-with-seed' (the 'seed' referring to a central vantage point, the 'I', through which reality is perceived). This level embodies the perspective of the 'I AM Presence'.

Brilliant Light and Light forms are perceived, viewed from the centralised perspective of the 'I AM Presence', rather than from the diffused, indefinable, global vision of the seventh body. From our incarnated perception in the third dimension, aural perception of this body is akin to seventh-body perception: a similar deep throbbing or humming. Here, one experiences a sense of majesty, spiritual ecstasy and fulfilment. This level of sensibility on the spiritual plane is similar to emotional feeling at the lower levels of the personality self, only broader and finer, such as the feeling of goodwill, virtue and pure joy in the heart.

When a person's consciousness in embodiment attains the vibration of the causal body, it reaches the same range of frequencies as the Higher Self, the same as the Conscious or Christ-like personality. This is the range at which the mind and feelings express themselves in harmony with the frequency of the spiritual heart. This higher transmuted version of the personal self allows us to embrace a higher state of Being.

It must be understood that this body is not equivalent to the Higher Self, nor to the soul. The Higher Self is a Conscious frequency of Intelligence, and the soul is an energy field and state of Being that uses all the dimensional bodies. The sixth body itself is an energy field that resonates with the needs of both soul and the Higher Self, embodying a perspective with a broadened understanding of who and what we are. For this reason, it has been termed the causal body.

The Fifth Body:
The Higher Mental Body

THE FIFTH BODY: THE HIGHER MENTAL BODY

The shape of the Higher Mental body is more compact and spherical than the two higher bodies. This body harbours a distinct Intelligence, capable of managing all levels of reality. It resembles electric blue webbing.

When Consciousness is activated at this highly developed level of perception, the embodied human perceives his or her own and others' guides and spirits, which appear beautiful and radiant, even godlike. Aurally, here one tunes into one's inner voice and knowing, in partnership with the Higher Self. This is the level where one may gain inspiration and prophecy, where it is possible to see and hear voices and infer meaning. Here, one gains a sense of mastery over the physical vehicle as a unitary experience of the three lower bodies, directly connected to higher forces, imparting strength and certainty.

The Higher Mental body (Mind) acts as a bridge between the higher and lower bodies and has a distinct existence apart from the other bodies. It is a function of Intelligence that reaches beyond dualism, having access to all that we have ever known or been, and all that has ever existed on this planet. This energy field enables you to understand the karmic forces behind actions and become a superconscious discerner: the proverbial watcher.

Let us take a moment to understand that all bodies or states of Consciousness operate separately but also simultaneously. For example, right now, you are here in all of your bodies. Like a television station, your consciousness is tuned into one channel, so you cannot fully grasp that you are also attuned to other levels of reality. You are understanding these words, for instance, through the ability of the lower mind, but your physical and emotional bodies are also involved. Explore what your physical body is sensing and what your feelings say about what you are reading. Notice how your Higher Mind comprehends holistically. Become aware of how your spiritual bodies are 'humming' in a kind of remembrance of what is happening at this moment.

You are, in fact, always in touch with the higher sensitivity you have at the causal level, and with the exquisite vastness of your electronic body. If you can experience all of these things while reading this, you can imagine how much you are also experiencing while talking, dancing, loving and even sleeping!

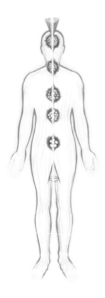

The Fourth Body:
The Etheric Body

THE FOURTH BODY: THE ETHERIC BODY

In the Inner Alchemy system, this body is placed in fourth position (a middle position), although in relation to the physical body, as seen in the illustration on page 47 depicting the layers of the body, it appears immediately next to the physical body. This particular energy field links to all the lower bodies involving the administration of physical resources.

The etheric body is an exact replica of the physical body, but where the physical body is made of matter, the etheric is composed of subtle substance, made up of lines of force. This subtle substance is pre-material, lighter, highly impressionable, and bears the imprints of previous experience in other lives, as well as influence from the stars. Its colour is a very pale silvery-blue, almost white.

The lines of force that make up the structure of the etheric body manifest themselves inside the physical body as energy pathways. This is reflected in the Eastern system of *nadis* or meridians. The energy pathways link together different points within the organism and also serve to connect the body to like points among the other bodies and the Universe.

The etheric body is closer to physical existence than the higher bodies, and thus serves as a link between the dimensions, particularly between the third and the seventh dimensions (which will be clarified in Part Five). The emotional and mental bodies act as instruments for the etheric energy field in out-of-body experiences, a phenomenon also known as astral projection. In this kind of experience, the astrally charged body is attached to the physical body by a silver cord.

This body contains traces of karmic experience accumulated over the past. These impressions shape and mould the etheric body, which, in turn, shapes and moulds the lower mental, emotional and physical bodies we use in daily life.

When consciousness is attuned to this energy field, it perceives more sharply than the physical faculties, as etheric vision heightens the ability to see beyond the density of the body and physical objects. Aurally, this body is capable of enabling telepathy and it has a keen sense of hearing. Sensorially, it evokes more intense stimuli than those found in the physical body. Physiological and psychological gender distinctions (which are absent in the higher bodies) are present for the first time at the level of the etheric body.

The Third Body:
The Lower Mental Body

THE THIRD BODY: THE LOWER MENTAL BODY

The third body corresponds to the lower mental energy field. Like the other bodies, it is a frequency of Consciousness. It is perceived as the shape of the body, composed of pale golden emissions of force.

The seat of the lower mind is the physical brain, a linear force that reflects the consensus of facts as knowledge or information.

The lower mind, like the mass mind that it reflects, operates through emotionally charged beliefs, judgements, superstitions and assessments, employed with a sense of righteousness, directness and personal will. Lower-mental energy is typical in business ethics, and the stock market in particular, where intelligence is used linearly and strategically.

This level reveals a collectively constructed personal consciousness that builds the thoughtforms the emotional field then animates and brings into manifestation. In itself it is devoid of feeling, sensation and even sensitivity. I will discuss this body in greater depth within the section on the power of thought in Part Three.

THE SECOND BODY: THE EMOTIONAL/ASTRAL BODY

The emotional body is a multicoloured, easily agitated, water-like energy field surrounding and interpenetrating the physical body. It is capable of expanding to a large circumference. Everyone knows how a highly emotional, volatile person is capable of filling up an entire room with their mood emissions.

This body has the same properties as water, with currents, whorls, vortices and eddies; and, like water, it can be refreshing, cool and nourishing, or heavy, stormy and disturbing. The nature of this particular energy is tremendously dynamic. Emotions gather substance and stir thought into expression. This body has also been called by some the 'astral' (meaning 'star-like') body, when used to project emotions. Emotions can become so intense that, before we know it, we are swept away by them, pulled into some emotional whirlpool that is difficult to subdue or control, especially as it will tend to travel towards the object of its desire.

The Second Body:
The Emotional/Astral Body

The emotional body has been the target of massive experimentation, particularly during the encounter and growth groups of the 1960s and 1970s. It is the body through which we may experience ourselves as relational agents experiencing others: where we feel ourselves feeling others.

The emotional body is not limited to time and space. It moves with ease and agility. Lovers know the feeling when their loved one is thinking of them or when their loved one has been unfaithful. They know this intuitively through the sensing mechanisms of the emotional body, which resemble antennae and easily attach themselves to their objects of affection.

A person who is emotionally dependent is easily bored and needs to create drama after drama to remain interested in life. Conversely, a person with a harmonious emotional body is a delight to be with. It is the intuitive vessel that can feel with the heart of the Spirit-self and transmit that Love emotionally to all of creation.

This body and the dynamics of feeling and emotion will be discussed in more detail in the section on chakras and in Part Three (on the power of feeling, see page 108).

THE FIRST BODY: THE PHYSICAL BODY

This is the ordinary physical body. The building of this body is a result of Spirit's capacity to draw substance (matter) from the Earth. This assures that the human being is committed to the evolution and safekeeping of the Earth; what we do to our bodies, we do to the planet, and vice versa. Physical bodies consist of the same dense matter as the Earth and reflect the planetary status of the moment. For instance, as the Earth's climate changes, the temperature of our bodies changes too. Practising ecology with our bodies goes hand in hand with ecological concerns for the Earth.

Not everything that is manifested in the physical body has its origins in personal past history: this body carries ancestral and collective history as imprints for each human to refine. The quality of Consciousness in embodiment, or the quality of a person's life, can help transmute much of the 'pollution' that has been generated throughout time.

The physical body reveals our emotional and mental attitudes. Practices such as Reichian and neo-Reichian therapies, bioenergetics, Reiki, and many more, concern themselves with reading and working with body types shaped by personal use and preference. Some may read a person's character by the way the shoulders sit, by the slant of the hips, by the angle of the legs, by the way they hold the feet or the shape of their toes and by the set of the jaw or face. The body is a map, which may be read by a trained practitioner. Everything shows up.

The physical body exists only in third-dimensional time and space. It can only be 'here' as an absorbing 'now' experience of material reality. When a person is focused on physicality, he cannot perceive other realms of activity. The vibration of this level is slow and restricted to dense sensory stimulation and attunement to earthly forms.

The number seven plays an important part in the energetic dynamic present in manifest reality, including in the human energetic anatomy – there are seven bodies, but there are also seven rays and seven primary chakras. In the following section I address the role of the seven rays, followed by the seven primary chakras.

The First Body:
The Physical Body

THE SEVEN RAYS

There are seven varieties of energy responsible for the existence of all life on our planet. These are the 'Seven Rays', which some refer to as the 'Seven Sacred/Divine Flames'. The descriptive terms referring to a ray or flame are metaphors. In essence, a ray is a name given to a particular type of energy expression with the emphasis placed upon the quality that it exhibits. A ray follows a directional impulse towards our physical world. When it contacts the gravitational pull of the Earth, its magnetism causes it to transform into a flame, creating the upwards motion of enfolding fire.

The seven rays are the building blocks of the Universe: they are the basic emanations from Source and imbue all of creation. These vital rays carry frequencies and qualities of divine Light in order to direct, ignite, dissolve, temper or define planetary affairs. This includes the human being: we are constantly shaped and informed by the frequencies of the rays. These rays give meaning to the world of matter and serve the urge towards evolution.

There is a distinction vibrationally between what is described as a ray versus a flame. At their core they are of the same fundamental emanation and can be likened to different colours on a spectrum, merely different manifestations of light.[1] Each body of expression and psychological constitution of the personality is determined by one of the seven rays.

Reference to the seven rays can be found in teachings throughout human history, including in ancient Egyptian and Vedic traditions, Christian iconography, and, most recently, in the New Age wisdom, introduced through the writings of Helena Blavatsky, Alice Bailey, Rudolph Steiner and others.

Each one of the rays manifests a particular aspect, or spectrum, of qualities. They project force, and as they enter into the physical atmosphere, they colour that atmosphere. Each ray resonates a quality, colour and even a musical note.

As discussed previously, Source is an undifferentiated energy field of the highest frequencies, containing all uncreated life, and the human being is essentially a spark of Source at its core. The Elohim can be

> A ray follows a directional impulse towards our physical world. When it contacts the gravitational pull of the Earth, its magnetism causes it to transform into a flame, creating the upwards motion of enfolding fire.

---

1 Some esoteric energy healers use the 'lower' versions, or frequencies, of the rays to work on the lower four bodies of an individual, and the 'higher' versions of the rays (i.e. the 'flames' of the same core ray) to work on the higher energy bodies of an individual. In Inner Alchemy, we tend to use flames for the lower bodies and also for the finer light bodies, with some exceptions.

considered a collective name for 'God'. Their creative Intelligence (Consciousness) is responsible for the emission of the seven rays with the full spectrum of frequencies.

The rays determine energetic function through the qualities of the human bodies and the chakra system (discussed shortly).

The soul ray of an individual, in our teachings, does not change with each incarnation. It is the ray of the interdimensional or conscious Self; the hallmark of individual essence.

A personality ray shapes temperament and determines individual life purpose and the aspirations that compelled us into incarnation. It changes according to incarnational purpose for each lifetime.

Rays colour emotional, mental and physical bodies, lending them attributes that the Self has chosen to work through prior to embodiment. They determine the manner in which we complete our life's purpose and also vary in every lifetime.

The rays influence attitudes, desires and *modus operandi*, creating the environment for individual expression, creativity and uniqueness. Not only our strengths and virtues, but also problems and vices in the personality makeup respond to the influence of the rays.

This is what the science of esoteric astrology, based on the study of the seven rays, teaches us. The system of soul-personality typology in esoteric astrology (also known as esoteric psychology) can help us identify the ray composition of an individual. Some esoteric astrologers, and also some particularly skilled energy healers and workers, are able to determine an individual's ray composition. Knowing which rays influence which aspects of the personality helps the human being to know their Self, to serve themselves consciously to identify the current life purpose and to aid their evolution and service in the world.

Rays qualify the soul, the Spirit-self, the personality and all of the human bodies (fields). They play a vital role in that unseen part of human psychology.

I shall go through the rays and their qualities one by one below. Before doing so, note that there are three primary rays and four secondary rays. The first three rays are the primary expression of qualities from Source: Will, Wisdom and (Divine) Love. These form the basic Father/Mother–Son–Spirit trinity. The remaining four secondary rays emanate from the third of these primary rays (the ray of divine creativity as the emission of Love).

THE FIRST RAY: WILL OF GOD

The first ray represents the Father–Mother aspect of the basic trinity. It is the force that impels life (activity) forwards. It is the quality of pure Will, which develops into strength, determination and leadership, and instils protection, power, initiative and faith. Its colour is blue, from indigo and cobalt to cornflower blue: strong, cool and penetrating, primordial and infinite.

The first ray invokes power, will and abundance, and is used to break up matter and help integrate it with Light. This ray rules leaders, executives and people who 'get things done'.

It is perceived as tremendous power in the form of a sword, a blue flame, a bolt of lightning or electricity. In visualisation, it may be used in different shades of blue as a strong protective shield over people, places or things, and even parts of the body (particularly around the throat chakra, its home base on the physical body). Its force is most imminent at the level of the causal body.

THE SECOND RAY: ILLUMINATION, OR WISDOM THROUGH LOVE

The second ray of the trinity represents the Son–Daughter quality in relation to the Father–Mother aspect. After the initial propulsion of force from Source, this force reconsiders itself; it evaluates, enlightens and teaches. It is the directing Intelligence which illuminates, and, as such, inspires discrimination, discretion and discernment. Its colour is yellow, like the Sun, representing illumination and intelligence.

The second ray refines the mind and clarifies the intelligence of an individual, providing a balance between the first and third rays; between Power and Love. Invoking this ray can soothe human activity, particularly the nervous system. The second ray may be visualised as pale golden or brilliant yellow gold, the latter serving to accelerate our vibration and give us access to higher dimensions. It is often evoked as golden liquid Light, as sunshine, and can be used as golden oil over the nervous system, or as a golden seal over the solar plexus.

This is the ray that represents the planetary activity of both Jesus and Buddha and their mission on this planet. It rules teachers, education and students. It is active in any walk of life where there is a need for practical, compassionate understanding and wisdom. The second ray colours the Christ Consciousness (another term I use for the soul), which we could say resonates in the heart centre in the body.

THE THIRD RAY: DIVINE LOVE, OR INTELLIGENCE OF THE HEART

The third ray represents the creative action of Spirit: the Holy Spirit aspect in the trinity. Where the roles of the first two rays are to create and to comprehend existence, the third ray concerns itself with the pure play and infinite creativity stemming from wholeness that enables manifestation. This ray is divine experience as the power of Love – the sustaining, cohesive force of the Universe. It births the remaining four of the seven rays (including overseeing all nature and planetary life). Its colour is pink, from deep magenta to pale rose.

The third ray is used to penetrate where sheer power would shatter. As its quality is that of the sustaining force and harmoniser, the third ray sustains, purifies and raises the human frequency and the world. It draws forth the good from people.

It dismantles patterns obstructing inner or self-love and is useful for toning down angry or hate-filled people by inducing the softening activity of the soul, which is Love.

As a source of inspiration and peace, the third ray rules artists, arbitrators and peacemakers. St Francis of Assisi perfectly embodies the qualities of brotherhood and goodwill of the third ray.

The following four rays originate from the third ray, generated from Source, the central pool of Spirit.

THE FOURTH RAY: HARMONY THROUGH CONFLICT

The fourth ray is called the ray of harmony through conflict, not because it fosters adversity, but because it promotes a stability that can only be achieved through the experimentation of polarity or duality. Ideas are born, and, when applied to life situations, forms are created through a process of trial and error.

The colour of this ray is white, crystal or the transparency of water, representing its commitment to maintaining purity and harmony. It is the colour of purity seen around angelic apparitions, the same as the ascension flame that surrounds the body during transmutation and transition.

This ray deals with the expansion and contraction of the original impulses from Source, as that contraction brings forth further expansion. Its qualities instil integrity and purity through all of life's testing grounds. The fourth ray rules builders, architects, engineers, musicians and artists.

One of the wonderful uses of this ray is as a stream through the brain, linking our thinking to the soul. The seat of this ray can be found at the base of the spine in the human body. Its fluid crystal colour is the substance of the silver cord connecting the etheric body to the physical body at the astral level. It is also the texture of the Tube of Light invoked in the Master Practice.

THE FIFTH RAY: SCIENCE AND TRUTH

The fifth ray involves the systematic application of cosmic order, and through it we understand the exactitude of the Universe and the pure mathematical accuracy of the laws of creation. Representing truth in all its aspects, this ray characterises scientific endeavour. Its qualities are concentration, precision, justice and dedication to service, and it instils these values to aid those serving the Light. The colour of this ray is green.

Since it is also the ray most frequently used for healing, this ray rules vocations not only in science (e.g. scientific researchers and inventors), but in healing too, such as nursing, medicine and healing in general, where structural precision is implied.

As a flame, it is used to transmute limitation and develop inner vision. Its force is most imminent at the level of the lower mental body, and its seat is at the level of the third eye.

THE SIXTH RAY: DEVOTION

This ray imparts spiritual nourishment, vitality and the sustaining power of peace to uphold manifestation. The sixth ray inspires a return to Source through devotion and service. Its role is to hold the peace, and it is closely linked to human emotion and its spiritualisation. This ray is a ruby-gold colour.

As a flame, it is used to transmute limitation and develop inner vision. Its force is most imminent at the level of the lower mental body, and its seat is at the level of the third eye.

The sixth ray can be visualised and used as a laser to penetrate and shatter emotional condensations. It can be pictured as a boiling ruby oil, which opens up to the subconscious; or as a ruby ray, which dissolves density. You may visualise it as a ruby cylinder enfolding you, sheltering you from projections and negative influences. As a form of protection, it seals off negative aspects of the lower world until they can be transformed.

Since its qualities are spiritual vitality, peace, tranquillity, healing, impersonal love and ministration, this ray rules priests, healers and all professions where unconditional devotion, mercy and forgiveness are called for.

The use of the sixth ray was prevalent in biblical times and during the time of Jesus's life. It is a very intense ray, particularly as it affects the emotional body and its activities through the solar plexus. Its use has been largely de-emphasised and transferred to the second primary ray, the yellow-gold ray.

—

The use of the sixth ray was prevalent in biblical times and during the time of Jesus's life.

—

THE SEVENTH RAY: FREEDOM AND CEREMONY

The seventh ray is violet and its characteristic is that of cosmic 'spring cleaning'. It serves as a transmuting fire, and a purifying, healing, regenerating force, leading to the qualitatively different style of life now emerging upon the planet. The transcendence this ray inspires is from individual to global consciousness, from the personal to the impersonal, from the mundane to the spiritual. The violet ray is the most active at the moment, promoting alchemy and enabling conscious transmutation or requalification of matter. It is the colour for mastery over the physical plane, visualised as a violet flame or pillar of fire.

This ray evokes ritual, or rhythmic activity, such as invocations, chants, decrees, sound and the spoken word, generating greater momentum or energy to enable power for transformation. Its qualities include the purification, sublimation and redemption of existing forms and their energies, ruling those involved in service of a higher global order, and diplomacy.

This ray is seated in the etheric body, and works through the second (sacral) chakra, affecting all levels of physicality. It facilitates integration of the soul and the Spirit-self within our physical vessel.

Our age is marked by a transition to the cycle of the violet ray, shown by the influx of the ascended master teachings of St Germain, the celebrated alchemist of European history and master of the seventh ray.[2] The prevalence of this ray is also characterised by the upsurge of ritual, ceremonial magic and ancient practices, particularly those of Druid or Earth worship.

Although in this book I focus only on the seven rays outlined above, there are other rays coming into activity – the gold and silver rays for instance – which serve to raise the frequency of our atomic structure for interdimensional purposes.

When considering which rays influence your psychology, ask yourself which colours you have an affinity with and which colours repel you. How do different colours affect you? Make a chart of your reactions. Which ray type do you think you fall under? For instance, a first ray person, ruled by divine Will, will show virtues such as strength, courage and an ability to effect real change, but they may, more often than not, exhibit obstinacy, pride, arrogance and many other vices on this spectrum, and should learn how to embody virtues typical of other rays, such as humility, tenderness and tolerance.

The rays are used in meditations and exercises in alchemical practices in order to sublimate matter and bring harmony to form. Opposite is a recommended beginning meditation practice using the seven rays.

Understand that the rays exist in another dimension of Consciousness altogether, not in our usual third-dimensional reality. As with our Spirit, there is no 'place' where the rays may be found. They are part of that eternal no-space within us, which will be better understood when you read the chapter on multidimensionality. As with our own Presence and the Tube of Light in the illustration of the Master Practice, to us, the rays 'appear' to descend from a fathomless space beyond and above us. In truth, both our Presence and the rays are within us, as is All That Is.

The meditation is an excellent one to record and listen to at leisure as many times as you wish. As preparation, you might want to find sheets of coloured paper in the seven deepest shades of each ray. They should be large enough to tape onto a wall before you, helping you imprint the visuals of each colour. When you are able to transfer the impression of

> When considering which rays influence your psychology, ask yourself which colours you have an affinity with and which colours repel you. How do different colours affect you?

2 See my book, *Divine Alchemy*, for more details on rays and masters.

colour from without to within, you may close your eyes and begin with the visualisation suggested below.

In Inner Alchemy, the rays and their corresponding flames are the foundation of our work with Light. This meditation is given to offer a direct experience of the rays and flames in order to understand the qualities they bring to humanity and to the Earth. As Light springs into being, it acquires consistency and definition through the dimensions. Pure Light is transformed into qualities and substance and permeates matter.

In a gentle, almost affectionate manner, without worrying if you have 'got it' or not, I suggest you explore the ways these forms of Light might affect your body, mind and feelings. You will have an opportunity to apply them in the fiery form of suns and colour later in this book.

For purposes of simplification, the meditation is conducted from the perspective of the third-dimensional body/self, where Light as rays appear to shower down upon you, at times becoming liquid and at other times fires upon contact with matter.

 ## MEDITATION ON THE SEVEN RAYS

Do the Master Practice as outlined in Part One (see pages 21–5) as preliminary preparation for this meditation on the rays.

THE FIRST RAY: THE BLUE RAY

From the Presence within and above emerges the first of the seven great rays of creation: the blue ray.

Notice how all the shades of blue, from deepest navy and indigo to sky blue are contained within it, appearing to spill down and fan out onto all of creation, including onto your own physical form.

Allow yourself to see and sense the activity of this ray.

Receive the ray as if from a radiant spotlight above you. It appears magnificent, with silvery specks, representing absolute power and divine Will, imposing authority and presence. The blue ray enfolds you, yet as it reaches the ground it ignites into blue flames. The blessing of the blue ray and the blue flames is one of shattering imperfection in order to clear the way for new forms.

Allow yourself to see and sense this ray with its corresponding flame.

Notice the difference between the impact of the ray from above and the flames from below on your body and your mind.

Explore how each one affects you. How do you experience this power? How does it reflect in your own use of will, force, leadership and authority? How may you best use it?

Feel strong and whole and independent within its embrace. Allow yourself to be powerful and to *know*. Affirm the purity, wholeness and perfection you experience.

THE SECOND RAY: THE YELLOW RAY

From the Presence within and above now springs the second of the seven great rays of creation: the yellow ray, in all its shades, from the deepest gold to the palest yellow. The yellow ray is sensed as a sparkling cascade of golden specks, like the effervescence of a sun.

Recognise solar qualities within you as Source. Remember the times you have brought light and joy to others.

Notice how the Light of this ray evokes illumination and wisdom. It is the colour of Intelligence, in perfect equilibrium between Power and Love. It stands for a refined mind as inspiration for peace.

How would you be if you knew you were a sun? Surround yourself with the light of the sun. Breathe it in. Feel it.

Sense the solar luminosity as pale gold, becoming liquid golden Light as it pours over you, saturating your brain, coursing through your spinal column and strengthening your nerves. Allow it to refine the grey matter of your brain and quicken it with higher Consciousness. It may remind you of the quality of great teachers such as the Buddha or the Christ. How would you be, if you acknowledged that you too are wise?

The First Ray: The Blue Ray

Incorporate the principles this ray stands for: caring for humanity without pride, gently and invisibly instructing, guiding and correcting. Become a brother, a sister, a son, a father and a mother to all through Love and through example.

THE THIRD RAY: THE PINK RAY

From the Presence within and above springs the third of the seven great rays of creation: the pink ray. Observe all its shades, from the deepest rose to the sheerest touches of palest pink pouring over you and spilling down and over all creation. As it descends, notice how it acquires consistency and definition, how it transforms from pure Light to eventually nourish matter.

Feel the smoothness of this ray as it relaxes, blends and enfolds you so that the divine plan might unfold. It is nourishment to all of nature, and it holds you in Love's safety, softening sensations and emotions so that you might function intelligently. This ray is associated with motherly love, the purity and potency of a love that allows you to be and to know – it is divine Love.

Ask and feel: how do you experience the qualities of this ray in your life?

This ray directly affects the heart centre in the middle of the chest. It represents the activity of the Holy Spirit, that creative expression of Love in you.

Allow it to spread from your heart and out onto your entire body and aura, gently, deeply; compassionately dissolving all crystallisations of ego through the sheer force of Love. The teachings of peace become manifest in the dynamic fullness of Love, making forgiveness and understanding possible.

Breathe it in! Feel it penetrating into the cells of your body, healing you and making you whole. Radiate this quality to others.

THE FOURTH RAY: THE CRYSTAL-WHITE RAY

From the Presence within and above springs the fourth of the seven great rays of creation: the crystal-white ray.

The white ray appears brilliant as a crystal sun and represents absolute purity. It is the force that allows us to sustain the divine plan without distortion and underlies impersonal service to humanity.

This ray directly affects the heart centre in the middle of the chest. It represents the activity of the Holy Spirit, that creative expression of Love in you.

It is the Light-substance of your own Tube of Light and maintains the divine pattern in the body. Its force also liberates the soul from the hold of the body at the moment of death.

This ray emits the qualities of harmony and beauty through the resolution of opposing forces, the polarities that underlie the structure of matter. Accept the power of harmony within, assuming integrity through purity.

See the activity of this ray as an expression of creativity. Feel this crystal-white ray radiating into all your cells, its fire purifying, re-qualifying and quickening.

Recognise this purity in you, as you are.

Determine to assume responsibility for the force and power of the crystal-white ray with courage and dignity, so that you may become an agent in the preservation of sanctity everywhere.

THE FIFTH RAY: THE GREEN RAY

From the Presence within and above springs the fifth of the seven great rays of creation: the green ray. Notice all the shades of green, from deepest forest and olive to palest lime emerging within and spilling onto all of life.

Green is the ray of fertility, defining nature, truth and science as manifestations of ordered Intelligence. It puts us in direct contact with the Mind of divinity, inspiring the systematic activity of cosmic law. It inspires abnegation, concentration and consecration to the service of the Light, ruling over all expressions of the Law of the One, such as materialisation, etherealisation, levitation and healing in general.

As a Light-substance it nourishes life. As a flame it is used in transmuting activities, addressing the development of inner vision and the correct functioning of the concrete mind.

Attract this ray into your physical self now and allow it to penetrate deeply as emerald foam into your brain; may it bring you the power of discernment and correct discrimination. Accept its energy radiating your mind as it links to the heart and brings you the ability to understand form, measure and the workings of the Law of the One with precision.

Affirm yourself as a constructive, productive and discriminating divine Intelligence.

Know that your own Presence is the only power, intelligence and substance in your world.

> Attract this ray into your physical self now and allow it to penetrate deeply as emerald foam into your brain; may it bring you the power of discernment and correct discrimination.

THE SIXTH RAY: THE RUBY RAY

From the Presence within and above springs the sixth of the seven great rays of creation: the ruby ray, manifesting in all shades of red from the lightest to the deepest crimson and maroon, fanning out onto all creation.

The ruby ray becomes both liquid Light and a flame as it contacts matter, inspiring devotion and impersonal Love that affects, transmutes, protects and corrects the lower emotions. The ruby ray appears majestic, speckled with golden iridescence and provides spiritual nourishment, radiating the qualities of piety, tranquillity and the healing powers of the priesthood. It is the ultimate force that sustains peace in the world.

Allow yourself to be impregnated by this ray and recognise how it affects your emotions.

Sense its quality deep within you as your own bloodstream and the fluid of life in the chamber of the heart. Accept its blessing into each cell of your body as you accept life itself.

Visualised as a balm, this ray seals and dissolves all crystallised negativity. Let it work on and through you freely, dissolving all traces of the unconsciousness of the past.

Learn the true power of forgiveness and correct devotion so that you may become a healing force among humanity, in true humility.

Accept the ray, visualised both as a balm and also as liquid, as both of its forms seep into all your bodies, consecrating you as a priest or priestess of the Light.

THE SEVENTH RAY: THE VIOLET RAY

From the Presence within and above springs the last of the seven great rays of creation: the violet ray. Become aware of its descent and the ignition of a fiery field around you arising from the Earth itself, bringing freedom through refinement.

Violet is the ray of transmutation through obedience and application of the universal principles of vibration, which underly ceremonial magic and ritual.

This ray teaches us mastery over the physical plane, affecting all levels of matter and facilitating the connection and collaboration with the Self. It acts through rhythm, sound and the spoken word.

Bathe yourself in the power of this purifying, transformative ray that spills over into your world, your relationships, and your affairs, into your country and into the entire planet. Liberty means breaking the chains of self-imposed limitation. Be grateful for the grace that comes from this ray.

Saturate your body with the violet ray and call it into your world. Sense its effect over you now as you embrace all of humanity.

INTEGRATION

Arise to your full stature and glory and accept the powers invested in you with the tremendous joy of freedom. Allow your body and personality to fuse with your Being and with Source.

Feel yourself crowned by the divine powers in you: will, wisdom, divine Love, harmony and creativity, science and truth, devotion and inspiration, order and rhythm, and the power of transmutation.

Affirm the power of Light in this and all worlds. Recognise how Light becomes manifest and the divine plan is revealed to whomsoever has the will to know and to be: affirm, 'So Be It'!

THE CHAKRAS

The chakras (also referred to as 'centres') are focus-points of energy and cone-like vortices contained within the etheric body that act as receivers and transmitters for the rays. The chakras process energies and colour human activity. They function through the endocrine glands that affect body functions, mental balance and emotional integrity at the physical level. They are also windows to interdimensional perception. The chakras are a reflection of the level of consciousness a person employs, and thus they may be used either constructively or discordantly, according to the level of consciousness held by the individual. Like all energy, the chakras themselves are neutral and they manifest the result, rather than constitute the cause of behaviour. Sometimes they are overstimulated; sometimes under-stimulated, just like the glands they rule. They are never entirely blocked or closed.

The chakras are many in number. Systems such as acupuncture and *shiatsu* allude to as many as three hundred or more foci. Others teach there are as few as three major energy vortexes. For our purposes, there are seven major chakras.

The seven major chakras are loosely related to the seven bodies, but their activity is mostly concerned with Earth life and development. The

—

The chakras are focus-points of energy and cone-like vortices contained within the etheric body that act as receivers and transmitters for the rays.

—

lowest chakra relates to the affairs of embodiment in matter, and the highest, or seventh, concerns itself with the leap from the material to the cosmic dimensions.

Mastery of the chakras implies embodying each of them in conscious awareness in daily life. Chakras are not things: they are energy openings to universal forces through which we, as active consciousness, receive and emit energies. Once we awaken to the fact that we are the ones who control and use them, and not the inverse, then we are on the path to their mastery.

The following illustration reveals the position of the seven major chakras, including frontal and posterior vortices.

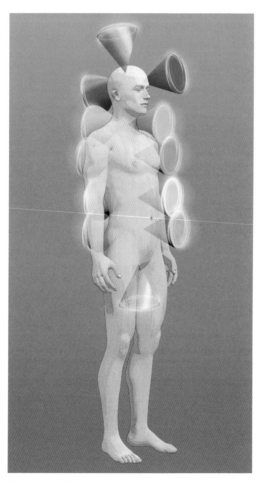

The Seven Chakras

The first chakra is also referred to as the base or root chakra; the second – the sacral; the third – the solar plexus; the fourth – the heart; the fifth – the throat; the sixth – the third eye; and the seventh – the crown centre.

There is a certain interrelationship between the seven chakras, the seven rays and the seven bodies/fields. The following two tables summarise this interrelationship.

THE CHAKRAS AND THEIR CORRESPONDING RAYS

Chakra	Ray
First (base) Colour: red	Fourth ray (harmony through conflict) Colour: crystal
Second (sacral) Colour: orange	Seventh ray (freedom and ceremony) Colour: violet
Third (solar plexus) Colour: yellow	Sixth ray (devotion) Colour: ruby
Fourth (heart) Colour: green	Third ray (Divine Love/Intelligence of the heart) Colour: pink
Fifth (throat) Colour: blue	First ray (Will of God) Colour: blue
Sixth (third eye) Colour: indigo	Fifth ray (science and truth) Colour: green
Seventh (crown) Colour: violet	Second ray (illumination/wisdom through Love) Colour: yellow-gold

THE SEVEN BODIES AND THEIR CORRESPONDING CHAKRAS

Body	Corresponding chakra/s; attributes
First body *(physical)*	Seat at the base of the spine, in the area of the base chakra. The densest bodily sheath, acting as repository of the substance of all the bodies. Transmits all the energies from the rays through the chakras (represented by the endocrine system). Exists in third-dimensional time and space only.
Second body *(emotional)*	Seat in the area of the pelvis and the stomach, as it acts through a combination of the second and third chakra energies. In conjunction with the third body, it translates feelings into actions on the physical plane, drawing on the necessary substance for manifestation. Responds rapidly to stimuli with sensitive antennae. Responds to finer vibrations; enjoys intensity and change. Its feeling capacity ranges from animal passions to unselfish love. Not limited to time and space.
Third body *(lower mental)*	Seat is the solar plexus, in the area of the third chakra. The logical or concrete mind. Translates thoughts from higher planes for the purpose of implementation on the physical level. Builds thoughtforms largely from the mass-mind. Subject to illusion and control.
Fourth body *(etheric)*	Connected through a silver cord to the physical body. Contains the Light pattern body, which holds astrological energies and is the blueprint for all the chakras. Also the mould of the physical body: contains the etheric records. Coloured by mental and emotional activity. It provides an opportunity to learn mastery over our impact in the world. This body is the bridge between upper and lower vibratory frequencies (dimensions and body fields).
Fifth body *(Higher Mental)*	Seat is the throat and third eye area, the position of the fifth and sixth chakras. Mind beyond dualistic thinking: home of intuition and knowing. The discriminatory faculty of the superconscious but can be subject to illusion. Acts as the link between Christ Consciousness/soul and the personality.
Sixth body *(causal)*	Seat is in the area of the third eye,[3] at both the sixth and seventh chakras. The perfected Self (and as such is in affinity with the soul/Christ Consciousness). The storehouse of treasures and talents from Source.
Seventh body *(electronic)*	Home of the Spirit-self, and therefore not confined to the chakras. Its field extends at least thirty feet (nine metres) over the top of the head and around the body; thus, it is somewhat associated with expansive capacity of the seventh chakra. Essence: individualised God-presence or Source. It radiates pure unqualified energy for use in all bodies.

---

3 The third eye is, in fact, the joint activity of the pituitary and pineal glands, which are very close together. The pineal gland has no real power; it is a centre for the reception and fine activity of Light (called *akasha*), whereas the pituitary is a cognitive centre.

The qualities, functions and location of each of the spinal chakras will be outlined one by one, as follows. Understand that although each chakra function is described separately, they work together as a whole.

With the exception of the base and the crown chakras, each chakra has a dual function; outward or extroverted (worldly) activity and a counterpart of inner or introverted (spiritual) activity, and this will be discussed in the descriptions of each chakra. A chakra's 'worldly' activity means its role in organ regulation, for example, or its effect on the personality. Its 'spiritual' activity means its role in managing higher-body energies or enabling higher-dimensional contact, or in developing non-physical powers such as foresight. The root (first) chakra pertains to worldly activity (survival, physical matter), whereas the crown (seventh) chakra deals with higher consciousness and spiritual questions.

THE FIRST OR BASE CHAKRA

The first chakra is located at the base of the spine. The functioning of the first (base or root) chakra determines our connection to the Earth and to matter. The experiences of the base chakra revolve around physicality, security, strength and stability. It is the anchor of Spirit.

When this chakra is activated by personal desire, the individual seeks to satisfy the craving triggered at the physical level. Once satisfied, the impulse recedes. With consistent drainage of energy from this chakra to fulfil personal impulse, the satisfaction never rises beyond its initial intensity, leading the individual to operate according to, what I call, the 'itch' syndrome. This is what happens at the instinctual or animalistic level of existence.

Raw sex, equivalent to animal lust, passion devoid of individuality and tenderness, is a typical manifestation of the 'worldly' activity of the base chakra; the drive for instant gratification, focused exclusively on the self. The main objective at this level is survival, where self-needs such as food, sex, security and sensation are imminent. When, however, the individual desire is activated by higher aspirational levels, such as pure feeling or unconditional Love, a delay of satisfaction occurs at the lower frequency levels until the higher need is quelled. The satisfaction may even be transferred to another dimension altogether, whereby the initial lower stimulus would be sublimated.

As the centre responsible for invoking and creating a life form, the essential power of this chakra is one of extreme purity. Mastery over this centre can only be achieved through purity of mind and action, and the acknowledgement of the responsibility that comes with the perception of oneself as a spiritual embodiment in partnership with Earth and its forces. The individual needs an integrated, healthy base chakra for all Earth-plane activity, much as a tree needs sound roots in order to be able to soar higher into the heavens.

The base chakra is the seat of the most intense physical energy in the human body. Along the spine there is a particular kind of tissue responsible for holding the body in shape. When this tissue is not working properly, disease takes over and the body begins a process of deterioration. The wilful misuse of this chakra results in numerous spinal and haemorrhoidal problems on the physical level; a loss of resources or control on the emotional and social levels; and a sense of alienation on the spiritual level. These problems provide lessons surrounding the right use of will and the correct focus of attention. The aspiring alchemist should notice where attention is being focused, and whether positive or negative attributes are being expressed in order to choose how to clear, refine and expand beyond instinct.

The colour that has been connected with the base chakra is red, which activates the motor mechanism at the densest levels, propelling it towards experience. The colour of a compromised chakra appears in varying stages of muddiness and distortion. The colour of the purified chakra, however, appears white, the same colour associated with this chakra's ray: the fourth ray. This ray and chakra are closely associated in the way their activities involve form-building, purification and refinement. The fourth ray triggers the adrenal glands (the fight-or-flight mechanisms), the kidneys (fear) and the spinal column.

THE SECOND OR SACRAL CHAKRA

The second chakra is centred in the physical body, around the reproductive organs. This is where indwelling Consciousness seeks to experience and relate to the outside world, including other people. This chakra has much to do with the exchange of energies, as it is associated with emotions.

> The base chakra is the seat of the most intense physical energy in the human body.

Emotional training involves expanding the capacity to receive and to give. When this capacity is blocked, the experience sought is solely one of pleasure or pain. A caricature of an individual stuck at this level would depict an emotional addict: those who seek to assault the senses by overindulgence in personal interactions and intensities. Physical imbalance at this chakra surrounds the reproductive organs, urinary system and the spleen.

The individual's attention at the second chakra integrates with both social and personal identity. When in a state of equilibrium, the energy feels stable, balanced, present and available to others in a very physical and emotionally responsive way.

This chakra can have a water-like nature, which ranges from turbulent oceans to placid, mirror-like aspects. The individual whose personal focus of consciousness is fixed at this level (rather than at the higher chakras) has a tendency to orient themselves towards preservation; in other words, towards planning for the future, rather than enjoying the flow of existence in the present.

This chakra is ruled by the forces of the seventh ray, which generate and restructure matter. The colour that energises this centre is orange; the colour of the purified chakra will reflect the lavender tones of its associated ray.

THE THIRD OR SOLAR PLEXUS CHAKRA

The third chakra is located at the solar plexus. Through this chakra, the individual learns the lessons of power and control through domination and submission, leadership and group consciousness. Many experiences may pass before mastering the dynamic of the solar plexus, which affects the entire nervous system, the liver, the gall bladder, the pancreas, and the stomach. There are primitive brain cells within the bundle of nerves located in the solar plexus area, and it acts as a sort of 'secondary brain', independent and not subordinate to the thinking brain.

With this chakra, one learns how to manage one's own power in the world and within oneself; in other words, learning cooperation, or balance between activity and passivity. The lessons in the context of this chakra occur through power struggles for sensation and security, and through jealousy and possessiveness, which often result in heart

The individual's attention at the second chakra integrates with both social and personal identity. When in a state of equilibrium, the energy feels stable, balanced, present and available to others in a very physical and emotionally responsive way.

attacks and ulcers. Physical imbalance affects the upper digestive system, pancreas and the gall bladder.

The individual who has learned to integrate their energies at the level of the solar plexus learns to express themselves physically in an appropriate manner and gains access to clarity and a sense of foresight. The sense of clairsentience, of being able to 'tune in' to people, places and things, comes from the intensified use of this centre, as does the ability to project the astral body (and maintain the memory of it) through the etheric levels of reality.

The element associated with this chakra is fire. The main ray operating through it is the sixth, promoting the refinement of emotional generation and service. The sixth ray and the solar plexus can generate power and its misuse, such as competitiveness and domination, which may also manifest as naiveté and the veneration of authority.

The vitalising colour for this centre is yellow. The colours of the rays that feed it are ruby and gold, the coloration of the sixth ray.

THE FOURTH OR HEART CHAKRA

The fourth chakra is located at the heart centre in the middle of the chest. This chakra is responsible for compassion and selfless love, and transcendence of judgement, prejudice attachments and dualistic thinking. The energies of this centre affect the heart, blood and circulatory system, the vagus nerve (which affects parasympathetic control of the heart, lungs and digestive tract) and also the thymus gland, which is responsible for the proper functioning of the immune system.

The heart centre is the seat of the Higher Self. At this level, emotions arise from empathy and deep understanding. The individual spontaneously generates a sense of impeccability and creativity, feeling nourishment within and radiating that quality to others.

With this chakra, Consciousness has moved beyond the self-involvement of the second chakra and the ambitiousness of the third, and now finds itself in relationship with its environment and Spirit. The ego, that sense of separation from others, begins to dissolve. At this stage the Self seeks to integrate the upper and lower forces and bodies within itself, and also the right- and left-brain functions. This is a meeting place of dualities, represented in some traditions as the star of David (a symbol that joins both upright- and downwards-facing triangular forces). One is also often immersed in a sense of timelessness.

Positive attributes associated with this chakra include tolerance and trust in the higher aspects of the Self in action everywhere. Negative reactions reflect a sense of emptiness, often manifested as suicide, falsity and superficiality.

The representative element for this chakra is air, with its lightness and its spaciousness. Its ray is the third major ray, Love in action. The colour for this ray and the purified functions of the heart centre is pink, but the vitalising, balancing frequency for the functioning of the chakra is green, the colour of harmony and balance.

THE FIFTH OR THROAT CHAKRA

The fifth chakra is centred at the throat, influencing expression and communication, hearing, telepathy and all uses of sound and of the word, including telekinesis. The fifth chakra rules the thyroid, the bronchial and vocal apparatuses, the lungs and the alimentary canal, as well as inner hearing (clairaudience). As the originator and modulator of sound frequencies, this is the centre most used in the practice of Alchemy for invocation and the use of power words, mantras, decrees and formulas.

This centre is particularly important because it is also close to the meeting place for the three upper chakras, what the ancients called the *bindu* or 'jade gate', which is the junction for higher faculties. The powers collect at the base of the brain, making a loop from the centre of the throat, through the third eye, the crown and back down to the base of the skull.

When this throat centre has been integrated, the voice takes on a melodious tone, harmonious and beautiful, conveying the range of human emotions and aspiration, and evoking higher truths. The energy at this level nourishes through sound, much like a mother's gentle lullaby, as the individual receives resonance from above, enabling survival and recreation. This centre has also been called the 'cornucopia' centre: what is voiced here in alignment with Source is manifested.

Mastery of the lower-vibrational needs and impulses of the lower chakras is necessary to maintain the higher-frequency awareness at this stage. At this level in sustained, integrated consciousness, not only is the individual able to move interdimensionally, recreate themselves and manifest their highest intentions, they are also able to lengthen their life.

This is the centre responsible for rejuvenation and longevity, connected directly with the activities of the causal body.

When energy runs through this centre but a person is unable to integrate themselves with it, they may go through periods of intense confusion between inner and outer reality, to the extent of tuning others out of their awareness, and appearing self-obsessed and introspective. As temporary as this might be, for the individual this is experienced as worldly failure: they just cannot seem to pull themselves together.

On the purely physical level, dysfunctions of this centre include vertigo, anaemia, allergies, fatigue and asthma, as well as improper oxygen uptake and metabolism of calcium.

Two elements have been associated with this centre: one is wood and the other is light. The first conveys the sense of inner sound[4], and the second, the awakening of higher powers relating to the base of the skull. This centre is ruled, coloured and activated by the first ray: the blue ray, and the colour of this chakra is also blue.

THE SIXTH OR THIRD EYE CHAKRA

The sixth chakra is seated at the third eye, the 'all-seeing-eye', the centre of visionary foresight and clairvoyance. In this chakra's worldly aspect, it rules the intellect; in its spiritual aspect, it provides inner vision and intuitional inspiration.

In the physical body, the third eye rules both the pituitary and pineal glands, the left brain, the left eye, the ears, the nose and the nervous system. It is interesting to note that the pineal gland contains vestigial retinal tissue, hence its association with the third eye. The third eye is the centre of the integrated personality and the pituitary gland is the 'master' or controlling gland of the endocrine system.

Here the individual is faced with higher forms of order and will, including the management of thoughtforms (covered more extensively in Part Three), psychic balance and the integration of the *yin* and *yang* elements of body and personality. Here is where the lower mind leaps into modalities of the Higher Mind. The Christ-self (Higher Self)

> The sixth chakra is seated at the third eye, the 'all-seeing-eye', the centre of visionary foresight and clairvoyance.

---

4 The concept of 'inner sound' is reminiscent of the practice in Tibetan and Zen Buddhism, whereby two wooden blocks clapped together create a hollow sound that spreads over the head – an 'inner sound' that is equivalent to the acoustic experience of the throat chakra.

becomes operational when the heart, throat and third eye energies have been mastered. Here we enter into the realms beyond time and beyond our own individual karmic load to participate effectively in the third dimension as service.

When integration is not possible, expression becomes illogical or over-intellectual. The person seems 'spaced out', forgetful and fearful, particularly of the future (which involves planning and ordering). Avoidance of the lessons of this centre may manifest as introversion.

The element associated with the third eye is the primordial substance of Light, known to some as 'alpha'. The ray that rules this centre is the fifth ray of science and truth. Its primary colour is green. The spiritual colour of this chakra, however, is indigo, which will heal, activate and stimulate the faculties of the third eye.

THE SEVENTH OR CROWN CHAKRA

This chakra rules the pineal gland, the pituitary gland, the upper brain and the right eye. This chakra is the master 'control panel' for the initiate of Inner Alchemy, and mastery of this chakra is the ultimate goal for the student in connecting to the divine Presence in the Master Practice. The seventh chakra feeds cosmic life into the individual, which happens in a spontaneous way that does not require conscious evocation. The full potency of this chakra cannot fully emerge until the lower centres have been mastered.

At the crown centre, the individual may attain synthesis and feel a genuine 'at-one-ment' with Creation. Here, they gain knowing beyond mere information from the true Source of all life and connects with the soul.

The energies operating here are extremely sensitive and delicate, are of a very high frequency and require a high degree of personal integrity, purity and harmlessness. If a person who does not possess these requirements should happen to hyperactivate this centre, they will have the experience of fantasy, or of feeling controlled or possessed. In this way too, the negative manifestation of the energies of this centre can be faithlessness, coming from belief in ego and separation.

———
The energies operating here are extremely sensitive and delicate, are of a very high frequency and require a high degree of personal integrity, purity and harmlessness.
———

The crown chakra is connected to the causal and electronic bodies and is activated by the second primary ray: the ray of wisdom, perception and action at the highest levels. The colour of the crown chakra is violet, whereas the ray it is governed by is yellow.

The table opposite summarises the attributes and deficiencies of the seven major chakras. The table also outlines the interrelationship between the chakras with the rays and bodies/fields, and the organs and body parts associated with each of the chakras. It also details what manifestations of mastery of each chakra may entail. For instance, an individual with mastery over their solar plexus energies may exhibit strong leadership skills, and as someone who is rarely 'rattled' by adversity yet does not fall into patterns of obsessive control over or domination of others. I repeat here that mastery of the chakras implies having conscious awareness of your energies; therefore, examining your emotional, mental and physical needs is a useful way of understanding which chakras may need extra attention.

KEY ASPECTS OF THE SEVEN MAJOR CHAKRAS

Chakra	Positive manifestation	Ray	Deficiencies, needs[5]	Associated bodies and physical organs
First	Use of personal will; Purity; Commitment to the planet; Responsibility; Security; Grounding	Fourth	Alienation; Jumpiness; Violence	Physical (first) body; Kidneys; Adrenal glands; Spinal column; Sense of smell and sensations
Second	Invocation; Sensitivity to vibration (supersensitivity); Individuality; Balance between the social and the personal	Seventh	Hysteria; Sensuality (pleasure/pain)	Emotional (second) body; Sense of taste; Reproductive system
Third	Mobility; Personal control; Peace; Fearlessness; Generosity; Balance; Ability to set limits; Orderliness and cooperation	Sixth	Disorganisation, inability to say 'no'; Tendency to power-trip: control through domination or submission; Jealousy	Emotional (second) body; lower mental (third) body; Nervous system; Sight; Gallbladder; Pancreas; Stomach
Fourth	Divine Love; Tolerance; Forbearance; Trust; Being 'in touch with self'; Unconditional Love; Timelessness; Joining of Consciousness and matter	Third	Sense of emptiness; Suicidal; Acting 'nice'; Judgemental	Electronic (seventh) body (the awakened heart is the doorway to the spiritual realm); Thymus gland; Circulatory system; Cardiovascular system; Vagus nerve; Touch
Fifth	Divine Will; Power to create; Expression and communication; Hearing; Telepathy; Time and space travel	First	Confusion; Alienation of others	Causal (sixth) body; Sense of hearing; Thyroid gland; Vocal cords; Respiratory system; Alimentary canal
Sixth	Third eye; Concentration and consecration; Clairvoyance; Order and will; Foresight	Fifth	Illogical; over-intellectual; Spaced-out; Introversion; Forgetfulness; Fearful of the future	Higher Mental (fifth) body; causal (sixth) body; Left brain; Left eye; Ears; Nose; Nervous system; Pituitary gland; Pineal gland
Seventh	Invocation; Knowing; Christ Self; No limits; Cosmic Consciousness; Oneness; Power of transmutation	Second	Faithlessness; Sense of being controlled or possessed	Causal (sixth) body; some interaction with the electronic (seventh) body; Dimensions beyond the physical; Upper brain; Right eye

5 Caused by a lack of integration of the chakra's pure attributes.

Recall that the etheric body acts as a container for all the chakras. Furthermore, while the bodies and chakras may be associated with one another, there is no cut-and-dried direct link between them that prevents certain bodies from interrelating with certain chakras: for instance, the link between the fifth body and the fifth chakra does not prevent the fifth body from interrelating with the first chakra. All energy systems cooperate and work together. Similarly, the electronic body does not have a seat in any one chakra – not even the crown – but interacts with an awakened heart chakra, which is able to serve as a doorway to spiritual existence.

MINOR CHAKRAS

As mentioned previously, there are hundreds, perhaps thousands, of energy foci within the physical body and around it, including points within the mental, emotional and spiritual bodies. These points have been used by spiritual disciplines (in the various Vedic and yogic practices), and ancient scientists and healers. They are created by criss-crossing energy lines. The major chakras are created by the intersection of twenty-one energy lines; the minor chakras arise at the intersection of fourteen energy lines; and the lesser ones are created by seven lines. Acupuncture and *shiatsu* maps outline the location of these centres and the energy meridians upon which they are situated. To the left is an illustration of the twenty-one minor chakras and where they are located on the body.

From the alchemical point of view, perhaps the most important of the minor chakras would be at the hands and at the feet. The hands serve to bless and to transmute and are an important tool for the alchemist. Transmutation of physical substance occurs largely through the sense of touch. Similarly, our feet may also bless the Earth upon which we walk.

DYSFUNCTIONS

There is no 'good' or 'bad' chakra; none are 'higher' or 'lower' than the others. All chakras are needed for the spiritualisation of earthly experience. There are only finer and denser frequencies, like musical notes or hues of colour; each equal, beautiful and necessary. Improper integration of any chakra leads to dysfunction and, ultimately, disease in the body. To be a physically, mentally, emotionally and spiritually healthy

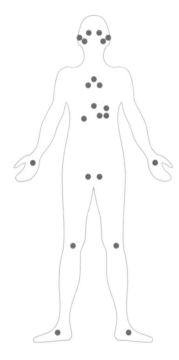

The 21 Minor Chakras

being, one must integrate lessons and allow the proper flow of energies at each and every one of the chakras.

Disease is caused by the inability to absorb, transmute or integrate energetic frequencies. Psychological problems are the demonstrations of a partially blocked chakra. When an energy is sent out with discordant qualifications upon it, it leads to physical or psychological problems. All of this happens unconsciously.

Having mastered the lessons of the right management of the energies at each chakra, we automatically transmute the substance or matter that is associated with a chakra and releases the energy into subtle energetic pathways along the spine. In Ayurvedic medicine and Vedic traditions these subtle pathways are called the *nadis*. They feed into the nervous system, affecting the endocrine system and eventually the cardiovascular system, i.e. the blood.

INTERDIMENSIONAL CHAKRAS

This chapter on chakras would not be complete without mention of the five out-of-body energy centres, less known for being less accessible to us.

We observe the true intricacy and perfection of the human energetic anatomy in the way the out-of-the-body chakras work. They open dimensional doorways to the planetary matrix and beyond. These networks spread far and wide and these centres link us to all creation. In esoteric teachings, it is believed that the farthest star in the Universe responds to the slightest signal of a single element, such is their connection, just as a heart is capable of instilling peace everywhere, and prayer affects all of life. These human, planetary and galactic circuits gestate and circulate life throughout the Universe and we are one with them.

Before being able to perceive the effect that these chakras have upon us, biophysical integration of the seven primary body chakras and their psychological influences must occur. The focus of attention needs to shift from the illusion that we are separate entities, dealing with external reality, to experiencing ourselves as part of a global field that embraces many elements simultaneously. Wider, more subtle fields of activity are involved, which we refer to as dimensions in the next chapter of this book. Out-of-body chakras link us to multidimensional life.

The out-of-body chakras are dimensional stations that lead to Being states. They may be accessed in meditation but, as suggested above,

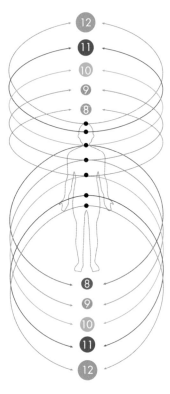

The Out-of-Body Chakras

become useful only when you have comfortably managed higher-dimensional frequencies and can sustain holistic awareness. These frequencies access both matter and consciousness as creative and constructive elements of Creation, focused on building, healing, repairing and accessing new potentials and forms of living in collaboration with higher entities, angels, guides and masters. When you tap into them, you become a co-creator with the architects of Creation.

When you wish to experience a state of oneness with humanity at the ordinary level of reality, your vibratory state would echo that of the eighth chakra rings. Next, at a slightly more expanded frequency, at the ninth out-of-body chakra rings, you would contact the fields of probability. The same applies to the spectrum of possibility that unfolds within the energy range of the tenth chakra, slightly more accelerated and diffused. Here, access to the fundamental building blocks of Creation – i.e. matter and thought – is gained. The eleventh chakra points you to a state of greater humanity, embracing hierarchy and all that pertains to the Human Model of evolution, while the twelfth, as maximum acceleration available to the Human Model, taps into total silence and Oneness beyond manifestation, as pure scintillating essence.

The illustration to the left depicts how, according to holistic perception, each chakra in this system appears in a pair of rings centred below and above our physical body consciousness. The circular pattern illustrates energy vortices, which work as rings, rather than focal points. They maintain an important relation with the seven spinal chakras, which at this point function as dimensional doorways.

These chakras may be accessed through the practice of colour breathing, as described below. Colours are inhaled into the pelvic cavity, then absorbed via the Figure of Light and the Sun Presence as per the Alchemical Alignment, and then exhaled by combining both colours (frequencies) and directing the stream of Light upwards and out through the front of the head, setting the vibratory frequency of the corresponding out-of-body chakra. Visualising the colours is enough to trigger their frequency; you need not involve or focus on the bodily chakra directly.

The information here is given only as reference. It is applied in advanced energy work at my School. For now, it is interesting to note how the higher function of a body chakra opens up to possibilities and probabilities.

Refer to the illustration on page 84 again: notice that the eighth chakra circles below and above the body. This field of activity is related to the higher combined functions of the throat and solar plexus chakras. The frequency set off by the lower ring is accessed through inhaling the colour copper linked to the throat chakra, whereas the upper ring is accessed through a silvery-blue shade, linked to the solar plexus.

The ninth chakra rings both coincide with the frequency of the heart chakra in the physical body and respond to the colour green.

The tenth chakra rings resonate to the joint activity of the solar plexus at the lower end, corresponding to a light orange colour, and at the higher end with the throat, which is also a light orange colour.

The eleventh chakra rings respond to rose-pink at both extremities, at the lower end resonating with the base chakra and at the upper with the third eye chakra.

Finally, the twelfth chakra rings resonate to a pink-gold shade both at the crown centre and at the lowermost centre below the feet, as shown in the illustration.

POLARITY AND MOVEMENT OF ENERGY THROUGH THE CHAKRAS

Everything pertaining to physical embodiment is polarised: the seven chakras demonstrate a sequence of polarities, where each has either a positive or a negative charge. The charge of each chakra is different for men and for women, where what is dynamic for one, is receptive for the other. This facilitates dynamism and merging at each level for purposes of growth and expansion. The negative polarity denotes receptivity and introversion; the positive denotes impulse and extroversion. In women, the first, third, fifth and seventh chakras are negatively charged, while the second, fourth and sixth are positive. In men, the polarities are reversed, whereby the first, third, fifth, and seventh are positively charged for men, and likewise the second, fourth and sixth are negatively charged, as illustrated in the diagrams to the right.

Notice how in women the odd-numbered chakras display a negative charge, while the even-numbered chakras have a positive charge, and vice-versa for men.

The chakras also work in pairs. For example, the sacral and throat chakras, the solar plexus and the third eye chakras, and the heart and

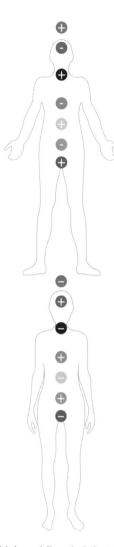

Male and Female Polarities

crown centres work together. Both the sacral and throat chakras pertain to creativity; both the solar plexus and third eye chakras relate to vision and intelligence; and both the heart and crown centres access cosmic dimensions. In each of these pairs of chakras, the higher chakra expresses a higher function and the lower chakra a lower function – i.e. the fifth (throat) chakra expresses creativity on a spiritual level, whereas the second (sacral) expresses the same function at a lower frequency level, pertaining more to the physical realm.

As mentioned above, the chakras (besides the crown and base) have a dual function in matter and in Spirit, meaning their activity manifests itself in physical and in spiritual dimensions. The chakras also embrace this polarity, or dualities, within themselves, with the major convergence of dualities occurring at the third eye and at the heart. The heart is where all the energies of the chakras converge to facilitate the experience of the electronic body.

It is in the domain of the heart, integrated, full, potent and pure, where the electronic energies of the Spirit-self abide as accessible content. It is within the heart where we hear the voice of our Higher Self and see its Light, where we receive insight, vision and gain a deeper understanding of that which is. It is in the heart that we are present to both our physical and personal selves and to our cosmic, interdimensional potential. All bodies, all chakras, all powers converge here.

The secret art of Alchemy is seated within the realm of the heart, and the highest powers are reserved only for the very pure in heart.

The powers of Light transcend all darkness.

> It is within the heart where we hear the voice of our Higher Self and see its Light, where we receive insight, vision and gain a deeper understanding of that which is.

ENERGY CIRCULATION

Having explored the three main facets of our energetic anatomy – the bodies, rays and chakras – we may now look at how they facilitate the transmission of energy into, out of and around our anatomy, and the techniques that allow us to work with energy.

The practice of transmutation in alchemy involves generating energy through the vehicle of the alchemist themselves. In traditional Taoist alchemy, this was done by circulating energy through the various energetic circuits in the body (such as the *nadis* or acupuncture points) in a systematic way. In Inner Alchemy, the energy is also circulated, but it does not happen via any physical channels. Energy circulates through the body's lines of force, and the chakras, as the body's energy centres, are absolutely crucial in affecting this energy circuit.

At present, our body centres tend to be absorbent, instead of radiant. Humans accept only that which they selectively desire, curtailing the otherwise spontaneous magnetic and radiating quality of each centre. The heart chakra is partially obstructed in most of humanity, preventing the possibility of authentic and practical spirituality. We would do well to facilitate the generation, circulation and then radiation of energy through our chakras and bodies.

Similarly to how Taoism uses a microcosmic (i.e. bodily) orbit, Inner Alchemy creates an alchemical circuit, such as in the Master Practice, and draws cosmic energy downwards into the planet itself via the individual organism.

Taoist alchemy and Inner Alchemy both propose to transmute the lower into the higher to embody the higher. The illustration, right, is an example of the Taoist microcosmic orbit, and how energies may be circulated around the body for optimal results.

One often sees reference to an upwardly moving energy current through the spine experienced in the refinement (i.e. spiritualisation) process. This is commonly referred to as the rise of *kundalini*.[6] The essence of the *kundalini* circuit was explained by ancient Taoist alchemists and by Indian yogis. It consists of the circulation of energy through the chakras, up and down them in a continuous looping motion, which serves to activate the chakras and link each progressively with the energy of the first. This continually intensifies the energy by building up the momentum through circulation. The increasing intensity of this visualisation stimulates the *kundalini* circuit into activity and often forces a passageway for the movement of energies in the body.

Inner Alchemy does not restrict itself to the circulation of energy within the body, but it teaches how to draw energy from both the Earth and the heavens, as shown in the Master Practice. This Master Practice is the process by which we may activate a second type of circuit:

The Microcosmic Orbit

---

6 *Kundalini* is a Sanskrit word that literally means 'serpent-like'. It has been used to describe the wave-like movement of energy in different parts of the body, but is best known as the yoga of the ascending current of force through the spinal column – Kundalini Yoga.

the spiritual circuit. This is the most direct and safest circuit, and my preferred method of energy circulation. It is formed by linking the personal self to the God-self through feeling, visualisation and affirmation. After grounding with the Earth (more on this below), one connects the bodily lines of force with the cosmic lines of force to create, what I have come to call, the Alchemical Alignment, or the Master Practice. This consists of collecting the energies of the lower chakras at the heart centre, where they are transmuted into Light. From the heart, the force generated proceeds to the throat, third eye, and pineal centres, ultimately connecting with Spirit-self, which returns its energy as a downpour.

There are three distinct journeys that Consciousness takes through the body. The first is the so-called *kundalini*: the more generally understood stage of ascending force through the chakras. The second journey is almost coincidental to the first and consists in the re-descent of pure Consciousness into matter. The third movement is that of full integration of Consciousness in matter, with the acceptance of the lessons imparted through each chakra. This final movement is perceived as an ascent towards spiritual perfection while performing in the world. Many Lightworkers today are at the re-descending stage, consciously embodying Light right down into the cellular level, opening to the activity of cosmic force on collective matter and imbuing matter with Light.

Once the initial upwards impulse has been satisfactorily completed, the pathway for the *antahkarana*, or rainbow bridge between matter and Consciousness, is formed, where each chakra becomes infused with Consciousness. The *antahkarana* remains to be tested, sealed and confirmed on the downwards journey. The difficult and painful journey back into density involves learning to hold the Consciousness of the higher powers in daily life.

On the descent, the individual may again face the temptations of the first cycle of ascension and fail many times. The descent is now linked to personal physical consciousness and moving from the third eye to the throat and heart, for example, is not as easy as it was on the ascending journey, where aspiration led the way. Now, on the inverse journey, Light must be brought down into the chakras and integrated for concrete third-dimensional use. The person is obliged to immerse themselves progressively into material reality devoid of the loftiness of the higher dimensions. 'Clear sight' in this part of the adaptation process is often not readily available. It remains as a subliminal memory, which makes the matter of 'trust' all the more difficult and necessary.

The entire re-descending journey is the implementation of inner ethics in the personal world. What might appear as 'sacrifice' is actually the application of our 'sacred-office'. In this process, we come to understand the real meaning of transcendence and sublimation. Ultimate death of the unconscious aspect of personality leads to ultimate rebirth and the process of ascension. When we at last integrate back into the lowest chakra, we once again regain the clarity of higher power.

It will be interesting, and in fact necessary, as an aspiring alchemist, for you to notice your emotional tendencies and their variations from day to day to determine which chakra is most active or which needs awakening. You need to notice where you have been focusing your Consciousness, and whether you are expressing positive or negative attributes from a given chakra. You then have the choice of clearing, refining and expanding beyond your own automatic behaviour.

Chakras, like everything else in the energetic anatomy, manifest the result of intention and sustained focus: these manifestations are determined by the quality of attention, i.e. the personal focus of Consciousness. The activity of the chakras is mastered once the individual is able to use energy with awareness, accessing it freely without repression or self-indulgence. Without awareness, all elements in the body may express raw instinct and operate unconsciously.

Please note that the functions of Consciousness are never fixed. You always have free will, while inner or outer circumstances create upheavals, reversals or accelerations of energy. Watch the rhythm of your sleep and the foods you crave, and you will be able to flow more easily with the natural cycles and needs your body dictates. Your physical, mental and emotional bodies speak to you. You would do well to learn their language and see to these needs as tenderly as you would to those of a child.

Once we have a better understanding of the energy dynamics at the level of the chakras, rays and bodies, we can begin to project healing love and energy to harmonise any imbalance and establish the atmosphere of peace and cooperation we are all craving.

The practice of Inner Alchemy is absolutely safe. One step leads to another. Each step guarantees the next: we cannot proceed unless we

—

Chakras, like everything else in the energetic anatomy, manifest the result of intention and sustained focus: these manifestations are determined by the quality of attention.

—

have mastered the first. We cannot partake of the powers of Light unless we ourselves have become Light. The individual is the Source of cosmic energy. It is a journey from self to Self through work on personality, discovering spiritual reality and identity.

ENERGETIC TECHNIQUES, MEDITATIONS AND EXERCISES

Inner Alchemy practices 'enlighten' the physical world, including the body. Their main objective is to raise the frequency of the human being into an instrument capable of communicating and acting within worlds of Light as well as matter. A body of Light-matter, receptive to Spirit at every level, is constructed in the course of the application of alchemical practices. The practices in the rest of this chapter are among a few of the techniques taught in Inner Alchemy that enable us to ground and protect ourselves, integrate Light in our bodies, and become an instrument of Service.

GROUNDING

Integration of Light within our bodies starts with our relation to matter: the first step to doing this is grounding ourselves.

When the physical body has been refined sufficiently through alchemical practice and transformation of the personality, it rises to a level where it is able to access and use the etheric body. This instrument, in turn, is able to access higher bodies and states of Being, depending on the level of sustained Consciousness, and the health and conscious level of their chakra system.

As the proportion of Light in matter increases and is anchored in matter, the physical body becomes more receptive and healthier. Matter is then able to act as a container and an emitter of fine Light frequencies through its etheric counterpart, which becomes a conscious, agile vehicle for service.

In the meditation traditions of the East, particularly India and Tibet, physical energy is grounded (or earthed) via the base chakra into the body of the planet. The physical posture used is sitting with crossed legs. The purpose is to achieve total inner silence and emptiness: inactivity. In the Egyptian tradition, on the other hand, as well as in the martial arts, grounding is done standing, or seated on a chair, with the knees and elbows held at a right angle, allowing for grounding through the soles of the feet.

For the purpose of inner work, one seeks to ground oneself: locating the body in time and space to secure re-entry, identification and stability. The entire body should be grounded, as taught in the Egyptian and Western Hermetic traditions, and in Eastern martial arts. This enables the individual to move and actively use their body in the world, as Service, linking inner and outer reality and applying spiritual principles in the uplifting of humanity. Service consists of prayer and thought formation, the generation of Light-substance as blessing and physical action in the world; an activity that involves physical transformation as well as spiritual awareness.

 THE HORSE POSTURE

You need to activate the energy flow within the first and second chakras and the lines of force coursing through your legs. One of my favourite ways of doing this is through soft stimulation, such as Tai Chi and Aikido. Running and hard physical exercise, while strengthening the muscles of the legs, do not provide the delicate awareness needed to avail yourself of the energy flow coming from the heart of the Earth.

You might simply like to hold the horse posture used in the martial arts for as long as necessary to feel the awakening of the *hara* – the Japanese name for the energies pooled at the navel centre.

The Taoist alchemist considered the martial arts an essential practice for the creation of the immortal vehicle, the maintenance of vigour and youth, and the generation of vital power needed to put into effect the practices of alchemy.

Please use the illustrations to the right as a physical guide to performing the horse posture, alongside the accompanying text to aid you in your visualisation.

After holding this posture for a while, you will begin to sense a trembling in the legs. This is the same trembling that is induced in Western bioenergetic stances and serves to generate the orgasmic reflex (or 'orgone' energy). You may sense a feeling of heat in the legs and may be tempted again and again to stop. The awakening of this energy, as Wilhelm Reich (the 'discoverer' of 'orgone' or biological energy) knew, triggers the locked imprints within the base and sacral chakras.

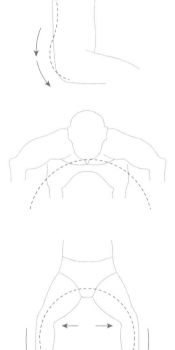

The Horse Posture

If you can hold the posture through the trembling, you will begin to sense an upsurge of energy flooding through you. At that point I suggest you consciously visualise your solar plexus connected to the centre of the Earth. Do this by visualising your legs as the two corners of the bottom plane of an upright triangle, whose apex marks the location of the solar plexus chakra. Extend the lines of force beneath your legs into a second, inverted triangle, whose apex is located in the centre of the Earth, so that the form roughly follows a diamond shape.

 ## GROUNDING CORD VISUALISATION

Another visualisation that is helpful for grounding, particularly if you are unable to use physical means of generating the vital energy flow, is to use the image of a grounding cord. This is a fairly standard grounding procedure in the West.

This grounding cord resembles a tail protruding from the tailbone and is an extension of the central energy circuitry within the body itself.

Visualise a grounding cord of energy emerging from your tailbone and extending into the core of the planet. See the core of the planet as a radiant, golden, crystal-like heart centre, emanating a soft pink glow.

Draw sustenance from the Earth's core as a child does from its mother. Feel the Light rising up your grounding cord and nourishing every atom and molecule of your body.

As you sustain the visualisation of points of Light in the centre of each atom of your body, your body grows in luminescence and so does the body of the Earth. Feel the solidity and the security of being anchored. Let your body rest in that feeling.

 ## FIGURE OF LIGHT GROUNDING

The grounding technique used constantly in Inner Alchemy is the figure of Light, which is based on practices used by the Essenes, a Gnostic sect. The full set of practices is contained in *Armour of Light*, two booklets by Olive Pixley. The basis of this exercise is the visualisation of a Light-double of the physical body mirrored below the feet. This Light-body serves to anchor physicality directly into Light and acts as a natural protection against the absorption of negative particles from the Earth

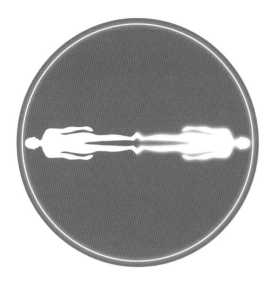

Figure of Light Grounding

and the environment. It is tremendously powerful. Before attempting the
visualisation, as outlined in the text below, please refer to the illustration
above. The technique is as follows:

Begin by lying down.

Sense the figure of Light at your feet, an exact replica of your physical
form, only in brilliant Light.

Sense the contact of the Light-body with the feet and allow that contact
to energise your feet, then draw from it upwards through your body.

End by sealing the connection with a circular beam of Light projected
from the right side over your head, around and over the head of the
figure of Light and back to close the circle over your own head. This
visualisation should be done quickly. Its purpose is not only to energise
the physical body in Light, but to expand the capacity of mind so that it
is able to register instantaneous contact with Light. The process works
to quicken your mental faculties, and so should be done in a flash. I
find the relationship with my own body of Light expressed this way
to be comforting. It also serves the purpose of creating the balance or
grounding tension necessary for the creation of the Alchemical Circuit
created in the Master Practice.

PROTECTION

You have already been using protection in the form of the crystal Tube of Light from the Master Practice in Part One. For those of you who desire additional protection, I outline two helpful visualisations below.

Ancient occult literature points to three 'psychic gates' through which energy enters the physical body: the coccyx, the kidneys and the back of the head. Each of these acts as a passageway for interdimensional energies to flow into us, but each passageway can also let in undesirable energies from the environment. Psychic self-defence practices teach us to guard these areas through protective visualisation.

Many traditions have long upheld the visualisation of the cross of Light enclosed by a circle. A favourite visualisation of mine is that of a revolving disc of golden Light placed behind the solar plexus. This covers the area of the kidneys and is not only protective, but also soothing to otherwise disturbed emotional energies. The illustrations on pages 162–3 may be used as guides for these protective visualisations.

The human organism protects itself automatically in most cases. When the individual is acting through the personality, however, over-activating a particular centre – such as misuse of the sacral chakra, the solar plexus or even the third eye centre – there is little that protection techniques can do. One of the safest and easiest ways to restore the chakras is through the use of colours. Look for colours that you resonate with: primarily green-, indigo- and magenta-coloured lamps are wonderful. Finally, of course, if you need healing, there is always the Earth (the healing green of nature), which is the best and richest harmoniser of all.

HEALING AND THE HEALING CIRCUIT

The Inner Alchemy School teaches that healing energy comes from Spirit. It descends through the upper chakras into the *bindu* at the base of the skull. From there it proceeds to the heart. If the healer uses the laying-on-of-hands technique, their shoulder and hand chakras will be especially open. If they are silent or far away, the radiation occurs through the energies projected through the healer's higher bodies.

Everyone's touch, even everyone's footsteps, imprint energy upon living things. Therefore, everyone is a potential healer, because everyone is a battery – a conduit for energetic frequencies.

Many traditions have long upheld the visualisation of the cross of Light enclosed by a circle.

A healing circuit may be formed through the use of the wrist, the soles of the feet, and any number of the chakras. Just as the feet are an extension of the base of the spine, the hands are an extension of the heart. A healing circuit is formed by lines of force linking the heart chakra with the minor chakras in the palms of the hands. One healing system may make use of the entire body, while another may channel pure Light-substance, directed out of the body by projecting thought. Some may advocate radiating pure Light/Love as an expansion from the heart chakra; others from the power centres, which are the lower chakras associated with lower body energies. Some use physical touch, while others use energetic projection as a form of absent healing.

The ancient alchemists created their lodestones (the magical alchemical instruments) by charging them with energy invoked from other dimensions, requalified with the help of elemental energies and channelled into substance through physical touch (via the five fingers of the hand). This is how, in the Middle Ages, a material substance, such as coal, was thought to be able to be refined into a diamond, or lead into gold. It is thought that the molecular structure could be altered by the expert manipulation of the alchemist's own vibratory frequency. The vibratory rate of the atomic structure was raised through the medium of the alchemist's body and channelled through the hands. This lodestone could then be used to recalibrate other substances as well.

Think of the implications of alchemy on rejuvenation and healing. Energy-balancing systems have a profound effect on the human energetic structure, including right–left and inner–outer polarities. Organs, as well as the chakras and bodies, have positive or negative polarities. By matching the poles, and not sinking too far into one polarity or another, one brings balance. Harmony is the magical ingredient responsible for all healing.

An embrace is one of the most healing acts, particularly one given out of an overflow of love and an abundance of physical (i.e. vital) energy. The energy simply leaps into the depleted person. Energy always seeks balance.

It is important to know your strength, your constitution and your energetic make-up. Know what your healing abilities are. Not everybody is a healer on the physical level.

When I put my hands on somebody, I am in touch with their Higher Self. From this perspective, I am aware of my connection to my own God-self. I allow that force to come through me in whatever way is

—
Think of the implications of alchemy on rejuvenation and healing. Energy-balancing systems have a profound effect on the human energetic structure, including right–left and inner–outer polarities.
—

needed. By virtue of having a body, I am in authority over physicality, but energy-balancing will happen spontaneously and bring about healing in certain instances. Healing itself cannot happen without intentionality, without some form of prayer or invocation: healing happens out of the partnership between matter and Light.

When an individual is not able to receive touch (either physical or auric), the energy can be projected through thought. Whereas physical substance is not approached directly, the emotional body is. That can trigger a certain restructuring at the physical level. By the time the individual leaves a session, they feel relaxed and uplifted.

Whenever I do energy balancing work, I never know how long my hands will remain in a certain place. Usually the person falls asleep, which is the most sought-after state of consciousness, as the mind (which is what normally interferes in the healing process) is laid aside. Their brainwave activity is slowed down and, at that point, the forces that work through me are able to bring about the balancing, aligning, vitalising, recalibrating or relaxing of the physical body. The process of harmonising prior to transmutation begins.

The lines of force on the body provide the basic framework for healing. They create the pathways that enable the alchemical work to occur by balancing the polarities of Light and matter. This work is usually divided into:

Transmutation
All healing and recalibration from lower into higher expressions.

Manifestation
Enabling physical or non-physical manifestations.

Etherealisation
The purification of density and its restructuring into Light forms.

By the very fact that I am in alignment with the forces of Light through my living and through my conscious invocation, when someone comes through the door, they will be affected by the vibrations of Light.
Everyone can do this.

Star of David Meditation

STAR OF DAVID MEDITATION

This is a good healing meditation using Light.

To heal yourself:

Visualise a large golden Star of David, made of bright yellow gold, just before you. See this star made of brilliant golden fire. Notice the aura of brilliant white Light surrounding it. You may use this illustration to guide you.

Notice in the centre of this star a brilliant sphere of white: a pulsating white sun, which seems to be far, far away, stretching into infinity. Walk towards the star in your mind, walk through it and into the Central Sun, the nucleus of Source that we may try to define in spacetime understanding. Merge into it, absorb it, let it absorb you, your body, your energetic fields.

Be still and know.

To heal another:

Bring the symbol of the star within your own heart chakra. Be with it.

Sustain its intensity.

Visualise the physical form of the person you wish to see healed and place it within the Central Sun.

There are many beautiful and powerful visualisations that may be used to attract the Light force needed to bring about spiritual healing and alignment, and even physical restructuring.

Explore the forms and colours that inspire and uplift you.

BREATH

The practice of Alchemy, as well as of many other esoteric and metaphysical disciplines, involves the conscious use of breath, which carries life force throughout the body. The more deeply and more fully we breathe, the better, more vital and healthy we feel. Breath quickens the blood and energises the organism. It is perhaps the simplest way to change emotional states and eliminate body tension.

A balanced breath will create or maintain a balanced physical vehicle by equalising the right and left sides of the body, the brain and the nervous system. The steady flow of oxygen in and out of the lungs will flush out any obstruction, fixation or block that may be in the mind, the emotional body or the physical body, and can change the overall frequency of a person. After a few minutes of balanced breathing, we feel more relaxed and integrated, and therefore, more receptive to finer perceptions.

Chants, mantras and most forms of singing and recitation will force a person to take deeper breaths, thereby increasing oxygen intake, retention and exhalation. Singing, particularly of devotional songs, is one of the easiest ways of opening the door to spiritual forces.

Another of the practices advised in the yogic system is the retention of the breath, both on the inbreath and on the outbreath. As you practise this, you will notice that as you hold your breath with full lungs, not only do you have a feeling of bursting, but you also begin tingling immediately from the increase of oxygen in the lungs. When you hold your breath after exhaling, with the lungs emptied of breath, you experience the feeling of collapse bordering on fear, and yet this also leads to this tingling feeling. Your emptied lungs force you to breathe in more air. The full breath might be construed as the fullness of life or birth: the empty breath might be seen as emptiness or night, the aspect of dying. We are constantly dying and being reborn.

It is not possible to breathe fully and be angry or sad. Become aware of how you breathe when you are in one of your moods and you will see that you are holding your breath. Some emotions necessitate that you breathe more air in than out; for others the reverse will be true. In some emotional states you will be breathing more through the mouth, in others through the nose.

There is a purpose for both nose and mouth breathing. The Sufis have a system of breathing according to the elements. Each breath will provoke the feeling and integration of an element within the body. For example, breathing in and out through the nose intensifies the purification of the earth element. The mouth breath intensifies the experience of the element of air. Breathing in through the nose and out through the mouth produces a feeling of water and in through the mouth and out through the nose intensifies the fire flow through the body. Using these different patterns of breathing, they are able to balance the body and transmute emotional states into balanced, positive states of harmony and creativity.

Breath contains life and Light. It also carries the qualities of the individual. Breath is a conductor that serves to transfer all sorts of energies, as well as to protect us and to awaken Consciousness. In the hands of a skilled energy master, breath can be used to disperse or ignite energies within the energy fields of the body. When the breath is further qualified with sound and consciously directed, its scope is even greater.

Breath, for us, is the fuel which catalyses the energy process that culminates in transmutation. Inner Alchemy draws from many disciplines – and not only when it comes to breathwork – and adapts these to individual need.

Breath regulation is one of the fastest ways of balancing brainwave patterns and entering higher states of consciousness. The method that I often use requires breathing through the mouth in greater and greater quantities, much as in rebirthing or Shugendo practices, or in holotropic breathwork. These are powerful methods of reaching energies and forces that may be used in alchemical work.

The journey through intensified and directed breathing practices is the journey through the different states of consciousness, from the intensely physical and emotional to the mental, higher mental and spiritual states. This happens through accelerating the rate of vibration of the entire being: the blood, the cells, the brain and the entire energetic circuitry. Open-mouth breathing facilitates this better than nostril breathing because it affects the entire cellular structure. Nostril breathing was used in the past, but in many it tends to induce out-of-body states, which disconnect us from the physical recalibration process.

———

Breath regulation is one of the fastest ways of balancing brainwave patterns and entering higher states of consciousness.

———

With breathing we eventually enter into partnership, however momentarily, with our Higher Self. We can enter into realms of Light ordinarily unavailable in waking states. With proper guidance through those states where we would normally lose consciousness, we may perceive other realities.

REVIEW

The basic energetic anatomy of the human being is a highly delicate apparatus, much too complex to be monitored consciously. Relax. You do not need to monitor all of yourself. You are your own master, creator and bookkeeper all in one. You are in this third-dimensional existence to explore and master detail. You are here to live fully at all the levels possible in this dimension. You partake of the highest and of the lowest forms of life. Within you, the elements live and multiply and, in turn, create and evolve.

The only thing you need to do is to be present within yourself and within your faculties as they evolve and expand. If you want to work overtime, you do so out of your own free will. When you remember to play some of the time too, life becomes an exciting adventure where higher and greater frequencies and experiences are forever within reach.

The alchemist knows themselves and knows that their reach is infinite, particularly at the level of spiritual evolution. The alchemist knows the supremacy of Light over technology, over matter and over the lower mind. The alchemist has intuited the Creator in the deepest recesses of his being. The alchemist has chosen to partner with the Creator in service to the Light. The alchemist uses all the aspects of themselves (their entire 'family of Self', so to speak) to help them co-create, transmute, heal and bless their immediate world, their environment and their planet.

The alchemist's journey to a higher level of Consciousness has several steps that they must work through. The first step, while becoming aware of the blocks within the personality, is enhancing flexibility or restructuring the personality, which I will go through in more detail shortly.

The second stage, often coincidental with the first, is the exploration of the personal self through time and space in meditative practices. This may happen naturally but is enhanced by the knowledge of the energetic

> The only thing you need to do is to be present within yourself and within your faculties as they evolve and expand.

anatomy and how to handle it. As an aspiring alchemist, here begins the conscious journey of identifying with your divine heritage. You deliberately ignite the fire within the heart and initiate the arduous path of taming the instinctual reactions of the lower bodies. As you progress, you access the higher chakras and through them other realities and other levels of Being.

Then begins the third stage of exploration into multidimensional existence.

All of the stages outlined above are made possible only through the activity of Spirit. As we grow in awareness of this fact, in deep humility and gratitude, the power of Spirit intensifies. For the Spirit-self is, in fact, the only presence acting in all things. This is the secret to the art of Inner Alchemy.

THE HUMAN FACULTIES AND PERSONALITY MASTERY

Part Three outlines the three human powers: the power of feeling, thought and the spoken word. This chapter guides the reader towards mastery of these powers, which leads to mastery of the three lower bodies: the physical, emotional and mental bodies. It also examines lower astral phenomena and the impact of negativity.

THE HUMAN
FACULTIES

The three basic human powers, as
mentioned in Part One, are the faculties
behind the dynamic of creation or
manifestation. These are the power of
thought as mental activity, feeling as
sentient connection and the spoken word
as vital resonance.

These powers are qualified by the individual through intention and
attention and activated by sense perception via the bodies and chakras.
They are the motor power behind the lower-self personality and its

physical, emotional and mental perception. Through the human faculties, humanity affects the world and determines the course of individual life. These three faculties interrelate with one another, creating greater and more complex fields of influence, attracting, rejecting and conditioning global life.

Thoughtforms are, in essence, creations; they are the building blocks of the world around us. Thoughtforms are formed when an image (a thought) is constructed and is imbued with human vitality (emotion), thereby giving it personal meaning. These thoughtforms resonate and come into coherence with others, and together they build up the consensus of opinions in the world around us. Thoughtforms have a life of their own, feeding on their creator. They are never dissolved, only transformed.

One must be attentive to the influence of thoughtforms, since the networks of attracting and rejecting ordinary thoughtforms can lead to low-frequency 'miscreations', which pollute the world around us and veil higher consciousness.

If one's access to higher consciousness is obstructed, then it is impossible to perceive the world neutrally, and in particular other people, as they are. Very often, when relating to other people, we do so through a bundle of thoughtforms as opinions, beliefs and evaluations that relates to another bundle of thoughtforms. Recall an unpleasant experience with someone you know who was reacting in exaggerated manner to a minor inconvenience. It is likely that what you witnessed was their thoughtforms playing out: such as anger and envy mixed with thoughts of self-pity, self-righteousness and so on and so forth. If you reacted with anger to their behaviour, this is in all likelihood a case of your own thoughtforms engaging with and reacting to theirs. If later you look back at the episode, and think, 'What came over me?', it may be that you are feeling the discomfort that is caused by witnessing dissonance between one's true Self and one's thoughtforms. We confuse them with authentic perception.

We see 'through a glass darkly'. Usually, our minds are filled with thoughts and memories at a subliminal level beyond our awareness. When we look, we are most often unable to see what is there. Instead, we see representations of memories or projections.

> Thoughtforms are, in essence, creations; they are the building blocks of the world around us.

Lost in Translation[7]

Consider the illustration above: although light-hearted, it exhibits everyday blocks to understanding others. When interacting with another, too often we do not listen to our truth behind a social facade, or the truth of what someone is trying to convey. Personal 'pollution' acts as a barrier. This is a classic case of communication being 'lost in translation'.

It is unfortunate that we do not perceive the other as the higher Being of Light they are, and others do not recognise this in us either. This leads to misunderstanding and invariably to the frustrating feeling that we are irrelevant, even when we are somehow shouting to be heard.

The veil to true perception is arguably one of humanity's biggest obstacles. It damages relationships with other people, with the outside world and with the Self. One of the most effective ways to lift this veil is to embark on the task of disempowering thoughtforms. Separating emotion from thought allows us to unveil the true root of behaviour. Having achieved this, it is possible then to see others, and the world, for who and what they truly are, rather than as we 'think' or 'feel' them to be.

> It is unfortunate that we do not perceive the other as the higher Being of Light they are, and others do not recognise this in us either.

---

7   Tribute to the artist: I have reproduced here a cartoon by Maria Barbara, aka Rainer Galea, Fluid Ink and the Phantom Scribbler, who passed away in September 2020. Maria had a love of cartooning from an early age and here she was able to portray the veils of separation between us with light humour and humanity. I honour her and her work.

Until a person can differentiate their dynamic of perception from vested interests, fears and defensive attitudes, it will be impossible to see, meet or comprehend human behaviour. Understanding the behaviour patterns and power of the three lower bodies is essential.

What this means is that whatever happens physically, mentally or emotionally will have either originated in, or caused ripples across, any of the other two bodies. Psychology is all about understanding this interrelationship between these energy fields, but to date it has not fully grasped the underlying differences operating that are determined by personal preference. Inner Alchemy helps us understand that the personal focus of consciousness (PFC) determines the quality of the creation that manifests according to personal or higher Will, allowing us to understand one another and act accordingly.

Let us now observe how the human faculties are used, beginning with the qualifying power of the emotions, i.e. the 'feeling blanket', which determines perception and conditions that we believe to be real.

THE POWER OF FEELING

Few people ask themselves, 'What is feeling?', 'What are emotions?' or, 'How do emotions arise and how might we manage them?' There are plenty of therapists and psychiatrists telling us how to control our emotions by chemical or hypnotic means, encouraging us to analyse them *ad nauseam* or to substitute them with something else. Most mainstream psychological methods do not really explain what emotions are and where they go, whether they are related to the body or if they arise from thoughts. Fundamentally, we might ask: 'What purpose do they serve?'

Have you ever stopped to consider how you use your emotions and the effect they have on the world around you, or how the emotions of others affect you? Are you controlled by your own or by the emotions of others, or do you artfully handle them? How? Are you at the mercy of your emotions or do you manipulate them knowingly? Can you discern good from 'bad' emotions, motivations, intentionality and values?

Emotion is a personal but also a collective phenomenon. Humanity moves in an ocean of emotions, generated by the astral (emotional) momentum of the past and by the present attitudes and beliefs of multitudes all over the world. Human emotion is perhaps the single most important factor in determining the quality of spiritual development. All of creation, from the human to the cosmic, responds to it. It colours and determines the quality of all life.

EMOTION AND FEELING

Emotion is a human phenomenon, whereas feeling is a *capacity*.

At the highest levels of Being, Love is the energy of cohesion, prevailing in Creation as sentience. Feeling is a creative, self-generated faculty. Human emotion stems from the pure feeling of Love, as the myriad of permutations and distortions of Love. Deriving as they do from an absence of Love, emotions are also manifestations of fear.

There is a world of difference between feeling and sensation. Sensation is the activity of intelligence in matter. Feeling does not arise within physical matter; it resonates with it. The body has its own instinctual reactions or emotions. These do not necessarily get processed by the mind, but instead are instinctive reactions such as aversions, avoidance, fears and physically-based addictions or habits. We also have psycho-physical reactions or emotions, predicated on personal history and defined as our 'psychology'.

Feeling amplifies energy. Thus, as a bearer of intelligence, the human being has the ability to envision something and give it energy through feeling. When a person views something as beautiful, this object of attention actually becomes beautiful; when they view something as ugly or fearful, the reverse becomes true. What we behold evokes a feeling in us, be it a novelty of the present, a repetition from the past or a constructive inspiration.

We qualify whatever we look at. Through our emotions, we are constantly bestowing a quality upon everything in our environment by the way we interpret it. The more people see something in a certain light, the more that which is viewed will conform to the way people see it. When enough people in a locality think and feel the same way, cultural idiosyncrasies and beliefs are formed. This mass feeling creates emotional trends and vortices of energy that, built together as they are by humanity, act with tremendous impact upon the individual, impinging upon their own energies through superstition, suggestion or even a form of hypnotic control.

If enough people see sex as evil, for example, then sex will manifest as something forbidden. If enough people see death as fearful, then death will be dreaded. There are many shared conceptions such as these, including the attitude about the process of ageing and decay. Our life span is short at this time, not only because of pollutants and stress, but also because of the consensual belief that we deteriorate with age.

The energy of the emotional body, in its pure and uncontaminated state, looks and feels like a scintillating mist of fine colours, much like the colouration of soap bubbles. Thoughts give emotions a context. When this energy is qualified personally – modified, intensified or frozen – by the individual, it takes on a different density and coloration. The energy becomes deeper in hue and muddier. The colours no longer operate through Spirit as they do in their pure state. They now reflect the selfishness or wilfulness of individual desire. At this point, the energy currents inherent within the emotional body, become agitated and turn into active vortices. Every time an individual feels a certain way, they deepen the groove. This vortex acts like a whirlpool, magnetically drawing in like energies, colouring those energies and then radiating out, affecting everything in its circumference. Before knowing it, they are projecting anger, fear and sadness through the power of the momentum of their emotions. The individual loses control over themselves. The vortex serves to stimulate, agitate, seduce or otherwise engulf the human being in negativity, such as irritation, dissatisfaction, frustration, lust, greed, pride or domination. This is the result of habitual and unconscious stimulation.

The emotional, mental and physical bodies of the personality are created from an etheric blueprint (the fourth body). This etheric blueprint contains the history of an individual's past lives, and the record of all actions, emotions and trends encoded in their cellular history. A human being's cellular history is the history of the lives and emotions of ancestors, which can manifest in their own emotional structure arising in the fourth body. As individuals, we not only have our own emotional conditioning to work through, we also have the cellular history of our ancestors to work through: our likes, dislikes, fears, doubts, pride and limitations respond in part to this history.

These ancestral records will not be modified unless you alter them through deliberate re-qualification. You alone hold the key, as they are a part of you. Unchecked, these impulses or compulsions continue to

The energy of the emotional body, in its pure and uncontaminated state, looks and feels like a scintillating mist of fine colours, much like the colouration of soap bubbles.

intensify similar characteristics as those of your ancestors in you, and add to the profusion of impulses generated by the age, culture and the individual life plan you choose, as well as seeds of past behaviour from your own past lives.

One must understand how important it is to work through emotions; to understand, face and conquer, so that the power of feeling may be freed to animate and enhance conscious creation. It is important to extricate oneself from the mass influence of energies and automatic habits, which coerce and sway the individual into inauthentic behaviour patterns, feeding a past momentum that may no longer apply to them.

In the past, people have attempted to master emotions by retreating or avoiding them in some way. In the East, this was and still is done through meditation and esoteric practice. In the West, this is typically done through mental forms of control like philosophy, affirmation or some forms of psychotherapy.

The cause of our present-day ills stems from a lack of understanding of the mechanics of the personality as an emotional compound. This compound has a mind of its own, so to speak, consisting of habits, impulses, unchecked or unexpressed desires, longings and aspirations – from the grossest to the sublime. In some psychological schools of thought, these impulses have been termed the 'ego', the 'id', the 'inner child', the 'libido', and so on. Usually, it is referred to as 'ego', meaning ego-centrism – that which separates a human being from Source.

It is becoming increasingly obvious that the way out of the pull of the emotions is not through philosophy or ordinary thinking, but through another, higher frequency: that of the activity of Spirit as pure Mind. Only higher frequency can alter the lower. The alchemist must recognise the power of feeling as the primary agent in the power of transmutation and creation of universes, from the personal to the cosmic. However, to understand the creation of universes, first one's own personal universe must be brought under control, particularly the interrelation of body, mind and feeling.

The heart, I remind you, is the 'abode of the highest living God': the 'I AM'. This voice of the heart is the Will of Spirit or divine Will. When you listen to the heart, you are attuned to Source, rather than personal will. This is perhaps what Jesus meant when He said, 'Father, if you are willing, take this cup from me; yet not my will, but yours be done'.[8] Here is a primal key to the art of transmutation: the power of feeling is amplified through a pure heart that expresses the Will of the Godhead (Source).

At this point you might now be able to answer for yourself the question, 'What are emotions *for?*'. They are to generate the Will of the Absolute through your own divine Presence, to create through the power of Spirit, to transform the whirlpool of emotions into the generating activity for transmutation of density that obstructs the Light. This happens by understanding who and what we are. It occurs as a result of conscious deliberate choice, by an act of Will; that is, by choosing to identify with our divine heritage, and by acknowledging unity with all that is rather than by reacting automatically to the physical laws of matter.

Loving and knowing are one activity. Your determination and choice stake your claim as a Being of Light manifesting the dominion and mastery that come from oneness with Spirit–Source.

To harmonise the emotions and generate feeling-vitality, my advice is to practise the Violet Flame Activation suggested in the opening pages of Part One (see pages 25–6) following the Master Practice (see pages 21–5), or do the Violet Flame Transmutation (see pages 151–3). As a natural side-effect in the cleansing process, you may have the impression that all density falls onto the ground like ashes and that a darkish smoke rises out of the spinal column. These are the substance of 'miscreations' that are being transmuted.

THE EMOTIONAL BODY

Emotions affect our entire body. The physical interface for the emotional body is the nervous system.

The impulse within the emotional body is one of desire. It longs for creativity through interaction with other energies; its nature is to reach, intermingle and relate. It yearns to embrace creation by merging with it, raise its own vibration and return to Self or Spirit–Source in its original form as Love.

Especially strong emotions, such as anger, fear or desire, project an image of ourselves that feels the object of its attraction. As with all desires, this self-projection is animated by the individual's own vitality.

---

8 Luke 22:42. *New International Version*

Be they conscious or unconscious, they deplete the physical body and draw from the body's reservoirs of vitality.

The emotional body, as a responsive network of the psycho-physical structure, is part of the planet. As a result of the largely selfish, adhesive nature of mis-qualified feeling upon the planet, the initially flowing liquidity of this body shows up as dense and sticky upon embodiment, adhering to like substances and creating an overall sense of heaviness.

The lower-frequency desires of this body thus coat the etheric body with density, slowing its vibration and pulling it magnetically down to the heavier Earth-bound frequencies. The experience of density at the level of the etheric double has been felt by anyone who has had astral out-of-body experiences in dreams. When the etheric double projects itself, it does so with a heavy sensation of moving as if through water and sometimes at a tilt.

Emotional intensity moves in cyclical activity. The emotional body especially responds to rhythm, particularly music. It loves the inspiration produced by art, nature and the excitement of the entire range of human expression. Through understanding that the emotional body seeks rhythm and responds in cycles, the individual can counterbalance the experience of sudden crashing that usually follows peak activity and avert the manic-depressive syndrome that characterises much social behaviour. In this way, they begin to establish the equilibrium that brings harmony and culminates in mastery.

Emotional thinking affects the environment in the form of judgements and accusations. We hate, dislike and are irritated by people and situations that mirror something within ourselves or from our emotional history that we have not come to terms with. As the usual energy field involved in relationships, the intensity of the compound energy field of two people's emotional bodies perpetuates the personal load called karma. All issues related to contractual and conditional giving, expectations and the many forms of manipulation operating in relationships are a direct result of the binding power of unchecked emotions. Much of the bonding that goes on in the name of ordinary love is extremely destructive. It may be perceived as thick, murky lines of force that tie people's emotional bodies together in a reciprocal swapping of power, attitudes and beliefs, to the extent that individual identity and sensitivity are largely lost.

—

Emotional intensity moves in cyclical activity. The emotional body especially responds to rhythm, particularly music. It loves the inspiration produced by art, nature and the excitement of the entire range of human expression.

—

The work of Inner Alchemy
at the emotional level
is to understand and
experience your own
attractions and repulsions,
your reactive as well as
responsive behaviour.

Doubt and fear are the primary gateways to negativity. If a person were to examine fear, for instance, they would see that it is based on a subliminal belief of being alone in an alien world, where they are vulnerable and frightened. That fear then transforms into doubt on the mental level and the individual ends up unable to trust themselves, let alone anyone else. Negative emotions are further amplifications of doubt and fear.

Everyone is caught within emotional mirages. Be sensitive and aware. Watch your expectations.

The work of Inner Alchemy at the emotional level is to understand and experience your own attractions and repulsions, your reactive as well as responsive behaviour. Observe your 'qualifications', i.e. the way in which you view reality through the filter of your own emotions and how you may redirect mis-qualifications into positive expressions. Ask yourself:

How am I feeling?

Am I responding to my environment or am I merely reacting to it?

How am I coming across? Am I successfully conveying the feeling that I have, or am I being interpreted differently?

How can I change the way that I perceive myself?

How can I change the way that others perceive me?

*What are my emotions about myself in my innermost privacy?
How is that different from how I connect emotionally in public?*

*How do I respond emotionally with my closest friends?
With a stranger?*

What are my distinctive likes and dislikes? How attached am I to them and to certain emotional patterns? Which ones am I addicted to?

What sort of people do I dislike and why? Do these people have traits that I am not acknowledging within myself?

Once these questions have been answered in deepest honesty, you need to act on what you have noted. Do this with your relationships, and note how you depend on others or others on you.

Interdependence is perhaps the most difficult lesson of third-dimensional existence. We co-exist with beings at all levels of consciousness. Attractions and repulsions are constantly being projected into the atmosphere. These attractions and repulsions constitute manipulation, which is employed by authority figures, parents, lovers, best friends, by the media and by educational institutions. Hypnotic control in the form of caring advice from friends and from psychics persuade and impinge upon our emotions. This augments fear, doubt and, especially, dependence upon authority and outside figures. When attention deviates from the innermost Self, personal power is relinquished.

The human aura is a most distressing sight, which is perhaps why it is merciful that most people do not possess clairvoyance. Vibrations, like the resonance they emit, travel to an object of dislike and return to sender with the same quality amplified. They then lodge in the aura, which depicts reddish and brown blobs, visual markers of stubbornness, selfishness and deceit in the lower bodies. Tears and wounds indicate places where a person has given away their power sexually, emotionally and intellectually. Here are lodged other people's energies, usually beliefs, which a person has adopted as their own. Personal energies are often dispersed in the auras of other people, whom we have manipulated in some way, and whose energies empower us instead of themselves.

The 'before and after' sequence of images, overleaf, illustrates an ordinary versus a 'cleared' aura. The aura serves as a visual representation of the inner work someone has undertaken on their personality. All energetic 'blocks' (negative thought patterning, addictions) show up in the aura. By working through these adherences and thoughtforms and therefore cleansing the emotional body, we may raise the rate of the emotional body's vibration and align with higher feeling at the level of Spirit.

The first image is of the greater dark aura most people have to a greater or lesser degree. It depicts someone who walks around hiding within their own illusion of self-containment, behaving automatically and in a self-centred way, surrounded by the negative thoughtforms (represented as clouds or a film over the aura) of worry and belief.

The human aura is a most distressing sight, which is perhaps why it is merciful that most people do not possess clairvoyance.

Dark, distorted aura, clogged with thoughtforms

Adhered thoughtforms, including attachments and influences

Cleansed aura

The second image shows how adherences stick to the physical body under the dark clouds of the general aura.

In the third illustration, the Light flows through and shines forth in a person who has worked on themselves, cleared themselves and who is becoming aware and conscious.

Extricating yourself from entanglement is called for in the first two images above, requiring a sort of peeling of your own skin and attitudes. This is the long and painful path of emotional mastery; it is critical, intense and unavoidable for spiritual evolution.

METHODS FOR LOOSENING AND FACING EMOTIONS

Several exercises are presented below. I designed them to help you understand how your emotions 'feel' on an energetic level and to aid you in the process of requalifying emotions and loosening emotional adherences in your energy field.

LOOSENING EMOTIONAL ENERGIES

The following method employs nonsense or gibberish talk. It is designed to bypass the mind's hold over emotions, allowing them to be expressed without intellectual content or meaning. You may wish to film yourself doing this to observe the visible difference in look and behaviour before and after the exercise.

Sit comfortably and alone.

Disconnect your phone and ensure that you can be as free as possible to express yourself, as this may include raising your voice.

Start rocking back and forth. Loosen your body and the mental hold over your thoughts.

Begin to make faces.

Start flapping your tongue and making noises, nonsense sounds like the sound of an engine: *'Brrrrmmmmmm... la la Ia prrrrtto o offa... Ia... Ia... mmmuuu... laggga.'*

Continue making these haphazard sounds and slowly build them into a nonsense language.

Dramatise the process: pretend that you are communicating with someone in this nonsense language and that you are telling a dramatic story. If any of the sounds you express start to have meaning and form words, it shows that your mind has got in the way. Change it.

Exaggerate even further by including gestures and your whole body. Disregard any feeling that you look silly or are acting in a ridiculous way. Stand up when the energy calls for it. You will notice the increase in vitality throughout your body as you loosen your hold over 'incomprehensible' emotional energies.

Continue the monologue, becoming more and more expressive, allowing for the waxing and waning of energy, and gently build it up again.

Become aware of the desire to communicate without any meaning. Feel the energy continuously swelling up within you. Give it a voice and gestures. Let the energy itself direct you.

Do this for about ten minutes and then stop. Rest.

Become aware of the emotions expressed. If you have filmed yourself, or have taken a 'selfie', you might notice how you now look, move or sound differently.

You will be surprised by the positive change in your aspect and in the experience of yourself. You have just shaken off a load of indecipherable and collective emotional imprints.

FACING EMOTIONS

The following exercise shows you how to transmute the negative expression of emotions into a positive expression. You may use anger, fear, sadness or any other emotion that comes up naturally, or explore those you have difficulty with.

When you have tapped into the negative quality of an emotion, allow yourself to find a positive expression of that very same energy. For instance, when anger is devoid of the personal defence mechanism that provokes it (i.e. its mental connotations), it is revealed as the driving force behind leadership: it is an energy capable of breaking through obstacles and reaching beyond into greatness. The transmuted force of anger, for instance, was arguably the driving force for many important leaders in our history, like Gandhi and Mother Theresa. Consider also the energy of fear. Fear and awareness fall within the same vibrational spectrum. Fear is an energy that summons antennae-like projections that produce greater awareness of surroundings. Used at the positive end of the spectrum, fear ignites finer sensitivity than what is 'usual' and enables caution. A greater sensitivity and awareness of one's surroundings can also result in empathy, i.e. awareness of the emotions of others. Thus, fear can be transformed into awareness, and anger into creative initiative.

Become aware of how thoughtforms and emotions are entangled, and may be disentangled, change the frequency of the emotional quality. In this way, a positive frequency is produced. The following exercises will guide you on how to use the power of transformation.

 ## FACING EMOTIONS EXERCISE

You must overcome all inhibitions that you may have acquired in your body and mind. Give yourself full permission to exaggerate.

Choose an emotion such as anger, fear, sadness or any other emotion that comes up naturally or you have difficulty with.

Take anger, for instance. It is irrelevant whether you are angry at someone in the present or in the past, or whether it is your anger or that of someone else. Summon the anger. Notice how it is triggered by a thought and an image. Intensify that sensation. Dramatise it, like in the previous exercise. Exaggerate it. Become aware of the energy within it. Forget about how you may look or be judged!

Tap into the quality of this emotion as a result of your experience directly. This will emerge spontaneously. Switch off mental connotations and feel the energy that remains. Discover the positive hidden behind that so-called negative emotion once you remove the negative labelling.

 ## OBSERVING THE EFFECT OF EMOTIONS

This exercise is to be done with a partner; someone you feel comfortable with and trust. There should be no holding back. The exercise is best led by a third party, so that both partners can be free to let go.

Sit facing your partner. Acknowledge and give thanks to each other for lending yourselves and your time to this experiment.

Pick an emotion or a negative characteristic, such as anger, greed, terror or deceit.

Each of you is going to play out this emotion before the other. You may not physically touch each other, but you must have full freedom of expression.

Decide who will be active first. The non-active person is to observe the other carefully while also observing themselves – their own bodily reactions and their own emotions – but they must not react or respond outwardly in any way (including laughing, or trying to stop, assuage or comfort the other).

During your turn as the active person, you should begin by eliciting a memory of a time or incident in which you were exposed to the particular emotion. For instance, if you are eliciting anger in this exercise, then remember a time when you felt this anger; feel the rage and indignation. If a memory does not come easily, then imagine a character in a book or in a film who had that experience. Evoke this with closed eyes.

Think of the images and events that triggered or could trigger this anger. Think of the injustice, perhaps. Intensify the anger within. Your partner might want to coax you into the feeling, if you have agreed to this previously and if you are having difficulty.

Keep building up the momentum. When ready, open your eyes and give yourself complete freedom to express the feeling verbally and through gestures in front of the other person. (Remember: the non-active partner has agreed not to react but to observe.)

Simultaneously, the non-active partner has been attempting to shield themselves from the energy. They may turn around, think of something else, do whatever they feel inclined to do *to not become involved* with the emotional energy coming at them. This part of the training is as important as the active part.

Sustain about three minutes of this intense expression.

A shift is induced by the person leading the exercise, who calls for an Alchemical Alignment with the receiver. The leader then calls upon the passive partner to open their heart and receive the energy, not as a negative qualification, but as pure energy instead.

The active partner should now involve the other person in their experience, surrounding them directly with the emotion in question, visually and emotionally.

A shift occurs spontaneously from the original emotion to a neutral energy. Both partners take note of their experience without discussing it yet.

Both parties notice the effects of emotion on the physical body. Allow the emotional reaction (crying, trembling, etc.), whatever it is, to subside before pausing and switching roles with your partner.

The non-active partner should take note of their own reaction. They should ask the following questions:

Who or what does this remind me of? In other words, what associations does this energy have for me?

What is my habitual defensive tactic? How do I respond? Do I run, hide or attack? Is this what I have done here?

What is my body experiencing? Pay especial attention to tension or tightness.

How do I feel now that I am aware of my reactions? Can I let them go?

Switch roles and repeat the whole procedure.

Only when both partners have had their turn, may you verbally share the experiences you had.

If unable to attain a peaceful state of neutrality easily, do your Alchemical Alignment (see the Master Practice, pages 22–5) again or the Visualisation to Spark the Brain (see pages 136–9) to bring yourself back to a state of balance and heartfulness.

Here is another meditation for spiritual balance.

RE-BALANCING THE BODY WITH THE THREE PRIMARY RAYS

This meditation serves all the bodies, but it is especially effective at the level of the emotional body.

The rays, as you may remember, are living energies that reflect pure cosmic qualities. They are known as the qualities of God and they are the constituent ingredients for all creation. Light emanates as beams or rays, but when it reaches the surface of Earth's physical density and acts upon matter itself, it becomes an etheric flame, such as the violet flame you are already familiar with.

At the heart of Being and Creation in general, in the form of the three primary flames, is the spark of Spirit and the seed of power for every activity. Within the physical form, at the heart chakra, is a miniature reproduction of this triune activity of Sacred Fire. This Sacred Fire is an etheric phenomenon that can be easily sensed and readily approached to charge, heal and balance yourself, strengthen your aura and irradiate qualities of perfection to everyone around.

In the remote past, at a time when the physical density of the human body was less dense, this triune flame was much larger and surrounded the body. With the densification of frequencies in modern times, the flame has shrunk to a much smaller size at the centre of the heart. The following meditation expands the flame back to its original size and brings about the harmony that is yours as a Being of Light.

THE MEDITATION

Sit down in a quiet, safe environment.

Bring yourself to a state of physical, mental and emotional stillness through the alignment induced in the Master Practice (see pages 21–5).

Visualise and sense a small flame within the centre of your chest.

Feel the activity of this energetic focus of inner Light and allow your whole attention to dwell within it. Go inside it. Notice that at the very centre of this brilliant core is a threefold flame. See it through the power of imagination. Activate it!

The first colour that strikes you is the bright yellow golden colour of the central flame: be in this; feel it.

The left flame is a deep pink with a magenta-coloured centre. Let your heart be embraced by that pink flame and amplify it.

The right flame is pale blue, with electric blue ribbons running through it. Now, let your heart be embraced by the blue flame, and expand it also.

Be with this three-tongued flame and notice it intertwine within itself, forming one magnificent flame. Become aware of a crystal sphere that seems to enfold the flame and cause it to give off a glow of multicoloured pastel light.

Now, as you focus within that flame, sense and see it grow brighter and brighter, and expand larger and larger. Continue this process until the flame completely surrounds your body and your aura.

Remain with this threefold flame and allow it to bring peace and balance to every part of you.

When you are ready to return to the ordinary world, enclose the flame into its usual size through deliberate, calm, centred breathing and visualisation. Hold and keep it inside as you would a secret treasure.

Take more deep breaths and ground yourself.

Allow gratitude for this Light in acknowledgement of your own Essence, your God-self. Having felt the magnitude of this power, permit yourself to bow in humble reverence.

CONCLUSIONS

Emotions originate within you and flow out into the atmosphere. People's individual emotional patterns are as varied as snowflakes. They reflect how finely attuned you are to yourself as Spirit, and consequently how you treat the environment and others.

Have you examined your behaviour from a physical point of view? Do you take the time to feel your body from within? I do not mean the tension and stress of athletic performance. I mean the gentle stirring of the breath inside you; the way your stomach feels when you overeat; or the way your body feels when you drug it with alcohol, tobacco and other poisons. Feeling yourself 'feeling'. What intentionality do you operate under when you are in close proximity to other bodies? Do you use or exploit situations or are you sensitive to the majesty of the life within?

As a third-dimensional being, you exist within an ocean of energy waves that continually animate recurrent thoughtforms. Within this reality, you have the powers to direct and recreate energy and substance through the conscious application of the Law of Light, or by allowing habits of unconsciousness to continue. The Law works whether you avail yourself of it or not. In Consciousness you create positive forms. In unconsciousness you perpetuate misery, lack and limitation, disease and strife. Either way, you are the creator.

Inner Alchemy advocates the deliberate and conscious application of the precepts of Light into ordinary daily life, beginning with your intimate life. Emotional life sets the foundation for everything that happens upon the planet and affects all bodies. For this reason, it is necessary to understand not only the principles underlying the

---

Emotions originate within you and flow out into the atmosphere. People's individual emotional patterns are as varied as snowflakes.

---

unconscious mechanisms of the emotional body, but also how to apply them constructively.

I cannot emphasise enough the tremendous power of the feeling faculty, especially as it applies to the projection of energy. Look at your moment-to-moment actions, thoughts and emotions to see the prevalence of automatic instinctual behaviour patterns. Fear is the seed feeling for all negativity, including the anger and violence that cloud our times.

People are constantly gossiping in the name of conversation. They give away their power through a misguided sense of loving and sharing. When people behold one another, they do so with greed and lust, possessiveness, jealousy and exploitation, instead of as unique beings of Light and Love and spiritual Power. When faced with injustice, they often retaliate belligerently with more injustice. In an era where so much lip service is paid to the virtues of surrender and 'turning the other cheek', peace and brotherhood, people misconstrue the messages by giving away more power to newer forms of political and religious authority.

Here and there friends of the Light are emerging. These are individuals who are embodying the teachings of Light, who hold to the vision of Light, who with great courage, gently but with unyielding firmness, hold the torch, lighting the world. Look for them.

But I also warn you, these are deceptive times. Things are not what they appear to be. You will know and see the 'real' only when you know and see your own Self as it is and as you have shaped it to be.

There are no teachers or guides, and there is no teaching. There is only *you*, in your wholeness. When you rejoice in fullness, you arrive home and everywhere at the same time. Only then you see others in the same light. Only then do you know the real meaning of power, the power of Light.

THE POWER OF THOUGHT

Thought is the primary impulse of being human: collecting sensations and feelings and putting them in context.

The power of thought goes hand in hand with the power of feeling. There cannot be one without the other, be it expressed or latent. Whenever there is feeling, there is an image, a trigger or a purpose behind it. A thought or idea occurs when an image or a series of images are

> I cannot emphasise enough the tremendous power of the feeling faculty, especially as it applies to the projection of energy.

created. Thoughts convey meaning when images strike a responsive chord in a person, who then responds to the images. This combination of image, plus feeling, leads to action and therefore a creation.

Thoughts are intention encapsulated into form. They encapsulate meaning. A thought is tangible. Clairvoyants and psychics know this well, as do parapsychologists who research extra-sensory perception and telepathy. Governments know it too when they apply astral propaganda and psychotronic warfare (psychic faculties to obtain information).[9] The media industry knows it also, when they create images, jingles and emotions that linger in the minds and feelings of the public. Thoughts are used without awareness. They are a tangible reality: they create negative, confusing imprints and massive traffic jams in the ethers. They pollute our atmosphere even without being voiced. They hold your own secrets, even from yourself.

We live in a world filled with double and triple meanings. The words say one thing, feeling conveys another, whereas the mind concocts yet another 'reality'.

Thoughtforms are composed of elements of the three lower bodies: physical, emotional and mental. Each person is surrounded by them, some stronger than others. Thoughtforms are formed of mental substance. Once an image is qualified by feeling, it is powered by vital energy. They surround the aura of an individual until the person stops giving energy to them. A thoughtform is held as long as an emotion animates it. Neutrality weakens a thoughtform.

The mental body is the field within which thoughts are stored. The field, frequency and manner of the mental body is linear and, in the case of the concrete lower mind, it is arrow-like. The frequency of the mental body is the same frequency of its component thoughts. When directed at another, thoughts can vary from acting as pellets launched at a target to heavy-duty ammunition.

—

Thoughts are intention encapsulated into form. They encapsulate meaning. A thought is tangible.

—

---

9 Astral propaganda is a kind of propaganda that was used, for example, in the Cold War. Images are projected by trained minds who are able to hold the focus long enough to imprint collective (or individual) consciousness, creating desire in people or coating ideas with fear and anger. Ordinary people do this all the time by holding in their mind a wish that involves something or someone else, until it somehow reaches the other and materialises in some way. It is also the basis for manifestation techniques.

Intelligence as thinking expressed at the level of the lower mental body, which is the level of detail, reflects the laws of matter. There is a regularity to it. It is definable. It can be defined by rules. It can be learned by rote. It demands neither flexibility nor spontaneity.

The mind moulds blueprints through visualisation. The lower mind and the Higher Mind operate on different levels. The lower mind uses the dynamics of the solar plexus and deals with outer reality. The Higher Mind uses the throat and third eye functions, although its primary source is the intelligence that lies within the heart. It deals with inner experience and with the aspects that bridge the inner world with the outer world. The upper chakras respond to finer frequencies; the lower chakras express lower frequencies of the thinking-mind.

All human powers are associated with, and serve themselves through, different chakra frequencies for manifestation at lower and higher ranges.

Thought as power is handled at both the upper and lower levels of Being: at one level ordinary thinking, at another the creative idea. Feeling (both emotion and sentiment) is what colours thought and its emission arises from the second chakra and also from the fourth (the heart). Feeling reverberates in the body tissue, stirring up substance and thus producing the energy that manifests as emotion. When this energy emanates at the highest level through the heart it mobilises higher feeling, or what I often call sentiment.

Consider the experience of 'feeling' associated with the second chakra, which deals with all types of energy exchanges between subject and object. It establishes relationships that reflect your emotional response or attitudes regarding the world and other people. This creates the subtle feedback that becomes like and dislike, opinions and even judgements. The second chakra is responsible for colouring our exchange with the world at large. Emotional activity at the level of the second chakra conditions matter by colouring it with your personal experience as interpretation. In this sense the second chakra manages or alters physical substance.

Each human power may express itself through one or all of the chakras and is not limited to any particular chakra.

Intelligence as thinking expressed at the level of the lower mental body, which is the level of detail, reflects the laws of matter.

THE LOWER MIND

For the purpose of simplification, I will speak about the lower mind as if it were an entity of its own, although lower mind is merely one way in which Mind is used, when directed by individual or personal will in daily life. The lower mind receives ideas from Spirit, interprets them according to its personal need or preference and implements them through a rational approach. This linear thinking is the natural way of third-dimensional life, where mind deals with detail.

The vision or understanding revealed through the lower mind functions solely from the perspective of the polarised physical world. Perception is divided into categories and pairs, which is the mind's way of comprehending duality. The mind erects systems upon these divisions: concepts of good or evil, right or wrong, with perception becoming narrow and one-sided.

The hidden files of the lower mind are those thoughts and memories that do not serve its immediate purposes, or that threaten to sabotage its immediate plans. This is how the subconscious aspect comes to be. These hidden portions of the lower mind are effectively disconnected from the whole organ, but are highly charged with instinctual emotional force, or libido. When consciously connected to feeling, these thoughts could prove dangerous, even life-threatening. Thoughts that are considered 'bad' are stuffed into the subconscious; those thoughts that are considered 'good', which, rather than originating from the Higher Mental body come from culture, are relegated to the superconscious.[10]

At the sub-planes of the lower mind, there are thoughts of domination and possessiveness, cruelty and sadism. At the higher sub-planes of the lower mind, there are thoughts of beauty, art, music and science. As such, lower mind fuels conscious, subconscious and superconscious aspects of the mind.

Understand that the mind, with the arrogance typical of the ego at the level of the lower mental body, will 'think' it has experienced, will 'think' it has forgiven and will proceed to act 'as if', to perpetuate the deceit that serves to confuse itself and humanity. This occurs through

—

The lower mind receives ideas from Spirit, interprets them according to its personal need or preference and implements them through a rational approach.

—

10 Here I use Freud's term, adapted for use in our vocabulary as subliminally active imprints that are of a higher vibrational quality. The subconscious and superconscious aspects are not 'better' or 'worse' than each other, they are merely thoughts originating from lower mind, of which the individual is not (yet) conscious.

lack of sensitive discernment of the environment. We will never come to understand the real workings of the mind unless, in deep humility, we understand reality beyond the scope of automatism of the lower mind. In order to reinstate the power of that highest, fullest aspect of Self, we need to recognise the lower as a tool for higher and greater force. The lower mind can be a wonderful servant, although too often an arrogant boss, who, left to itself, sits in judgement and exploitation.

Stop for a moment and examine your attitudes and beliefs. Be especially honest about your prejudices and inclinations.

Contrast what you think with what you feel, in areas in which you consider yourself weak or excessive.

A way to assess whether you are sending out double messages is to see how the world around you responds to your needs. Once you have understood the nature of your needs, are you manifesting them? Look at the reality of your immediate world. Does it fit in with your ideas? How often do you act on what you wish for? Is this authentic or does it reflect what you think you ought to do?

Not only do your three lower bodies, or aspects, need to be integrated and harmonised, you need to blend the energy at each level and manifest that integrity through physical action. Integrity shows up in your deeds and in a feeling of synchronicity with living things, not just in thoughts, however lofty they may be. Only then do you tap into the resources of the Higher Mind.

THE HIGHER MIND

The individual expressing themselves through the Higher Mind uses the faculties of the emotionally integrated lower mind. What at the one level appears as judgement, at another is discernment. What appears as arrogance, on the higher levels could be termed honour, integrity and fearlessness.

The inspirational activity of the Higher Mind reveals itself in thoughts of peace, brotherhood and goodwill. At this level, the whole is considered over the individual will. The language of the Higher Mind is primarily symbolic and abstract, embracing beyond personal consideration.

Higher Mind perceives beyond the rational. The student of Inner Alchemy must distinguish their mental faculty from mass mind and integrate the lessons of the emotions. At this higher level, the lower mind and the emotions move in harmony: the brain capacity expands to both right and left hemispheres, activating perception beyond duality. Whole brain thinking is the faculty of the Higher Mind.

When whole brain function is arrived at naturally, an entirely different state of Being emerges, which is qualitatively loving. The Higher Mental body is the result of an awakened heart. The direction of the individual's life – their energy and their attention – aligns with the level of the sixth, or causal body, the repository of all good achieved throughout the soul's lifetimes. The Higher Mind is the true intelligence of the heart. It is the realm of intuition and the 'knowing' that proceeds from accumulated inner experience. At the level of Higher Mind, the feeling nature within someone's heart has been refined from the heat of passionate intensity into the warmth of compassion and is ready to serve.

The actions of Higher Mind are inspired by compassion, love, understanding and forgiveness. The Higher Mind continues to avail itself of the mechanism of the lower mind, giving go or no-go decisions, but it does so objectively and impersonally. Its vantage point not only brings about the revelation of the individual's divine plan for life, but every possibility of fulfilment.

The Higher Mind is in partnership with the soul. The partnership will be as strong as the Consciousness poised at finer dimensions of Light.

In the Inner Alchemy School, we aim to co-exist in conscious and close proximity to the Higher Self, gaining access to creative ideas, forces and powers that enable us to rebuild the personality, the world and the planet.

Mind, tempered by purified feeling, turns self-indulgent reasoning into reciprocity and a greater vision of the whole. Mental activity is reduced but its frequency is accelerated, creating pockets of silence that attract far greater and higher thoughtforms. This also brings in the regenerative force from Spirit. This is the silence sought and achieved through meditation. Just as we create thoughtforms, as too do spiritual beings who release them as aids to humanity. You 'catch' these aids through silence.

Clarity is a virtue of silence and ultimate clarity is the experience of the highest frequencies, known as the emptiness of the Void or the Infinite All. In that overwhelming and humbling realisation, you come to know that 'I AM'.

—

The Higher Mind is in partnership with the soul. The partnership will be as strong as the Consciousness poised at finer dimensions of Light.

—

MIND ENERGETICS: METHODS OF ENERGY DYNAMICS

As in the pair exercise at the end of the section on the power of feeling (see pages 119–21), the following exercises demand your full participation and the commitment to explore, uninhibitedly, the energies within thoughtforms, which are usually subliminal. The three practices outlined below resemble the previous exploration of emotions, with the difference that here emotions are clearly propelled by thought.

EXPERIENCING THOUGHT PROJECTION

The three exercises that follow are best done in pairs, with a group of at least six people and led by a neutral party.

Sit facing your partner. Acknowledge the Light within each of you and verbally thank one another for the opportunity to explore the Self in a controlled environment of trust and cooperation.

You are now about to explore three basic energies that are commonly projected at you and that you often unconsciously project to others. These are emotional energies now charged with personal intent or thought. They are seduction, manipulation and coercion. These particular thoughts are heavily laced with egotistical, lower chakra desires.

THE ENERGY OF SEDUCTION EXERCISE

In this exercise both the opposite gender and same gender energy should be experienced so that it is in not confused with sexual advance.

Decide who will be active first. The non-active participant must not react. They should endeavour to observe themselves, their emotions, their energy fluctuations and their habitual impulse (avoidance or indulgence).

The non-active partner should shield themselves from the energy coming towards them. They should do this in the way that is natural to them. There should be no prior prompting. The whole point of the exercise is to discover how you protect and how you shield, however appropriate or effective this might be.

Now you, as the active partner, should elicit the thoughts that trigger the intention of seduction. The entire process is done without words and without touching the partner in order to grasp the frequency associated with this intention. Sounds, gestures and movements may be used as thoughts, sensations and emotional feeling are intensified. Notice the change in your breathing pattern and focus on it, making sounds. When ready, open your eyes and surround your partner with your energy.

Notice if there is any fear and go past it. You are exploring this energy in a loving environment. You are bringing it out of secrecy and into the Light.

Allow the energy to build intensely and continue to project it for about another two minutes.

Become aware of how you feel physically, mentally and emotionally.

Simultaneously, the non-active partner has been attempting to shield themselves from this energy. They may have turned around, be thinking of something else; whatever they feel inclined to do in order not to become involved with the manipulation aimed at them.

In the second phase of the exercise the leader calls for the Alchemical Alignment (see the Master Practice pages 21–5). The active partner continues to project seductive energy. The non-active partner now prepares themselves to receive the energy. The partner accepts the energy into the heart and only into the heart, transforming the emotional energy from lower stimulation into higher feeling. The heart here serves as the alchemical chamber or laboratory for transformation.

It is the receiver's deliberate intention that will determine the transformation. Both the active and non-active partner take note of their experience without discussing it with the other yet.

Roles are then reversed.

After both partners have had their turn at projecting, shielding and receiving the energy into the heart, they share their experiences with one another, noting the tremendous difference when energy was embraced by the power of consciousness in the heart.

POWER ENERGY EXERCISE

The process outlined in this section is identical to the previous one, except now the energy projected is that of imposed power: solar plexus energy.

Each partner, in turn, is to project the drive to get things done: this may be the experience of, for example, winning a competition; selling something; speaking up for a cause; or promoting a political campaign. Find the ways in which you apply these energies in your life. If you happen to be a fairly passive individual, then imagine being someone who is like this. Do your best to involve the other person in your scenario.

It could also be the energy of holding power or authority, or control over another person or situation.

The non-active partner is to try to resist in every way possible.

After about three minutes, the leader induces the Alchemical Alignment and the non-active partner (at a moment designated by the third party) accepts the energy into the heart, just as outlined previously.

Roles are reversed as before.

 INTELLECTUAL ENERGY EXERCISE

This time, the energy projected is directed from the lower mind, such as when persuading someone to do or think something, or when trying to win an argument through your ideas.

Put yourself in that frame of mind in which you are convinced you are right and the other is wrong. Mentally try to convince the other with your reasoning. Try to penetrate through whatever resistance they might have.

The non-active person shields themselves from this energy. At the designated moment after alignment, the non-active person accepts the energy into the heart. This usually requires that the receptive party visually bend the energy that is being directed from the frontal part of the third eye and see it entering in the heart.

Roles are also reversed.

Each of these exercises not only reveals your own psychology and the working of your mind, but the ways in which you unsuccessfully defend yourself. These exercises are not dangerous when carried out in supportive cooperation.

The technique provides excellent training in discernment and discrimination among the different qualities of energies that are mentally projected in conjunction with the chakras. Take note of the different sensations they each provoke.

Notice which of the three was the most difficult to send, to resist or to accept. Then notice what you experienced as sender when any of these three energies was received in the heart.

Herein lies the secret to your real self-defence.

MEDITATIONS AND EXERCISES FOR ENHANCED MENTAL POWERS

The meditations provided in the following section refine your power of thought, expand mental perception and raise the vibratory rate of your mental abilities.

VISUALISATION FOR WISDOM

This visualisation cleans and clears the brain of impurities and accelerates its rate of vibration.

Generate energy through the breath or through movement. When you feel filled with vital energy, and yet serene and aligned (as with the Master Practice), visualise a golden pyramid about three feet (one metre) on each side, pointing upwards, several feet above you in the centre of the room.

With your eyes closed, imagine a single eye within this pyramid. See crystal rays of Light emanating from the eye in all directions.

Sense the rays entering your own physical brain and opening the all-seeing eye of Spirit within you. Accept them.

Central Eye Visualisation

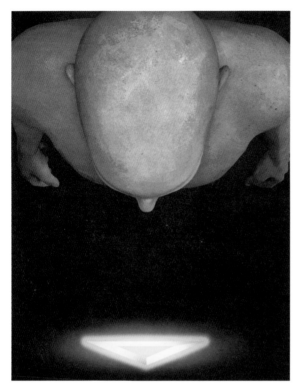

Step one of the 'Pi Yu' Exercise	*Step two of the 'Pi Yu' Exercise*

 EXERCISE TO UNITE HEART AND MIND

The following practice comes from Olive Pixley's repertoire of visualisations and meditations, and uses inner sound as well. Use the 'Pi Yu' illustrations above as a guide to this visualisation.

Picture a golden upright pyramid at a distance in front of you, at the same level as your third eye.

See the pyramid coming closer until it is flush against your forehead. Pull the pyramid inside your head to form a three-pointed base – one on each temple, the third towards the back of the head. The upper point is at your crown centre.

Step three of the 'Pi Yu' Exercise

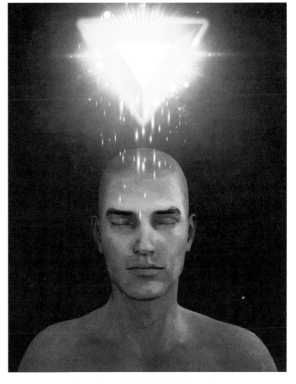

Step four of the 'Pi Yu' Exercise

Draw the pyramid in with your inbreath and use the inner sound (i.e. pronounced inwardly, wordlessly) *'pi'*, pronounced like the word 'pie'.

On the outbreath, to the inner sound *'yuuuu'*, visualise turning the pyramid inside out (like a sock) and imagine it rising, but upside down, base-side up. See the pyramid positioning itself over your head, with the point now pointing downwards into your heart.

The sensation produced is one of smoothness and a feeling of release. You might in time add a problem, a thought or a wish and imagine placing it on the base of the pyramid, just before you send it up to your Presence for requalification. Feel the Light that pours through from above into your heart.

Step one of the Golden Sun Visualisation

Step two of the Golden Sun Visualisation

 VISUALISATION TO SPARK THE BRAIN

This particular visualisation, see the Golden Sun illustrations above, is especially useful for interdimensional perception.

Visualise a bright golden yellow sun before you, the size of a plum.

Pull that sun inside your head. Sustain the visualisation of the bright golden sun within the brain, and visualise it colouring the grey matter of the brain in yellow golden Light. See your brain become golden.

Feel the sensation of this sizzling yellow golden sun within your head, and practise it sending out golden rays in all directions around you.

Step three of the Golden Sun Visualisation

Step four of the Golden Sun Visualisation

After a minute or so, follow the golden sun as it rises through the head and stops at a point about a foot (30 centimetres) above the head. Relax the head and sustain this picture and the accompanying sensation for as long as you can.

Allow whatever images appear within your mind to be there. Take note of them, without judgement and without trying to interpret them. Return to your usual reality in stages. Be sure to ground yourself thoroughly by filling the body with the presence of yourself as weight and density. When you are fully earthed back in your body, return.

'Ah Lah He Ay Veh' Exercise

 EXERCISE TO CLEAR THE MIND

This exercise also forms part of Olive Pixley's series of exercises to build an armour of Light.

In this exercise, a crystal white Light that stems from infinity is used to clear the mind (although 'infinity' may not be physically imaginable, you can picture this as a ray coming from above, as in the 'Ah Lah He Ay Veh' illustration above). It streams into your head and loops out to connect you with a symbol of the inner guide, teacher or Source.

The power of the Light streaming through the head washes the mind clean of all dusty thoughts accumulated during the day as you forcibly expel the air. Even though this exercise may be done at any time, it is especially helpful to do it at night. In the morning the mind awakens cleared of the previous day's frustrations.

This exercise forms the alignment proposal in the Master Practice (see pages 21–5). It is done either standing or sitting.

THE EXERCISE

Begin by connecting with the great Central Sun, through the awareness of your God-self. Invoke the forces of central Intelligence to descend. Call upon the visual image of your own Higher Self or that of a Master, such as Jesus, Buddha, Kwan Yin or of the Sun Presence, which represents individualised God-force.

On a deep inhalation to the sounds *'ah lah'*, bring in the Light, which is positioned just above and slightly forward of the head, entering through the throat.

On a forceful outbreath of release like blowing out air, to the sounds *'he-ay-veh'*, flash the Light through the head and out of the back of the neck, curving up and crossing the head from back to front, to issue out through the third eye as if flushing out all thoughts. Send the Light and its contents into the visualised radiance of the Christ-mind.

The head should be tilted upwards and this exercise should be done three times, whenever the need for clear thinking is sought.

Pronounce *'he'* as in 'see', *'ay'* as in 'day', and *'ve'* as in the way you would pronounce the first syllable in the word 'verily'.

THE POWER OF THE SPOKEN WORD

Who has not pondered the meaning behind the biblical statement, 'In the beginning was the Word'?

As outlined in the Introduction, the primordial Source is a nexus of vibration, from which all substance and all attributes derive. This Source is a state of Oneness. It is the universal sum total of as-yet unqualified energy. The instant the energy is qualified and becomes 'something', its vibration collapses. This process of qualification occurs through sound. From an oceanic, all-pervading humming (which is the primordial sound in *'Om'*, *'Aum'*, *'I AM'*), it individuates into notes. Each resonance vibrates in a unique way, breaking up into some kind of form (into parts). It becomes substantial. Sound is the precipitating activity that coalesces substance by gathering energy into clusters, which then mould into a form. Colour is sound as substance. Thus, you may understand how the rays build or create all that is through combinations of colour/sound frequency, thereby allowing Light substance and physical matter to emerge as form.

It stands to reason that just as sound creates, it can also destroy. This has been proved again and again by science in the last century. Ultrasound waves, for instance, may kill bacteria and cancer cells. Sonic booms can cause shock waves that damage surrounding objects. On a more poetic note, the opera singer Caruso's voice could break glass!

It is easy to forget the awesome vibratory power that lies in sound. The scientific field of acoustics is constantly revealing innovative new uses for sound. Scientists have long used sound to move small objects in the air, a phenomenon known as acoustic levitation. Apart from its technological uses, sound is a vital survival method in the animal kingdom and our primary mode of communication.

You utilise the same principles in creating yourself and your worlds. Not knowing how to use sound purely, you use the spoken word. A word is a sound that has been invested with meaning; it carries a thoughtform and a feeling. Tone is a qualifier that conveys feeling and colours the environment. When tone is injected into a word that carries intentionality, we have formulas such as 'abracadabra', or 'Be Still and Know', power phrases, incantations, decrees and affirmations, which bring about envisioned results.

The throat chakra, a vehicle for first ray activity, is responsible for expressing will: both personal will and divine Will. Will is the propelling force for manifestation and creation. The throat chakra can express bitter-sweet emotionality, romance and sensuality; it can express raw power, and even violence. When the throat chakra is at the service of the upper chakras, the sound produced inspires, uplifts, lulls and awakens. It also nourishes, imparting the will to live and transmitting warm folds of security as well as the dreamy spaces of Light and Love.

Once a thoughtform has been constructed, the Light-form counterpart of that which you wish to manifest physically is activated. You invoke the 'substance' of Light, following the formula for creation: sound, or the spoken, i.e. vibrated, word.

All words are invested with cumulative power or momentum. Magical formulas and incantations are invested with the accumulated energy from thousands of magicians and adepts from centuries past, who have created a powerful vortex for manifestation. Although we have retained the knowledge of some formulas, humanity has lost most of them and has mostly lost the deeper understanding of the dynamics involved.

Not knowing how to use sound purely, you use the spoken word. A word is a sound that has been invested with meaning; it carries a thoughtform and a feeling.

Here, as always, one has to thank the grace of Spirit and of the luminous presence, of the Masters, teachers and guides, who guard and inspire all. We must thank them for having sealed off the knowledge of the dynamics of the Law of the One from past civilisations that did not have the refinement needed for the correct ethical implementation of higher principles. One has to thank them also for having reopened that seal now. Now is the time to recreate and rediscover the workings of the Law in awareness of the divine partnership with Spirit.

MAKING THE CALL AND HOW TO APPLY IT

All substance, whether of Light or matter, follows the command of the Word. Before making the call or issuing a decree, an affirmation or a spiritual fiat, you must be in correct alignment with both Earth and cosmic forces through the Master Practice (see pages 21–5).

Alchemical formulas follow the same mechanism as in the Alchemical Alignment and consist of these simple steps:

Invocation

This means extending your physical life force – the powers of thought or visualisation, feeling and words – up to the God-self, connecting with that higher frequency in a way that reverberates back upon physical reality. Starting the call means formulating your intentions in a clear way.

Identification

In this step, identify that frequency of the God-self as your own, allowing waves of energy to gather and be sustained within the body. At the same time, affirm 'I AM' in whatever is invoked ('I AM serving my highest purpose'). In this manner, as Source, you project energy from the highest level down into matter.

Acceptance

This means re-descending into the consciousness of the physical body and embodying the Light experienced at the higher dimensions, where you have accepted your identity as a God-self within matter, fulfilling the call you have made. The acceptance of your identity is stated as a fact, which sets the mental blueprint for physical activity to follow and carry out the invocation.

Pay attention to this formula, for it will be the basis of much of your alchemical work and will be frequently referred to in the following pages.

'Making the Call' works according to the same principle as the dynamics involved in the law of supply and demand. You create a demand (what you are asking for) and it is then released (supplied) to you.

You are reaching for your Self, the highest Source, and then giving to yourself. You are coming from a place of centrality and wholeness, with focus, and using the faculties of Higher Mind.

Thoughtforms act as a magnetic drawing force. When you issue a decree or affirmation with power and conviction, i.e. combining the adequate intensity of feeling with visualisation to produce a dynamic living impulse, the visualisation congeals into a positive image within the aura. You set a pattern that physical matter must follow, and you begin to create your own world.

Everything in creation moves in cycles. Whatever goes out returns to the sender, qualified and multiplied by the force of its trajectory. A call compels an answer. This is the meaning behind Jesus' statement, 'Knock and the door will be opened to you'.[11]

The problem lies not in the answering process, but in the way in which the call is made. If projected through fear and need, it will return the same qualities to the sender. If projected in full consciousness, no miracle is too big. The projected energy, in this case, is that of Love.

THE BASIC ALCHEMICAL FORMULA

The following section serves to reinforce the Master Practice (see pages 21–5), now that you understand the power of feeling, thought and the spoken word.

To connect experientially with higher vibrational frequencies, one still needs to use third-dimensional vocabulary. Although there is, of course, no real map for the dimensions beyond our third, you may guide yourself through the use of certain visualisations and emotions, thereby translating multidimensional reality into third-dimensional linearity. The best illustration for Consciousness I have found is the vertical one, adapted for the Master Practice meditation presented in Part One. This

---

11 Luke 11:9. *New International Version.*

> Everything in creation moves in cycles. Whatever goes out returns to the sender, qualified and multiplied by the force of its trajectory. A call compels an answer.

illustration is as old as humankind upon the planet but was reintroduced to the public at the end of last century by the Theosophical movement and popularised in the 1930s by Mr and Mrs Guy W. Ballard. It is the roadmap used in the Master Practice and resembles the Inner Alchemy dimensional chart explained in Part Five (see pages 200–1).

As you visualise a vertical ascent of your Consciousness, you actually move the energy interdimensionally and effect a vibrational acceleration.

The individualised God-self is the highest vibrational frequency possible for any intelligence in embodiment. The pure sustained intensity of this dimensional frequency is something that is not available, or possible, in this dimension. The God-self is an interiority. It is a space that does not correspond to physical time-space, but precedes and accompanies heightened sensibility. Like the dimensions beyond and below the individualised God-self, it is experienced as simultaneous space within the Now. The fact that your experience of this God-self is coincidental and experienced as an energy frequency finer than this one indicates that your Being is part of it. You would not be able to experience that which is not a part of you.

In the following practice, the Source-point (the centralised position acquired by the focus of a person identified with Source) is located about thirty feet (nine metres) directly over the head when sitting or standing, and the same height over the body at an angle while lying down. There is no exact correlation between distance and dimensionality. This is merely an approximation.

As you ascend, there can be a sense of riding a supersonic jet during take-off. Before engaging on the 'take-off', you need to be wholly grounded in your physicality; sensorially, emotionally and mentally. This serves as the anchor. It is precisely the physical vehicle you want to charge to be able to transmit the higher frequencies around you with goodwill and blessing, and in so doing ennoble, uplift and refine for the good of all, shunning self-pleasure and gratification.

Next, locate the heart centre, because it is through the heart that you connect to interdimensionality and to Spirit. In esoteric traditions of the past, this was visualised as the sacred heart, or the abode of the sacred fire, the home of the Divine Spark. A multicoloured flame is formed in the heart that radiates in all directions, its radius in proportion to the degree of purity

> The individualised God-self is the highest vibrational frequency possible for any intelligence in embodiment. The pure sustained intensity of this dimensional frequency is something that is not available, or possible, in this dimension.

and spiritual development of the individual. This flame can be magnified and sustained according to your ability to sustain the frequency.

Within the sacred fire in the heart reside all the powers of the God-self and the faculties of Light. The sacred heart is an exact replica of yourself as essence. You might, at this point, consider that you are, in fact, a simultaneous reality – you are both a being of Spirit and matter – and understand how your physical self is a projection from the farthest dimension of Spirit-self.

Next, follow an energetic line, a beam of Light, extending from the heart upwards to the Source-point about thirty feet (nine metres) above, rising through the heart, throat, head and out; continue until you experience a focus of Light so intense that you can scarcely contain its energy.

The Light appears brilliant white and contains all the different rays and colours of the spectrum. As you consider your totality of being, you come to understand now the saying: 'I AM THAT I AM', meaning 'I AM down here in physical embodiment THAT I AM up there in Light-substance'. Saying this is an affirmation that establishes the Alchemical Alignment in etheric form, connecting the matter of your Earth body to the substance of your Light body.

The way in which you use the spoken word in Making a Call is critical, as is the visualisation involved. Notice the difference between what some people call prayer and an affirmation such as the one cited above ('I AM THAT I AM'). The common misconception about prayer is that the one praying is begging for something from an outside god: one is seeking help 'out there'. This implies that the individual is inferior, identified with limitations, temporality and third-dimensionality. Instead, with the use of the power words 'I AM', you affirm, make your claim and establish in word and in deed (your visualisation) that you and your Source are One.

When you Make the Call now, at the third stage of acceptance, you make the statement:

'I know that you and I are One. Where you are, there is no time and space. Everything exists in pure potentiality. As I speak in calling for the manifestation of your divine gifts and the fulfilment of your divine plan for me on this Earth, I know that this call is already fulfilled.'

Step one of the Alchemical Alignment

Step two of the Alchemical Alignment

Step three of the Alchemical Alignment

Step four of the Alchemical Alignment

You pull the seed idea, or affirmation, into physical reality. You are perfectly aware that you exist in two dimensions simultaneously and exert the powers over both the substance of Light and matter.

'Making the Call' and the Alchemical Alignment constitute the Alchemical Formula.

THE PROTECTIVE TUBE OF LIGHT

The protective Tube of Light is an extension of the Master Practice (see pages 21–5). The Tube of Light is an emanation from the God-self, that arises from invoked and sustained contact with the God-self. The Tube is an emanation that surrounds the physical self to resemble a tube or cylinder, enfolding the whole body.

The Tube of Light also serves as a tunnel or passageway for Consciousness through the dimensions. The Tube of Light helps enable an acceleration of the frequency we are able to sustain in the physical body. This acceleration resembles what the Self experiences at the moment of death with the separation of the personal concrete mind from the elements that compose the body. Both of these experiences involve a projection of consciousness as awareness.

At the onset of physical embodiment upon the planet, use of the Tube as a protective shield was an activity that was automatically sustained. As the centuries progressed, humans turned more and more towards personal and physical satisfaction, without any integration with spiritual experience. As a result of the frequency of their material investments, the resonance emitted from their bodies damaged the natural protective shields such as this one, culminating in their relinquishing of their God-powers.

Humanity has been operating without tangible physical protection through these very real 'dark ages' of the soul. This has made it prey to manipulation and superstition. Even where protective methods have been taught, they are often practised robotically, without inner understanding.

Step five of the Alchemical Alignment

People have also prayed to an outside god for too long, rather than acknowledging their Source.

Should you wish to regain the protection lost, you must turn to the Light and consciously rebuild the Tube of Light through the use of the three creative powers. The first step entails having faith in the power of the God-self, identifying with it, trusting the experience of it, remembering it often enough and applying it – in other words, you must *dare to believe* and acknowledge the power of Spirit. To rebuild the Tube of Light, your invocation might use words such as these:

'Beloved Presence of God, which I AM! I send my love to you and ask that you enfold me in your Light of pure electronic substance, which keeps me protected and insulated against all that is not of the Light and keeps me consciously sensitive to you within me.'

As you say these words (and I suggest you make up your own too), stay with them until you build momentum. You need to feel consciously what you are saying, experience the power of that feeling, and also the circuit you are creating. You also need to sustain the visualisation and make it so real that you would even want to raise your arms and extend them around you, sensing the thoughtform you have created through the power of Spirit and fully identifying with it.

THE EXERCISE

Feel and see yourself as the God-self.

As you look down, see yourself surrounded by a cylinder, like a large beam of Light you have projected as the God-self.

Send so much love down to your physical self that you feel as if your heart would burst. Visualise that love coming down and over your physical body, strengthening the cylinder of pure electronic Light-substance.

Then, come back down and feel yourself from the perspective of the human self, surrounded by this Tube of Light. You may want to use an affirmation such as the following:

'I AM a child of Light. I love the Light. I AM protected, illumined and sealed by the Light. I move in the Light and forever live in the Light. I thank you!'

Become aware, from this moment on, of the use of the words 'I AM'. Let these words serve as a reminder of the God-self, 'the God I AM'. You might like to say something like this:

'I AM the circle of protection around me, which is invincible and repels instantly everything discordant from my being and world. I AM the perfection of my world, now and forever.'

Always end with a statement of acceptance and a benediction, an expression of acknowledgement, gratitude and blessing. This may go something like this:

'As the Consciousness I AM, all time and space is one. As these words are spoken, it is done! I know it. I see it. I believe it. I accept it. I thank you!'

The experience here is one of humility, yet also power. In making the call for your protective cylinder of Light, as for all things, you exert your authority over physical substance and your responsibility for creating your world. But you also acknowledge your God-self and the power of Light that is Spirit. In the past we erred through employing either too much power – personally qualified power, remember – or too much humility. The first has made us ruthless, the second has rendered us ineffectual in the world.

The final phase of Making the Call is the seal, the acknowledgement that confirms the physical reality:

'So be it. It is done. Amen'.

THE VIOLET FLAME: ETHEREALISATION AND MAGNETISATION

Once you have fenced off your territory with the seal, by invoking the Tube of protective Light from the Godhead, you confront and change, re-qualify and transmute trends, habits, impulses, compulsions, beliefs. You may even transmute physical substance, like disease and malformations, malfunctions and projections. As already suggested in Part One, you do this through invoking the Violet Flame. The Violet Flame is the 'mysterious' frequency of transubstantiation and grace.

It serves this age, in which old thoughtforms are being dissolved and the substance of the planet is being transmuted. In this sense, the Violet Flame exemplifies purification and redemption, advocating transmutation and sublimation, which is, in effect, the raising of an energy to a higher frequency.

Inner Alchemy occurs when the Violet Flame is drawn into a condition or state usually with an intention to alter it. The Violet Flame addresses the intelligence within that substance, accelerating the substance so that it may leap into another vibratory rate to produce a qualitatively different substance altogether. This activity defines the human being in embodiment, a creator of forms, a Consciousness with direct access to physical substance, who by his or her very embodiment is in a position of authority over substance.

—

The presence of the Violet Flame will serve to bring up all the impurity or miscreation for review and re-qualification. This means you have to face what arises, look at it, deal with it physically, mentally and emotionally.

—

The presence of the Violet Flame will serve to bring up all the impurity or miscreation for review and re-qualification. This means you have to face what arises, look at it, deal with it physically, mentally and emotionally, while also regarding it from the perspective of the Higher Self and the transmutation process. In the case of physical disease or disturbance, you need to confront the causes behind the afflictions.

When faced and understood, miscreations are ready for release. The process here is called 'etherealisation', which is the release of the building blocks or electrons (both the physical and nonphysical kind), back into the formlessness of Source. This is, in other words, the process of dematerialisation. With the release of these electromagnetic electrons, a magnetic centre is created, which provides a space for Light to descend and recreate substance in its likeness – perfection. This part of the process is called 'magnetisation'. The Violet Flame is responsible both for etherealisation and for magnetisation at every level of substance, from the substances of Light to those of matter.

The Violet Flame has been called the flame of forgiveness and mercy. Seen from the perspective of the personal self it is experienced as grace.

The Violet Flame is a very important visualisation for Inner Alchemy work, which is why I outlined the Violet Flame Activation exercise in Part One (see pages 25–6). An illustration that you may use as a visualisation guide to accompany the following exercise appears on page 152.

 VIOLET FLAME TRANSMUTATION

The Violet Flame may be used in the process of transmutation in the following way:

- Visualise it enfolding your body. 'Feel' it, sense it outside your body and inside your body, in your solar plexus and so on. See it around you, swelling to cover your aura within the protective Tube of Light.
- Direct it into wherever you need it, physically, mentally, emotionally, and see it acting there, breaking up thoughtforms and dissolving substance. Watch what actions it takes, appearing at times to sweep, blaze, boil, spin and explode thoughtforms and all substance.
- Claim the transmuted energy. Send it out into the depths of the planet Earth, with love and forgiveness, with blessings and in goodwill.
- Test or check out its effects, acknowledging that the triggering thoughts, ailments or emotions are no longer there.
- Seal the operation.

Your affirmation of the Violet Flame, accompanied by the visualisation and feeling-sensation associated with it, is addressed to your own I AM Presence and may sound something like this:

'Beloved Presence of God that I AM, blaze now through and around me the violet transmuting flame. Purify and transmute in me and my world all that is not of the Light – all impurity, lower emotions, wrong concepts including negative etheric records of my lifestream – known or unknown. Keep this activity sustained and active. Re-qualify and replace all by purified substance, power of accomplishment and the divine plan fulfilled. I AM, I AM, I AM.'

It is not enough to pray vaguely. It is not enough to imagine. It is not enough to convince yourself that you have forgiven yourself or someone who may have wronged you. It is not enough to substitute wrong behaviour through imposing new, artificial modalities. It is imperative that you incorporate the new behaviour in the three energy bodies of the personality.

You will need to put your intention into physical form and to check your habitual thoughts to ensure that the old patterns are not recreated.

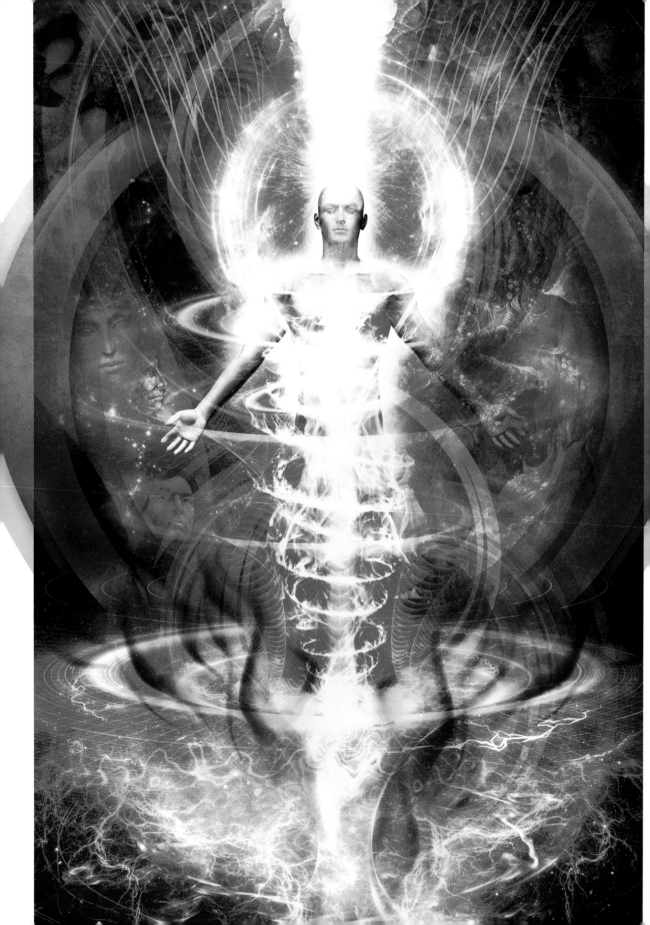

The way in which you prepare yourself for Light-work in Inner Alchemy is by doing the Master Practice and the Violet Flame practices daily. This protection tool separates you from the web of third-dimensional desires and thoughtforms, in order that you may transmute your own creations and proceed with your evolution and your life's purpose.

It is a good idea to practise protective shielding upon rising in the morning and upon going to sleep. When you visualise shielding at night before going to sleep, know that your physical body is held within the transmuting fire. Your consciousness, on the other hand, goes up through the Tube into the higher vibratory realms. Without this protection, you might get affected while you sleep by the surrounding psychic and lower astral forces that interpenetrate your world.

You may want to commune with your God-self often; acknowledge it, establish a dialogue with it and direct your thoughts as well as your inner vision vertically. Listen for responses, which will at first be vibrational but in time will come in the form of images and perhaps even words. Even if you practise nothing else but these two processes – the Master Practice and the Violet Flame practices – alchemical secrets will unfold within you automatically. You will gain access to higher knowledge and insight directly, without intermediaries.

Transmutation by the Violet Flame

1. *The Violet Flame is activated through visualization to form a vortex around the body.*
2. *The vortex sweeps downwards, rotating clockwise around and through the body.*
3. *As it circles down, the vortex picks up debris from the astral field within and surrounding the physical body.*
4. *The origin and meaning of these adherences stand revealed for self-processing.*
5. *The power of the vortex intensifies as it reaches the surface of the Earth and drags the debris down.*
6. *The load is absorbed by the Earth as astral debris, while the subtle residue is absorbed by the heavens as a darkish smoke.*

There will be times when you will be shown answers to questions or dilemmas in your life. Your personality will be exposed and revealed. The history of your individual lifestream will unfold. The Akashic records (the repository of all memory in the Universe) will display your memory in visual and tangible forms, and open dimensional doorways.

Each time you create the Alchemical Alignment through the Master Practice and project your consciousness into higher frequencies, you affect your physical cellular structure, recalibrating yourself in patterns of Light-substance.

SOUND PRACTICES TO EXERCISE THE POWER OF THE SPOKEN WORD

Sound practices are very powerful physical exercises that the student may use to enhance the power of the word. They vary widely: from playing with sound vibration, such as humming and 'toning', to repeating mantras and affirmations. I provide meditations and exercises below that utilise sound and also colour.

 HUMMING PRACTICE

Humming is one of the most effective ways of balancing yourself, as it resonates with each of your bodies. The vibratory activity set off by your humming redistributes the energy throughout your cellular structure as well. Momentum is important. Once you begin, you should stay with it for at least ten minutes.

Your eyes should be closed. Align.

Sit comfortably in a position you can hold without having to shift or adjust. Loosen your clothing.

Begin to hum. At first you will feel the vibration locally in the throat area and in the head. Allow the vibration to echo throughout your body.

Be inside your body, and gently, through the power of your visualisation and sensing, spread the vibration right down to your toes and the soles of your feet.

Feel your entire body pulsating.

Now extend your awareness to the space around you and feel the humming like an invisible membrane vibrating. See your physical body as a central cord, resonating and vibrating throughout the entire room.

If there is any area of your body that is unwell, direct the sound to it for a few minutes, using your hand to focus the energy if you need to, and then proceed to expand the vibratory activity.

You may intensify the activity by extending your arms out around you. Holding your palms facing upwards helps to give out energy; palms down helps to gather it. Explore both positions.

Qualify the outflow now with the energy of your heart. Send out, through sound and through your palms, your own individual quality of Being into the Universe.

Continue as long as you like. After you stop humming, sit silently (or lie) for as long as you need.

 ## GROUP HUMMING PRACTICE

This is very powerful process, particularly if you join hands in the group. The momentum builds much more intensely if the sound is held continuously, without breaks. Be sure there is always someone humming while others are taking breaths.

After about twenty minutes, a magnificent pillar of blue flame gathers naturally in the centre of a circle where people are humming. Within that pillar, you can place people or images of people or places you would like to heal or bless with this force.

 ## OTHER SOUNDS: TONING

Vowels are powerful in the way they transmit sound. Explore the quality of energy created by each vowel sound. Notice how you feel when chanting them. Notice how it feels when someone else chants them.

You might like to investigate the properties of 'toning' with one another. Do this in pairs or in threesomes. One or two people can do the actual toning while the receiver lies down, eyes closed, and experiences the effect of sound upon their body.

Chant each vowel softly. When doing it with another, be sure to harmonise the tones. Get really close to one another and to the area in the body you are focusing on. You might like to start with the area of the belly and move down the grounding circuit, through the legs and feet. Then you might want to try the healing circuit, from the heart and down the arms and hands. I suggest you do not tone around the head area. At this level, the individual can tone themselves much better.

Notice the different effect of each of the vowels. The sound *'ah'* will serve to expand. The sound *'eh'* is a bit deeper and rounder, creating a soft vortex of energy. The sound *'ee'* (as in 'we') is quite focused and seems to vibrate in a spiral formation. *'Oh'* penetrates and reverberates within. The sound *'u'* (or *'oo'*) goes deepest of all, penetrating the body almost like a laser beam.

Now explore different pitches.

Whenever you practise toning, be sure to talk and comfort the person who is being toned. Never create discomfort and always leave them feeling whole. You might like to end with a few minutes of silent laying-on of hands onto the person being toned. If there are three of you, one person can be at the head and the other at the feet, gently blending with the subject in loving intentionality.

The whole purpose of this exercise is to redistribute energy through the effects of sound upon your physical, mental and emotional bodies. Once you are familiar with the different sounds and tones, you may use them to harmonise or energise yourself as needed.

Explore the effects of chanting the powerful combination of vowels, which form the sacred word *'I-A-O-U-E'* in one long exhalation. Hear yourself. You will find that they sound like the sacred Hebrew name for God, 'Yahweh'.

MANTRAS

Words have an even stronger effect than sounds. There are combinations of words you can make yourself. I especially like chanting 'I AM' over and over again. The sound and the feeling, together with visualisation, serve to energise and harmonise. There are also the traditional mantras, which contain centuries of momentum and qualification, such as *'Aum'* or *'Om'*.

Explore sounds and sensations. When you have connected with yourself at interdimensional levels (as will be explained shortly in Part Five), you may discover your own resonance at different levels of Being. When you

— The whole purpose of this exercise is to redistribute energy through the effects of sound upon your physical, mental and emotional bodies. —

hear such a sound or name with your inner senses, chant it and discover its properties.

Here is an example of an extremely powerful Buddhist chant for the heart. It brings peace and stillness: *'Aditya Hridayam punyam, sharu shastru bina shaman'*. Get to the point where you can do it all in one exhalation.

Then there is one of my favourites, the Sufi affirmation, 'Nothing exists but God!', or *'La ilaha illa llah'*. There are many, many others – experiment.

SOUND AND MOVEMENT

Sound and movement are a potent combination for energy work, used by Sufi dervishes in the form of *zikrs*, which are mantras chanted in combination with movement and dances performed ritualistically, akin to many tribal customs.

The Sufis are perhaps the best practitioners of an earthy esotericism that unites body, mind and Spirit. If dance, chant, rhythm and devotion appeal to you, you would do well to explore Sufi practices, including the whirling dance of the dervishes.

I want to propose a simple practice to centre you that allows you to feel the power of sound and movement, in this case to centre you.

For this practice, it is best to sit cross-legged on the floor or on a flat platform. If this is not possible, then sit on a stool with your feet firmly planted on the ground, without tension. You must not have back support for this exercise.

After the initial humming practices suggested earlier, place both your hands at the level of the navel while continuing to hum. Begin to rotate your body in a clockwise fashion from the pelvic cradle. The back must be straight. The axis for movement is at the level of the navel centre. Become aware of your shoulders and avoid the tendency to slouch. Also avoid the opposite sway-back rigidity, which would prevent you from connecting with this centre. Continue for at least ten minutes rotating to each side. Then stop. Feel. Be.

You emerge feeling stronger and more centred in your body. Practise it and see.

THE NATURE OF COLOUR

Light manifests as sound and colour. Colour and sound can be used to affect your vibratory activity.

By exposing the physical system to the vibration of colour or its sound, you are able to balance the body. As you grow in consciousness, you become more aware of sound colours in the environment, clothing and music.

Colour affects behaviour. The best nourishment we can give ourselves is through green, the colour of nature. It is the middle colour of the spectrum, as well as being the colour of the ray affecting the heart chakra. It promotes balance and harmony.

You might like to take another look at the chart on the rays and their uses (see page 71), and to explore the effects of colour.

In using colour, as in Making the Call (see pages 141–2), you may invoke purity, healing, illumination of the intellect, abundance or many other things. In your Alchemical Alignment practice, you may witness colours emanating from Source without having to select or direct them, or you may project healing colours of your choice. All you need to do is affirm, 'I AM THAT I AM', identifying with the Presence and acting in its Name.

The colour of any ray may be used to effect change and can be used in conjunction with the Violet Flame practice. Surround, direct and enfold yourself with light and colour.

For many, the favourite colour used for the emotional body, after violet, is pale gold. Gold soothes, heals and stimulates healthy and peaceful activity at the solar plexus, the energetic coordinating centre for the lower chakras. The visualisation of a golden liquid Light descending from above is especially helpful, as is the visualisation of a golden shield placed in the centre of the solar plexus (see illustration, page 162).

Source expresses itself dimensionally as a sun. This sun radiates Light-life by projecting life force into matter to become life as you know it.

Light, in the physical sense as sunlight, reaches the individual through the pineal gland and the optic nerve. These affect the functioning of the brain and all our vital processes, including the nervous system and the pituitary gland, which in turn regulates all bodily systems. The effect of light and colour on our physical life is undeniably primary.

Colour affects behaviour. The best nourishment we can give ourselves is through green, the colour of nature.

COLOUR BREATHING

Another way of using colour that I have found helpful is to direct it through the different circuits of the body through colour breathing.

This is a method I developed over the years, inspired by the work of Petey Stevens. It is one of the fastest ways of attaining altered states of reality by affecting the vibrational rhythm of the physical body (matter) directly. If you find any difficulty in eliciting a colour, I suggest you use coloured sheets of paper as a visual aid. Pin the indicated colour on the wall and look at it as long as you need to in order to transfer and reproduce the impression with your eyes closed.

This technique works, not only because of the vibration of the colour combinations used, but also because vibration flows through the energy currents within the body.

Follow the same principles of colour as outlined for the rays, including ruby for strength, blue for peace and compassion, yellow for joy, orange for vitality, and violet for vision. Crystal, silver, gold and combinations of these colours also accelerate energy states.

I outline below the technique for colour breathing and provide an illustration as a guide. The colours you may like to use for a particular purpose may obviously differ to the image below. It is important to follow the direction of movement for the colours used: the colours enter the body at different points, but after blending with one another, they exit the body through the top of the head.

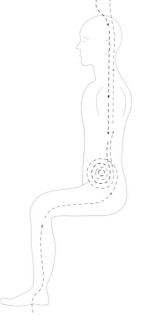

Colour Breathing

 COLOUR BREATHING MEDITATION

GREEN

Use two shades of green to begin with. Visualise a deep forest green for the Earth and a pale apple green for the cosmic Source. Draw streams of breath of forest green from the centre of the Earth, pulling them up through the breath through the soles of the feet up to the pelvic cradle.

Inhale to draw a stream of pale apple green from the Presence above you in the Alchemical Alignment posture and bring it down through the central part of the spinal column to the pelvic cradle as well.

Holding the breath ever so briefly, visualise the two shades blending within the pelvic cradle. The colours should blend without losing their individual shades. On the outbreath, project the mixture through the body upwards and out of the upper part of the spinal column towards the front of the head, just above the forehead, the same spot as in the Exercise to Clear the Mind on page 138. Do this for as long as it feels comfortable.

Each step, breathing from the Earth and breathing from the Source should be done slowly and with maximum awareness, sensing and feeling the circulation created by the entry of both colours into pelvic cradle.

The last stage should be a joyful release through the whole body out onto the aura.

Use the same process for other colours.

GOLD

Invoking gold brings instant energetic acceleration.

It is interesting to observe that, in a physical context, gold (the traditional material and colour used in Alchemy) is a combination of orange and blue. Orange, in many traditions, evokes the initial burst into Being – the Alpha, and blue evokes the extension of Being into infinity – the Omega. In the methodology of the Tree of Life in Kabbalah (the Jewish esoteric and alchemical tradition), gold denotes happiness and beauty. Invoking gold brings instant energetic acceleration.

Invoking gold in breath brings into our personal consciousness the golden flame of Light-life. It ignites the mind and purifies the blood. It is the flame of rejuvenation.

Invoking violet in breath (the other characteristic colour used in Alchemy) brings properties of transmutation to our physical system, primarily to the blood, thereby affecting the Light cells of all the bodies.

OTHER COLOUR COMBINATIONS

Experiment with breathing and directing the colour copper, envisaging it coming from the centre of the Earth for grounding, and do the same with turquoise coming from the cosmic Source for clarity. As you will discover soon in Part Five, this particular combination accesses a higher level of Being.

Likewise, explore purple from the Earth and lavender from cosmic Source, or light green from the Earth and sky blue from the cosmic Source. Each combination produces different effects. Investigate them for yourself without fear and enjoy the play of colour and Light running through you as you observe frequency alterations in your energy.

 ## PROTECTIVE VISUALISATIONS AND AFFIRMATIONS

It is always recommended to set a definite time and duration for a practice in order to set a routine.

Visualise a clear crystal-like skullcap and armour over the body. You might want to explore this visualisation further, using gold, blue or violet at other times. Use the illustration below as a guide.

Crystal Skullcap Protective Visualisation

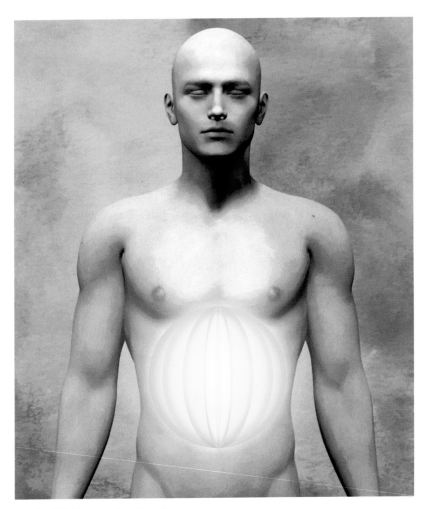

Golden Shield Protective Visualisation

Invoke the power of the blue ray by creating a sword of blue flame.

Hold that sword in your hand and swing it forcefully in criss-cross patterns, with the intention of cutting yourself free of any lines of force, or cords, sent to you or from you that may be keeping you bound and limited.

Invoke a cross of white fire and visualise it in front of you. It acts as protection. You may intensify the protection by extending that visualisation to include a cross at the back, both sides, above and below you – a total of six. Crosses of blue flame provide still stronger protection.

Visualise yourself inside a nine-pointed star, within the centre of a cross of white fire.

Blue Cross and Circle Protective Visualisation

Picture a shield of golden substance over your solar plexus, or a revolving disc of Light at the back.

Encircle your midriff area with a band of deep-blue flame. This also works well around the throat when used as light blue.

See yourself within a pearl of effervescent, flaming Light.

Invoke purity, in the form of a star, to descend into the structure of your brain, then see its rays go out from your head like a sun; do the same for the chest area. You might want to seal this with an oval of Light (outside the Tube of Light).

Picture a silver-blue sphere of Light within the throat.

See yourself within a pillar of Light that is coloured violet, white and blue. Then project that Light outwards in all directions, beginning with your immediate environment and stretching out over your city, your country and the whole Earth.

Invoke the golden flame and see it descend into your skull like a great golden liquid spiral, coursing down the centre of the body and into the centre of the Earth. Pause to let it flow into every nerve and every cell in your body. Bless your feet and make the decision to allow the golden current to flow through you everywhere you go.

Make the call for the dissolution of all your negative etheric records, that is the negative memories in your body, your mind, your emotions, in your environment, relationships and activities.

Surround your home, your car, your workspace, wherever, with a ring 'pass-not' of blue flame (a visualised protective circle of Light around an object or person, used in traditional cultures preserving 'old ways') or the crosses of blue flame. The following affirmations may serve as inspiration for making your own:

'I AM a white fire-being from the Central Sun living within this body of matter and expressing itself as perfection through every cell. I AM the presence of my God-self manifesting perfect health, youth, beauty, intelligence, poise and peace.'

'I AM the intelligence that knows everything it needs to know. I see through everything that is not of the Light!'

'Beloved God-self, which I AM, and all great beings of Light and Love! Protect me against everything that is not of the Light, especially all accidents, jealousy, injustice, gossip, discord, impurity, hatred [include anything else that you may need].'

'I AM the presence of my God-self, in perfect control over my mind, my emotions, my body, my affairs, my finances and my relationships.'

'I AM within the Light of the sacred fire of the Godhead, which is eternal security.'

'Beloved God-self, which I AM! As I leave my body in sleep tonight,

> Invoke the golden flame and see it descend into your skull like a great golden liquid spiral, coursing down the centre of the body and into the centre of the Earth.

fill my body and mind with rest and peace, with clarity and understanding, with all that I will require to do my day's work well, harmoniously and successfully.'

'See that I bring back into my waking consciousness the memory of what I AM so that I may use it in my everyday activity.'

Follow the seal procedure, outlined in the Alchemical Formula in the section on the Violet Flame (see pages 149–51), for sealing your affirmation.

Use these suggestions freely, without fear or a sense of obligation. You must not be bogged down to such an extent that you feel burdened. The insights you gain are from Spirit and evoke the power of Light. They are to be used joyfully and not begrudgingly, in deep understanding and not out of imposition.

Love is the best protection. However, by the same token, you must not be so complacent and naïve as to believe that being indiscriminately vulnerable and open to everyone and everything is being 'loving'. Love is foremost right action and discerning vigilance. Love involves consciousness and alertness. This amounts to discipline and obedience to the Law of Light, regardless of your chosen path.

The power of feeling, which in its purest form is Love, serves to generate the fuel or energy required for all activity, particularly that of creation. In order for the fulfilment of your calls to take place, and for that which you are calling for to be released, you need to believe and act in partnership with your Spirit-self, and exercise discernment in your use of the spoken word. This is a twenty-four-hour job carried on in your work, sleep and play, as it acts through your body, emotions and thoughts both in your laughter and in your sadness.

—

The power of feeling, which in its purest form is Love, serves to generate the fuel or energy required for all activity, particularly that of creation.

—

THE EFFECT OF NEGATIVITY ON THE HUMAN FACULTIES

In human beings, fear and doubt, as gateways for negativity, feed on the consensual belief that we are separate from the Godhead.

Fear is intrinsic to animal life. It is linked to the body and survival. It relates to anxiety about being hurt physically, feeling pain, not being able to survive and dying.

When you know that you are not the physical body, the mechanism upon which fear operates weakens. But the memory of fear is still imprinted in the cells of the body, as cellular or animal instinct. It is the way the body warns us of danger. When you cross the street and there is a car coming, the body instinctively reacts to avert it. When there is a threat looming in the atmosphere, you sense it immediately in the emotional body. You register oppressive or violent vibrations through premonition. The mental body also serves to alert you by intuitive flashes of deduction. These responses are part of the mechanism of the lower bodies, part of animal heritage and wisdom.

Whoever premeditatively activates these mechanisms does so with the purpose of gaining control over and manipulating people and situations. If you ask yourself who benefits from induced fear, you will understand how priests, politicians, the establishment and authorities have used fear for millennia. Fear creates bondage. When a person is afraid their partner may leave them, for instance, they relinquish their power, their authority as a God-being, their autonomy, and their independence.

Lack of physical resources is heavily laced with guilt and fear.

Doubt is a form of fear. It is something of an art to learn how to sort out the real fears, which are physical warnings, from the induced fears, which are terror-propaganda.

A good way of dismantling accumulated beliefs is to affirm: 'I AM Light', 'I AM divine protection', 'I AM truth, clarity, peace', and so on. By repeating a statement such as, 'the Light of God never fails!' or Jesus' statement, 'I AM the resurrection and the life', and believing it, incorporating it, we reprogramme our mental and emotional circuitry and gain intelligent distance from the animal nature.

It is surprising how people believe themselves to be a body, a name, a profession, a gender or a personality, instead of a Being. The discovery of Being marks a major step in freeing yourself from fear; or, more specifically, from the fear of fear.

The author Frank Herbert wrote, 'Fear is the mind-killer'. Fear opens the door to negativity, manipulation and outer control. Experiential and direct identification with the God-self is the only antidote.

> Doubt is a form of fear. It is something of an art to learn how to sort out the real fears, which are physical warnings, from the induced fears, which are terror-propaganda.

UNDERSTANDING LOWER ASTRAL PHENOMENA

Everything pertaining to personal emotion based on separation could be termed 'astral'. Astral activity is constant, especially at night when the conscious mind is off-guard and repressed and incomplete emotional drives take over. Astral experiences define wish-fulfilling dreams and nightmares.

The astral part of third-dimensional life consists not only of your own unresolved issues but also those of humanity that preceded you. There are millions of astral thoughtforms roaming over the surface of the Earth, seeking their expression through living beings. Every time someone experiences a negative thought or emotion, for example, an astral entity (see the section on the astral realm in Part Five, pages 204–7) finds food and a way for expression of its own desires. This is how archetypical images emerged, and gods and goddesses, demons and spirits were created and sustained by witchcraft and similar practices that prey on superstition and the belief in outer authority. A living human being links to astral influences that magnify their own fear and alienation.

The lower astral level is denser, thicker and heavier than an ordinary thoughtform, creating imprints that last as long as they are empowered by self-involved human emotion from people.

The oldest formula for the dissolution of astral phenomena from our lives is to claim the power of the Godhead as your own, to disengage from the dynamics that unconsciously distort reality and reinforce the belief that you are a mere mortal physical being. Set personal desire thoughts and emotions aside, particularly in preparing for sleep.

Stand in your power, directly aligned with the God-presence above you, within the Alchemical Alignment. Create and sustain that link. The more you create a habit of continuously perceiving the world as an extension of Spirit, the stronger your connection with Source power becomes, to the extent that this connection also carries through into your sleep. You will know that the connection has been deeply imbued, when you find yourself using its power in your dreaming.

In the middle of emotional turmoil, whether awake or asleep, you are immersed in lower astral phenomena; you will need to use power words in the Alchemical Formula identified with your divine Presence to command and impose the power of Light:

'In the name of God, the Almighty, I command you to be gone.
In the name of Master [name][12]
Through the authority of the God-self, which I AM;
With the power of Light;
In the name of Truth.'

Use authority to command everything which is not of the Light to be gone. If it persists, direct yourself to it and affirm with conviction and strength: 'You have no power!' Repeat this as often as needed.

And then, exerting the dominion of the purest and highest frequencies within you, declare:

'I AM the only power, the only substance, the only intelligence acting in my world!'

HYPNOTIC CONTROL AND SUGGESTION

No-one who recognises themselves as Self can be hypnotised. The fact that millions want to be told what to do does not give anyone the right to control them. Yet hypnotism is performed day in and day out, all over the world, collectively and privately, from leaders of state to their citizens, from husbands to their wives and vice versa, from parents to their children, because people do not acknowledge the power of Self as their true identity.

The voice of the collective unconscious, when controlled by the outer authority's vested interests, results in hypnotic beliefs and ideas. Hypnotic control is the result of mass thinking. If you hear something often enough, it becomes a fact. When people don't know who or what they are, when they want to be loved and accepted at any cost, because they don't love or accept themselves, what else can be expected?

The hypnotic effect of the collective is powerful. Subliminal messages are constantly bombarding the physical, mental and emotional bodies, stimulating appetites and instincts.

Hypnotic control works through the power of suggestion, which is the layman's hypnosis. It is offered most of the time in innocence, without regard to the effect it can produce, in other words without sensible

---

12 Choose the Master who resonates with you, e.g. Buddha, Mohammed, Saint Germain, among many others.

consideration, sensibility or foresight. People are constantly giving their opinions and others are constantly accepting them.

Whenever someone advises you or suggests you do something, stop for a moment. Remember your Self. Acknowledge where your power lies. Unfortunately, even the best of do-gooders will be offended when you don't listen to their advice.

A person must break free from societal imprints and from the habit of intruding upon others in the name of 'good advice', learning to respect one another and their decisions.

When enough people are willing to risk standing alone, when enough people are happy, blissful and ecstatic in their wholeness, without despair or need, or automatic, haunting fear, then hypnotic control is impossible. Once you enter the vertical dimensions of higher consciousness, hypnosis cannot happen.

To disengage from hypnotic suggestion, sit in the posture of your Alchemical Alignment. Then, imbibed by the power of Source pouring through you, an affirmation such as the following will help you:

'Beloved God-self, which I AM! Cut me free from all hypnotic control and suggestion. Clear my mind and feelings that I may see and feel and manifest you in my world.'

Inner Alchemy suggests a connection with your authentic Self in the form of dialogue or invocation. This offers protection from forces that bind, coerce and limit your perception of what is real. Without the Tube of Light and the use of the Violet Flame practice, you are just like anybody else, immersed in a sea of dense influence, confused and feeling powerless.

PSYCHISM

Psychism, or psychic power, operates under the principle of fear. Its influence through fantasy and suggestion, in the lower astral realm, is much stronger than is commonly believed. When a person lives in separation, everything appears to be a threat.

Psychic power is allied to lower astral reality, which is, in turn, intimately linked to lower chakra collective impulses and desires. These

—
A person must break free from societal imprints and from the habit of intruding upon others in the name of 'good advice', learning to respect one another and their decisions.
—

lower chakra impulses work through your own fears and desires, through emotional bondage and by mental impingement.

Personal desires continuously lead people to attempt to control their surroundings, unconsciously twisting words and meanings to serve their own self-centred purposes. A person swept away by personal desires manipulates and capitalises on people's increasing need to connect with spiritual phenomena as a means to feed off them and control them.

A black magician usurps Light, through varying degrees of malice, preying on ordinary people's egoic needs and fears.

CLEARING PSYCHIC DEBRIS

The following meditation activates higher psychic perception. This is used to invoke the activity of the higher chakras, to heal and to awaken the inner senses.

After appropriate preparation, lie down. Breathe long regular breaths for as long as you need to relax.

Align with and acknowledge your Self.

Feel your body melting onto the surface of where you are lying. Feel the weight of your body. Feel the ground supporting you. Imagine you are getting ready to go to sleep and you are finished with the day's activities. Let go of your hold over the chattering mind.

Feel the energy coursing through your body from inside, and from outside.

Imagine and sense a focus of Light in the centre of your chest, within the heart centre.

Colour this Light a bright apple green and watch, feel, sense it grow and glow to the size of a small sun, about three inches (about eight centimetres) in diameter.

Feel the pulsation of this bright apple-green sun within your chest, sending out ripples of apple-green radiation all around you.

Now sense this sun dissolving into vapour and slowly rising through the inside of your body, through the throat, head and collecting just above your head, about a foot (30 centimetres) beyond. Watch as it forms an apple-green cloud of radiation.

Hold that cloud for a few moments, and then sense the cloud dispersing down, over, under and around you, all the way down to the feet, enveloping you in a shroud of apple-green, vaporous radiation.

Next, allow your physical body to absorb that apple-green Light. Feel it sinking into your cells, all the way into the marrow of your bones, until it dissolves inside of you.

Now, following the same procedure as for the apple-green Light, draw from your God-presence a bright electric blue and see the bright electric-blue light arising within the centre of your throat. Let it glow and grow into the size of a small sun.

Feel the orbs emanating from this bright electric-blue Light – like the blue of a beautiful stained-glass window – as it goes out in all directions. Listen to its sound.

Now sense this electric-blue sphere of glowing Light dissolving into a mist of blue, and slowly, gently rising through your head to form a cloud of vivid blue just above you.

Hold the cloud there for a few moments and then see it spread over, under, around and down your body all the way to your toes, enveloping you in a mantle of bright, electric blue.

Feel this, see it, sense it, as it is drawn into your physical body and dissolves within the cells, the blood, the marrow of your bones.

Finally, sense a sphere of bright, almost blinding, white – a white as you have never seen before, without a trace of yellow, as white as virgin snow.

See this whiteness in the form of a brilliant Light within your head, at the area of the third eye, and fill your entire head with it. Feel there is a sun of brilliant purest white within your head.

Feel its orbs flowing out into all directions. Sense its pulsations; hear its sound.

Now gently witness the dissolving process as this pure white sun melts, and its vapour rises to form a cloud over your head.

Hold the picture of this cloud around your head for a moment, and then sense the cloud spreading out over, under, around and down your body. Let it blanket you, envelop you and hold you within a cloud of the purest white radiance.

Gently feel your body absorbing this white radiance, as each cell drinks of it and is nourished by it. Feel the cells being healed, raised and purified, until the whiteness dissolves completely into your body, all the way to the marrow of your bones.

Feel what you are now.

In that stillness, know 'I AM'.

Allow yourself to remain in this state for as long as possible. Upon your return, record your experience visually, sensorially and energetically.

Visually delineate your physical form upon returning. Define the space your body occupies and then feel its weight and density, its currents of energy, the sense of temperature, the conditions of the room, the textures, smells and so forth.

Breathe into the belly to come back to the awareness of the whole body. Move and squeeze the hands and feet. It often takes time to readjust. Give yourself the time to fully incorporate yourself.

In order to set the positive, joyful tone you would like to have in your world, a lovely procedure to follow at this point would be to dance, play a particularly happy melody and feel the magnificence of life, of being able to be here – and there and everywhere!

REVIEW

I hope you now understand the purpose of this section in the book. Personal energy management, which entails the management of the faculties available to us, is the key to tearing down the veils of perception that we so readily weave in the third dimension. Expanded perception implies holistic perception, being able to see your Self and the truth of what is around you. The thoughtforms that shape your personality and reality may be reshaped and requalified. As a result, a new way of life opens to you.

The purpose of conscious refinement of the personality is that it may align with the state of Being of the soul. Soul-connection implies a total requalification of your perception and reality, and it is on this precept that I would like to invite you to consider the consequences of the alchemical path, now that you are equipped with practical knowledge of your makeup and faculties and the procedures that make soul-connection possible.

Expanded perception implies holistic perception, being able to see your Self and the truth of what is around you.

The knowledge and practices in this section should help you in personality mastery and consequent alignment with soul and Spirit-self. The tools you are now honing are not limited, however, to third-dimensional reality. The third stage of the alchemist's journey consists of exploration of higher levels of Being: living in multidimensional reality, and this is the focus of Part Five.

But let me first compare for you key distinctions between an 'ordinary' human being and a 'soul-embodied' one, as outlined in the following chapter.

PART FOUR

MASTERY AND SOUL-CONNECTION

Part Four illustrates the differences between a soul-connected human being and an 'ordinary' human being. It provides a sketch of how soul-connection shapes the behaviour, and ultimately the life, of an individual. Thoughtforms that exemplify soul-connection are provided and may be used as affirmations.

MASTERY

Mastery comes by degrees. Self-mastery is not something that happens whenever you have insight or connections with the inner world of dimensional reality. It is not the result of occasional communion with the soul, where you clearly experience yourself under the aura of a greater life force than the vitality you are accustomed to.

Mastery demands practice. It requires that you deliberately change the way you perceive everything *all the time*. It suggests using the Master Practice (see pages 21–5) in little things daily. At first, you forget your intention and respond to triggers automatically, the way you always have, and your mind follows suit with its usual comments and assessments, including the onslaught of emotions. Gradually, you remember to apply the Alchemical Circuit more and more and start to wonder how you could perceive in a different way. You begin to intuit other perspectives, unveiling subtle and constructive emotions instead of being plagued by the usual thoughts and standard reactions, until one day the Alchemical Alignment becomes the most ordinary posture in the world. You see. You know. This is when your life and priorities start to change.

The key to mastery is the perceptual and energetic shift that occurs when you transfer your attention from believing that reality happens outside of you to understanding that reality is a part of you, and this understanding is integrated at a higher and vaster perspective. Mastery takes place when you are able to shift focus from your psycho-physical structure and open to a state of Being Light. Rather than a linear process, mastery is a holistic phenomenon. Its utter simplicity is frustrating, because thinking cannot make it happen, but in persisting and embodying Light, the fruits of mastery bring about a complete and irrevocable change in the way you handle life and the way that life responds, in kind, to you. Your body, personality and world are all a reflection of the image you have projected of yourself through your psycho-physical needs. Only Light, when managed by the fully conscious human being, has the power or right frequency to break through and dissolve the thoughtforms that clutter and forge ordinary life. Communion with Light teaches you correct management of life forces, beginning with your own subtle energetic anatomy, faculties and powers.

Mastery begins with the first step you take when you connect with Source, Spirit or Presence, and your entire body experiences a change of frequency. At first it seems that it is just a bodily experience and you do not notice that when you are vibrating at a higher frequency, everything shifts. You have access to a different point of view that reveals another way of thinking and another way of feeling. This is because, at this point, your physical body, where energies from all the bodies and dimensions meet, responds to your focus of attention now functioning at a faster rate of vibration and accessing higher powers that enable contact with all subtle forms in Creation. This unfolding of Consciousness is the ongoing process of Inner Alchemy.

The key to mastery is the perceptual and energetic shift that occurs when you transfer your attention from believing that reality happens outside of you to understanding that reality is a part of you.

I could not finish this book without giving you a clear picture of what to expect, parting from where you find yourself now, as an ordinary human being with beautiful instincts and a heart to match, who has glimpses of truth (or you would not be reading this book), who yearns for more, but who invariably falls into patterns that reveal loss of Consciousness, lack of self-respect, bouts of dark energy and so much more that you would rather not see.

To one degree or another, negatively charged personality traits are the burden we each carry as members of humankind. These commonplace and often fleeting thoughts and feelings lower our vibrational frequency and bring out the villain in spite of good intentions, while polluting our atmosphere. Having understood that our ecological programme begins with ourselves, a human being who has been touched by the grace of Light decides to embrace all of life in order to grow and bloom into a fully-fledged, soul-connected individual who can change this world simply by their presence.

Automatic habits determine the behaviour of the average human being, making them somewhat compulsive, speedy, hasty or impulsive, if not inordinately slow and evasive. A strong feeling of veiled childhood trauma separates them from others, even loved ones: a feeling of being different, unfit or even alienated, which creates dependence and consequently builds unacknowledged resentment. All this happens beneath the level of ordinary awareness. To survive, defensive forms of self-deceit arise, telling the individual they can take anything, do anything, that others' feelings or attitudes do not affect themselves. Inwardly, they fall prey to gnawing doubt and insecurity, suspicion, lack of faith and fear, which threaten their self-created image and status. Too often, human attention is placed on *doing*, and responding to the needs of others, instead of drawing from the substance of the inner being, which remains unacknowledged and not quite understood.

In this state of precarious consciousness and separation from the only source of Oneness possible, there prevails a concern with their own needs, which invariably leads to confusion of priorities and conflicting loyalties, producing stress or its opposite: apathy, confusion, anxiety and despair. In order to deal with the needs of life, an ordinary human being must have recourse to segmentation and categorisation of things and people, dealing with only one thing at a time and losing sight of the greater perspective.

Have you noticed that this also applies to you?

Such a degree of inevitable self-deceit leads to mismanagement of energies that function astrally without a clear centralised directing of consciousness. The person feels forced to implement, demand, and apply their own standards everywhere, no longer capable of flexibility or true empathy. Irritation arises. Everything extraneous is deemed irrelevant.

This behaviour fosters a high degree of absorption from other living things operating in like manner, and the person responds to horizontal rather than vertical impulse, shifting between attachments and aversions, blindly misusing personal will in an attempt to survive by manipulating the environment and imposing their notion of truth.

Let us look even more closely, now with a neutral mind.

The main characteristic of the ordinary human is a constant need to figure things out, looking for guarantees and evaluating the surrounding world. Armed for self-defence and with a sense of separation resulting in self-importance, everything is taken literally and personally. Degrees of imposed conditionality cover any genuine generosity and heart-based impulse. Minute attention is given to detail that invariably insists on continuity and preservation. Rigidity sets in.

Such a human being can be proud, judgemental, stocked with ready-made references, answers and formulas, unintentionally unethical and devious, bordering on the 'correct' but lacking in the self-confidence that a deeper connection with Self might provide.

The following summarises the (not always obvious) common underlying beliefs of the 'ordinary' human being.

> The main characteristic of the ordinary human is a constant need to figure things out, looking for guarantees and evaluating the surrounding world.

THE ORDINARY HUMAN BEING
- 'The world is dangerous' (instinctual gut feeling).
- 'People are not to be trusted' (lack of faith, heart-connection and discernment).
- 'We must compete to succeed' (comparison and testing with others to determine excellence or superiority).
- 'I must be 'tough'' (meaning impermeable and unifocal, i.e. insensitive).

- 'I must be self-sufficient' (physically provide for myself without having to depend on anyone).
- 'Only the fittest survive' (fostering personal will and brute force).
- 'Money is power' (equal to external privilege, influence and opportunity, as substitutes for inner authority and higher power).
- 'Nothing is easy' (implying that everything requires discomfort, effort and privation).
- 'What others think or say is important' (veiling insecurity and need of approval).
- 'Rules, social precedent and order must be observed' (need to fit in and follow externally imposed discipline erected on belief as tradition).
- 'Authorities (someone else) always know best' (parents, family, spouse, church, the boss; this sentiment exposes a profound insecurity and fear of standing revealed and found wanting. It also shows absence of critical appraisal).
- 'I cannot be alone' (a very deep, veiled fear of extinction and meaninglessness).

The ordinary human being might be drawn to aggressive gymnastics, such as speed and high-risk sports that generate adrenaline and muscle building, or fitness-training for stamina and resistance, enhancing sexual performance and physical image. This activity occurs while the mental and emotional counterparts are disconnected from the body and elsewhere occupied with daydreams, audio activities, conference calls or other forms of 'doing'.

The ordinary human being often seeks vicarious emotions that do not threaten their image of the self, living out intensities in films, stories that happen to others and other forms of distraction. Such a person cannot conceive of being alone for very long, and 'aloneness' usually involves some sort of activity such as reading or exercising in the absence of physical company. Silence is virtually impossible, and meditation must have an entertaining or distracting element for it to be 'useful' and not boring.

Relationships are a must, although often long-distance or only partially engaging ('doing' things together, for instance) that guarantee the illusion of independence. Absentee-relating at every level is an accepted norm, where time is of the essence and 'doing' is a priority. However, the individual's misplaced 'intention' and inner feelings assure them that

> The ordinary human being often seeks vicarious emotions that do not threaten their image of the self, living out intensities in films, stories that happen to others and other forms of distraction.

they do, indeed, love and care. Great demand is placed on vows and demonstrations of love and fidelity.

Relationships are based on magnetic attraction and heightened physical sensation, which serve to disguise the phantom of loneliness. A form of alienation arises in couples ('we vs them'), based on like–dislike biases and a need for approval and recognition. Like attracts like. These relationships are often superficial and recreational, including alcohol and light drugs as ways of escaping from themselves. Things must always be done together, often including spiritual adventures, which are later analysed and assessed.

The main mental trait of the ordinary human is to stake a claim upon their surroundings, looking for guarantees, comfort and convenience where their own or family needs are concerned. The ordinary human is easily upset by anything that gets in the way of immediate needs or calculations. Anything that appears different or in any way critical is taken personally. The average human being's way of showing kindness invariably imposes conditions and ownership. They can be subtly and unconsciously unethical, devious, bordering on what is 'correct', but lacking in the feeling of security and self-worth that a deeper connection with Self might provide.

If such an ordinary human being were to understand and apply the alchemical principles of Inner Alchemy, how would they change? How would they sense and respond emotionally? What kinds of thoughts would they have?

Such an understanding would imply a radical change. Imagine. Place yourself in the position of applying all that you have read and experienced here. Take a step into that space of intimacy with your Self and feel its nourishing warmth. Sense how you could come to live as a soul-connected human.

The soul-connected person becomes a blessing to everyone and everything, enabling peace and creativity. The aura, that compound of body, emotion and mind, acquires a rhythm of serenity and harmony, a sense of solidity, inspiring trust and transparency in others.

In a soul-connected human, behaviour is typically spontaneous and original. The soul-connected human enjoys the world and its personality, its body and life in general, and knows that it is not perfect. Not devoid of occasional sadness, their sensitivity often leads to frustration with surrounding conditions, where old, unchecked emotions may crop up. Nevertheless, this person is responsive and deliberate, oriented towards group and environmental matters. Such a person has built a transparent temporal identity, based on a clear recognition of its strengths and weaknesses. They never feel wholly alone, but instead are marked by a strong link with Self and Spirit-presence. Guided thus, the ability to see beyond the obvious through greater dimensional insight is possible.

The actions of a soul-connected person are addressed for improvement and self-correction upon a platform of higher values from dimensions of Being where they, too, have their being. Discernment and discrimination, together with an artful use of power (when necessary), replace any need to defend themselves or control others.

A soul-connected human is aligned in such a way that their nature is in obedience to the Law of the One. This is the result of conscious embodiment of the Alchemical Alignment, evoking truth and love, joy and serenity at will. Behaviour is qualified by a discipline that emerges from within spontaneously as the voice of conscience (soul). Through the application of the Law of Love (which is the Law of Oneness), wellbeing and goodness is assured, together with a state of discernment that has no place for distraction. Under careful scrutiny, habits and carnal desire are acknowledged as part of natural law which, when properly understood and administrated, can lead to joy.

THE SOUL-CONNECTED HUMAN

The following summarises some of the thought processes inherent in a soul-connected human being. See how they fit you now.

- 'The individual is a cell in the body of humanity, partaking of Spirit, a reality shared by all.'
- 'A person's personality is a composite of historical precedence, constituting a rather unsteady identity susceptible to faults and lapses of consciousness, together with a spirit open to opportunity given the right approach and circumstances.'
- 'The world is our own creation and projection; it is within our ability to shape and restructure reality.'
- 'Cooperation is essential to survival.'

- 'Evolution depends on individual flexibility, openness to change and acknowledgement of difference, in order to serve the divine plan for humanity and the world.'
- 'Every human being is responsible for themselves, called to do their part and to help and inspire others.'
- 'Physical and material reality depend on the awareness and degree of application of higher laws of Light through a conscious personality.'
- 'Money is energy and as such belongs to all, demanding ethical handling if it is to serve the good of all.'
- 'There is no need to worry about personal survival needs, as all is freely given by Spirit under the use of correct formulas of alignment and evocation.'
- 'Everything contains a grain of truth. Other's opinions are important inasmuch as they reveal levels of consciousness and enable the soul-connected individual to act or help accordingly.'
- 'Rules and social order have an important place in the physical order of the world, yet there are higher laws and principles that influence these and sustain creative initiative.'
- 'There is no greater authority than the connection with the inner Self who is capable of seeing and knowing all that is needed every moment.'
- 'Belief is transient and personal. Reality is based on change and adaptation.'
- 'I am never alone. Humanity is a community of like souls, both in embodiment and out of embodiment, linked to angels and higher beings.'
- 'Soul-connection is dependent on individual level of awareness and sensitivity.'
- 'Everyone has a place and a mission in the highest order of Being.'

In a soul-connected human, physical and emotional needs are acknowledged and held in appropriate perspective. Physical activity, for instance, varies with time, place, purpose and individual structure, and is always approached as an integrated whole that encompasses emotional and mental awareness. The physical body is sacred. A soul-connected person practises sports and all physical activity with fun, self-awareness and connection with surrounding life. Training is focused on gradual awakening of the body as temple of Spirit, responding to higher Intelligence. Vitality is fuel for creative endeavour. Sex is embraced as a joyous act of union, blending with another human being in the light of spiritual presence.

Emotions serve the soul-connected human as antennae, receptors and gauges of emotional climate and fuel for conscious creation. They are deeply sensed and most often expressed as gratitude and celebration. Relationships are based on conscious choice and kinship, built not upon need, but on the ability of each to stand alone and whole in order to share. They are based on a soul attraction that recognises embodied spirit, and on helping one another overcome life's challenges with greater sensitivity.

Under the direct influence of the soul, the personality, cognisant of its earthly duties, has an inkling of its 'mission' as it responds to attraction and danger, knowing its own capacities and scope of action. A soul-connected human is aware of their life-lessons and has a general grasp of their life-purpose, living the ideal of oneness, brotherhood and unity, through which they derive pleasure and meaning. The soul-connected person is aware of the needs of humanity at large, and its notion of service responds to its deepening perception.

Personal psychology arises out of an understanding of embodying family patterns, conditioning, and, through deliberate choice, a soul-connected being strives to reach universal values that embrace, include and transcend the personal self. There is genuine enjoyment of and command over one's personal array of traits and dispositions. A strong conviction replaces ordinary belief, revealing that the human being is the living temple of Spirit, bestowed with the capacity to activate and generate creative thoughts through the application of personal willpower linked to divine Will.

The mind is perpetually alert at different levels of communication simultaneously, responding to situation and need, perceiving possibility and probability in order to improve life conditions on the third dimension and link with higher intelligent guidance. This individual is fully aware of living within a protective circle of divine influence that matches their own level of awareness and action in the world. Such a person sees holistic patterns behind even the most common occurrences. Perception is keen and multi-levelled with heightened sensibility and intelligence. Understanding emerges naturally. Results arise from being, rather than doing. Life is lived without the fear of death or discontinuity, because eternity is experienced as the natural result of living fully in the present.

—

Personal psychology arises out of an understanding of embodying family patterns, conditioning, and, through deliberate choice, a soul-connected being strives to reach universal values that embrace, include and transcend the personal self.

—

REVIEW

The purpose of this section is to shed light on what mastery may look like for you.

As I hope I have made clear, although soul-connection legitimately and significantly manifests itself in an individual's 'concrete', third-dimensional reality, it cannot be achieved through ordinary, third-dimensional means.

You should now have a basic understanding of your makeup and the powers you possess to mould and create physical reality. The next stage of inquiry, however, will be to cross over the veil into the spirit realm. Living interdimensionally is the key to communing with Spirit, and for the personality to meet with soul.

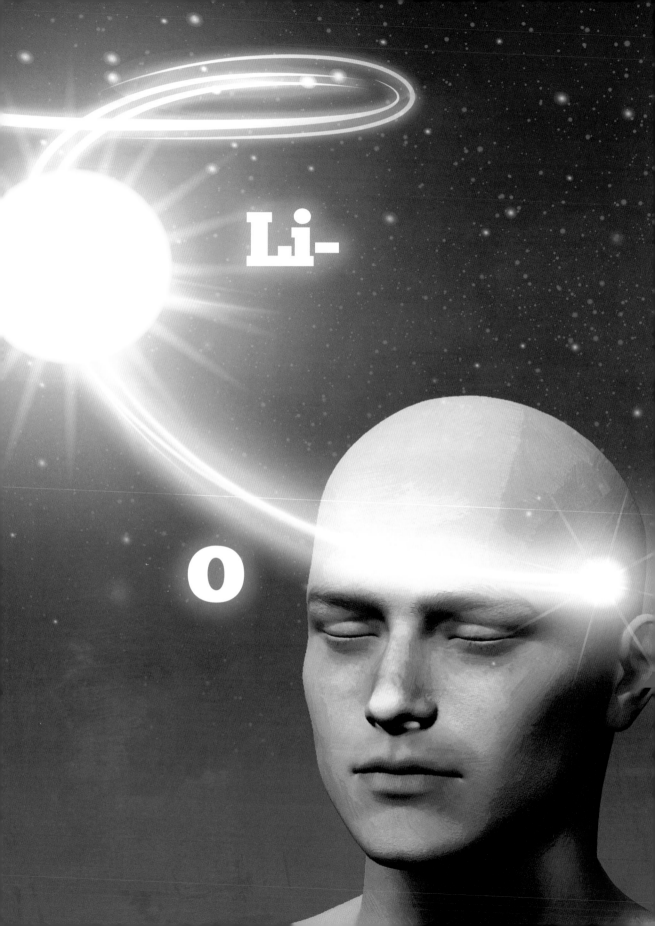

DIMENSIONS OF CONSCIOUSNESS

Part Five traces the Inner Alchemy system of twelve dimensional stages of Consciousness, and how understanding multidimensionality may give the reader greater understanding of Self and the physical dimension. It also describes dimensional beings, guides and masters.Meditations are provided for aiding the reader in navigating interdimensional dynamics, so they may align with higher frequencies of Consciousness and bring back insights from these higher levels.

INTERDIMENSIONALITY: THE CORNERSTONE OF INNER ALCHEMY

The journey of Consciousness weaves through different frequencies and dimensions that compel us to learn greater and greater management of human faculties and levels of Intelligence.

Inner Alchemy training in perception takes the student through three stages. The first stage has to do with defining Self in time and space. The second stage concerns itself with the subtleties of multidimensional reality. The third, which occurs simultaneously with the second stage, relates directly to the process of expanding Consciousness and connecting to Source.

WHY IT IS IMPORTANT

Knowing who you are in the physical world and multidimensionally makes a great difference to the way you perceive and handle opportunities in your life. The purpose of this part of the book is to acquaint you with the dimensions beyond the third and with new levels of reality, so that you may begin to transcend limitation, achieve freedom, and create yourself and your world with greater and evermore magnificence.

Each of us is a Being co-existing simultaneously in, what I have defined as, twelve dimensional levels of Consciousness, while also coursing through third-dimensional time and space. Each dimension of Being can be roughly translated as a capacity of Intelligence to handle elements that range from vast cosmic consciousness to the minutest detail. To experience the gradating scale of frequencies represented by these levels is to understand vibrationally and qualitatively in order to apply one's complete array of human faculties. This not only allows the individual to differentiate between the mental and emotional aspects of thoughtforms that pervade existence, hereby gaining clarity of perception, but also allows one in full consciousness to draw valuable information and abilities required to administer life.

The evolutionary journey into embodiment as Consciousness traces the projection from a formless state into progressively denser and denser forms, culminating in physical matter. As discussed in Part Two, the passage leads through various frequencies and levels of adaptation, or bodies. These energy fields, or vehicles, give the individual access to faculties at different dimensional stations, yet they also operate independently of personal awareness. These interdimensional faculties are usually taken for granted, and such perceptions are often attributed to chance, destiny, upbringing or cultural climate.

There are two aspects to multidimensionality. The first, or original, journey was enacted with the descent of Consciousness into embodiment. Levels of original Mind progressively coalesced into matter. The second, from the human perspective, is a transcendent experience while in embodiment, reaching upwards to the Source of power for clarity and creativity, beauty, truth and justice.

Godliness and perfection are the forever-living imprints of the original experience of Oneness. Surprisingly, the tremendous power of Oneness, the expansive faculty of thought, the fervent desires and the

> Knowing who you are in the physical world and multidimensionally makes a great difference to the way you perceive and handle opportunities in your life.

overwhelming feelings can be found in one's very own thoughts, feelings and desires in the here and now. In claiming higher mental abilities, one may start exerting the mastery already inherent, although unrecognised, at the level of the Higher Self and interdimensional life.

Everyone has access to these levels, but not everyone is equipped to handle the exalted frequencies of these dimensions, due to lack of dominion over the first three bodies of the personality. The acquisition of dimensional abilities depends entirely on the stability provided by work on the physical, mental and emotional self.

All of this is made accessible through the application of the Master Practice, with the acceleration of vibration of the lower three bodies to a higher frequency than the physical or astral dimensions. The Master Practice allows the student to invoke the dimensions consciously, by focusing on the points of Light in the body and accelerating this light nucleus at the centre of the atomic structure (see page 46). The purpose of this practice is to tap into information from higher levels and gain a wider perspective of ourselves and of third-dimensional life.

INTERDIMENSIONALITY

When you go up a mountain, you gain different perspectives of the surrounding territory. At ground level, you perceive individual activity. As you climb higher, your perspective broadens. Only from the summit are you able to see at a 360-degree radius and understand the simultaneous and disparate events that take place at the different heights and breadths of the terrain.

Such is the relationship between interdimensionality and the vast scope of the Universe. Each dimension offers a perspective of a form of life and activity. With individual evolution and the expansion of Consciousness, we may draw intelligence and abilities from our dimensional selves. If I were to try to portray what this reality looks like physically, I might say that dimensions form layers, like an onion. Each serves an evolutionary function and holds a vibratory rhythm that resonates with similar frequencies along a scale of growing complexity and clarity. Humans, through deliberate modulation of frequencies, can be in tune with all levels of existence.

If you question the existence of multiple dimensions of Being, share this experience with me for a moment.

One weekend, I had a walk in a park with a friend. It was a beautiful spring day, and it felt like the whole city was in the park. As we walked, it was as though we were traversing across different universes: in one area people were dancing; in another, sunbathing, mostly alone, book in hand; in another again, families were out walking their dogs.

Further along children were playing football, couples were practising yoga, old men were on benches feeding birds; the cyclists were in another world altogether, as were the runners. People from the wealthy areas of town mixed with people from poorer parts of town, people of different ages, backgrounds, ethnicities, sexualities, genders; there were beautiful people, artists, young parents, teenagers, grandparents, lovers and lone walkers. Each of these groups was living within a different dimension of Being that went beyond mere physical activity.

A dimension can be thought of as an inner location for like states of Consciousness that function in a specialised way. What determines the dimension a person lives in is neither money nor education, cultural heritage nor upbringing. It is the level of Consciousness. Why certain things happen to certain people is a result of a state of Being (often a result of habit, or karma). On the highest levels of Being, you choose the conditions of your life.

Interdimensionality is an inner phenomenon and relates to inner awareness and perception. Each dimension consists of a form of life and activity. These dimensions interpenetrate and affect ordinary third-dimensional life, depending on the extent of an individual's consciousness and consequently their access to the dimensions. It is not possible to infer the internal dynamics of the people in the parks; for instance, the level of consciousness of the lovers may range anywhere from the lowest chakras to the sublime, poetic heights of higher dimensional states, where the intelligence of the heart perceives Light and force of a transcendental nature.

The reality of these dimensions, or planes, consists of life forms and activities indigenous to them. By touching these dimensions, an individual may not only draw information from them, but also an experience through them: a person may anchor their consciousness in a dimension of higher mathematics, aesthetics, spiritual principles, musical

> A dimension can be thought of as an inner location for like states of Consciousness that function in a specialised way.

creativity, healing or clairvoyant faculties, depending on the frequency at which their vehicles of Being are vibrating. A student on the path of Inner Alchemy may connect to all of these dimensions by modulating their vibration to the levels at which these dimensions exist.

The dimensions of Consciousness can be thought of as similar to the human being's seven personal bodies of Consciousness. If we were to think of them as located in space, then we might imagine the dimensions as located not only around the physical body and interpenetrating it, but also in concentric rings around the core of the body of the planet. Each dimension encompasses the whole Cosmos in the perspective that it embodies. They are simultaneously experienced as inner and outer space. Understanding this requires a leap in thinking.

The moment we touch upon a higher dimension we are already in the body, or energy field, corresponding to it, at that particular level of Consciousness. The moment we wish to do or create something within the upper range of dimensions, we mobilise the particular body that we wear in that particular dimension, employing what looks like a similar Light form, or mould, of the physical body, or we tap into the corresponding higher mental and sensitive faculties. This is an advanced practice, which for a very few, may be triggered in dreams during special moments of connection with teachers. An 'ordinary human' would not be able to do this: at best they can gain information from their Consciousness vibrating in that dimensional range.

The first challenge that faces a person who wishes to know the nature of the Universe is switching from the perception of duality to the awareness of an interpenetrating reality that is much vaster. This interpenetrating reality is the common ground of Spirit in which everything lives.

Accessing fullness implies the modulation of Consciousness: from linear mental perception to a holistic one, graduating finally to a subtle sentience that is wholly and personally experiential, at the core of our Being.

To the naked eye, a body is a unit composed of parts. To the trained eye, the human form is structured in unified layers of fine substance, extending electromagnetically into an auric field, and beyond into an exquisite aquarelle of the softest particles of Light comprising the rainbow radiance of Spirit, such as those in the illustration of the Seven Bodies in Part Two (see page 47).

The ingrained three-dimensional notions of time and space between objects create a linear bias that demands continuity and fixity, leaving little space for simultaneity, probability and alternate reality. Only those individuals who rise above the range of dimensions, the human, may grasp the fullest extent of alternate expression.

In our normal range of activities, we use the *physical senses* together with the brain to perceive and evaluate the material world. At the same time, we are gifted with *subtle senses* that perceive in non-linear ways, and with *spiritual faculties* that capture invisible forces. 'Like attracts like'. We tap into each sensory level by vibrating at the same frequency, accessing physical, mental, emotional and spiritual phenomena. We participate in the processes of matter as well as those of Light, and ultimately in the full recognition of a transcendent phenomenon of inherent godliness.

By integrating the bodies of the personality, a guiding, inclusive Intelligence emerges that allows for the perception of other levels of dimensional activity without ego distortion, embracing the first principle on the path of mastery: placing personal will at the service of Higher Will.

The individual usually links to these states accidentally. For the student of Inner Alchemy, access and decoding are deliberate. At the Inner Alchemy School of Consciousness, our practice of energy acceleration, based on intensifying the Light within the points of Light at the centre of each atom, facilitates direct access to the dimensions by focusing on the human being's Light-nature.

It is important to note that the experiences of the dimensions delineated in the following pages are attainable for any student who engages in and practices Light-work. The meditation and energetic practices outlined, combined with spiritual discipline, can induce an acceleration of Light within our being that facilitates a recognition of higher levels of Consciousness, or Being, beyond that of the everyday, physical state. This expanded perception may be used to gain wisdom that can be integrated into lower, third-dimensional existence.

Some people experience interdimensionality as an aspect of interiority. Others experience it as something outside, like existing in space. For individuals of a feeling nature, the best interdimensional guidance might be reached through prayer; for those of a physical bent, through dance; for the person of intellect, it might come through science, deep thinking and the search for truth.

As you first tap into other dimensions, your experiences might seem futuristic and implausible. Remember, however, that interdimensional experience is available to everyone.

Crucially, the key is always vibrational. Dare to tap into your own energies. Explore consciously raising your vibration. Give yourself permission to see and know and remember experiences of other dimensions – especially at night, when you lose body consciousness and open to other states more easily. Draw from the alliance with the Higher Self, teachers and guides. Use visualisations and guided imagery to activate your chakras and the points of Light in your body. Believe in these dimensions as you believe in yourself.

INTERDIMENSIONAL DYNAMICS

The higher and more accelerated the frequency of other dimensions, the progressively more refined and diffuse they appear. The upper dimensions are compiled of pure-grade Light substance, which at the highest level is pure Light-intelligence as individualised Spirit-force, expressing itself as simultaneity and a vast, incomprehensible abstraction. The inhabitants of the upper dimensions are Light beings, who embody greater and greater wisdom. At the lowest levels is condensed matter, expressing itself in form and sequence.

The dimensions are reached through the seven human bodies as well as through the higher chakras. Remember that information from dimensions beyond the activity of the third is already flowing into material reality. Understand that all dimensions co-exist within the present moment and within the framework of third-dimensional life. It is ideal to keep our energy frequency high, as anything that lowers frequency will diminish our power and perception, limiting access to higher dimensions and to Light in general.

I shall now explore these dimensions one by one, addressing how they appear and how we, as human beings attuned to these frequencies, express ourselves; how Mind manifests in each dimension; and what we may draw from each.

Before I describe the twelve dimensions in detail, consider the illustration on page 198 as a visual guide, an 'interdimensional map' if you will, to the twelve dimensions.

Use visualisations and guided imagery to activate your chakras and the points of Light in your body. Believe in these dimensions as you believe in yourself.

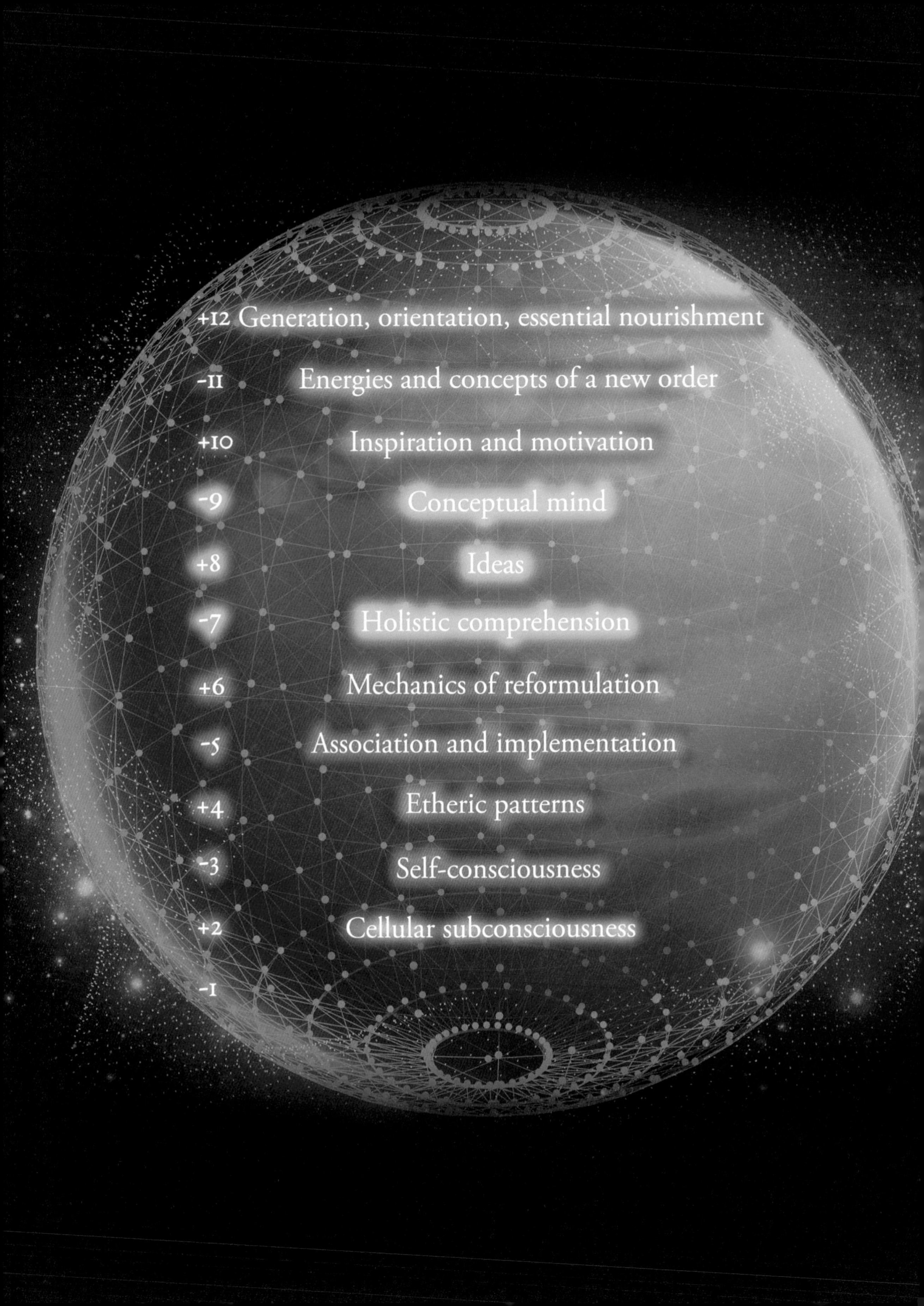

+12 Generation, orientation, essential nourishment

-11 Energies and concepts of a new order

+10 Inspiration and motivation

-9 Conceptual mind

+8 Ideas

-7 Holistic comprehension

+6 Mechanics of reformulation

-5 Association and implementation

+4 Etheric patterns

-3 Self-consciousness

+2 Cellular subconsciousness

-1

The Dimensions table on pages 200–1 defines different dimensions, their purpose and their expression of Consciousness. The first to the sixth dimensions in this table can be thought of as correlates to the physical dimension; the seventh to the ninth as holistic dimensions; and the tenth to the twelfth as transcendent dimensions, or the spiritual realm.

Note that in this table I have included the polarities of each dimension. While knowing about the polarities of dimensions is not essential for beginning students of Inner Alchemy, it may be useful to know that these polarities define certain effects. Negatively charged dimensions (the third, fifth, seventh, ninth, and eleventh dimensions), for example, indicate stations of consciousness where human beings experience multiple aspects of life and integrate these elements: in the third dimension, for instance, where we encounter beings at different stages of soul evolution; and the seventh, which houses multiple foci of activity from all dimensions and planets. The positive dimensions (the fourth, sixth, eighth, tenth and twelfth dimensions) offer a certain state of integration in the individual, and lead to the subsequent negative dimensional level.

In the table, the Roman numerals on the extreme left refer to phases of human development. The dimensions are divided into the four groups, according to the level of consciousness applied by a person.

The Interdimensional Map

THE DIMENSIONS

	Dimension	Purpose, use	Aspect of Consciousness	Expression of Consciousness, dynamic of Mind
IV	+12	Generation; Orientation; Essential nourishment	Pure effulgence; Formlessness	Meditation; Silence; Dynamic stillness; Accelerated Being-state; Fusion; Flashes of wisdom; Illumination fullness
	-11	Link to energies and concepts of a new order	Essential Intelligence as a state of Being	Aspiration to service; Self-offering; Contact with self-potential; Soul yearning
III	+10	Inspiration and motivation; Experience of ecstasy, fullness and peace	Supramental	Longing for peace; Union of opposites; Silence; Sense of possibility; Contemplation; Paradise
	-9	Production of concepts like form and measure for the implementation of formulas; Potential and impulse		Serenity without intentionality; Theoretical insight; Induction; Creational keys
II	+8	Ideas and their application; Eureka experience		Intentional focus; Inference; Truth seeking; Discovery
	-7	Holistic comprehension of the evolutionary process; Divine plan manifest and revealed	Non-temporal (holistic); Higher Mind; Time simultaneity; Higher astral plane	Philosophical thought; Intuition; Neutral mind; Global perception; Registry of human ideals; Simultaneous integrated perception of component parts

	+6	Mechanics of reformulation and assembly; Decoding centre for concrete mind	Abstract mind (global thinking); Lower mind (detail and sequence)	Creative flexibility; Intelligence; Discernment; Objectivity as a faculty of introspection and neutrality
	-5	Association and implementation of parts within a whole		Planning; Calculation; Speculation; Deliberation; Association; Probability; Logic; Deduction
I	+4	Evocation of etheric patterns; Construction of forms in order to materialise, dematerialise and restructure	Concrete mind (all mental faculties)	Reflection; Premeditation; States of dreamlike reverie
	-3	Identity and self-consciousness; Integration and development of mental faculties; Acquisition of knowledge (experience) of natural forces		Analysis and study; Observation; Experience of parts; Separation; Detail; Experience of life in matter as sensation and pulsation
	Lower Astral	Personal desire and egoism; Reaction/reactiveness		Psychic astral consciousness; Emotional waves; Automatic triggers of instinctual desire
	+2	Cellular subconsciousness; Life-death-renewal processes, i.e. illness, death, decomposition	Sensory syntony; Attunement with the environment	Resonance; Sound; Rhythm; Pulsation; Pressure
	-1		Pure pressure; Creative natural impulse as force	Elemental subconsciousness

THE MATERIAL DIMENSIONS: THE FIRST TO SIXTH DIMENSIONS

The *first and second dimensions* in the system represented in the table on pages 200–1 refer solely to the gestation of matter and do not involve human consciousness. They concern elements of nature, and their domain is the elemental dynamics of gestation, decomposition and recreation of matter. They resonate microcosmically as pressure, which gives birth to substance and movement, and is below the threshold of collaborative human intelligence.

The human body echoes this subatomic activity in the way that it senses textures, colours, sounds and rhythms indirectly through keen resonance of physical rhythms and pulsation. Certain beats, like those of the drum and other ritualistic, tribal instruments, emit pulsations that alter the frequency of brainwaves, allowing humans to tune into biological and geological consciousness. This is the very stuff of shamanism and is already well-documented. The drums and other ritualistic instruments used in shamanism evoke resonance within the lower dimensions of creation.

THE THIRD DIMENSION AND ITS RELATION TO THE FOURTH, FIFTH AND SIXTH DIMENSIONS

The third dimension works by attraction, repulsion and electro-magnetism, which are organic reflexes that evoke in us meaning and quality. The experiences of the third dimension are of stability and predictability. This is a dimension where accidents appear to happen; a place of relief and distraction. Humanity avoids contradiction, discomfort and uncertainty in the third dimension and trains for an endless cycle of challenges, success and conquests. The third-dimensional mind reflects the qualities of the physical senses, concerned as it is with survival and mastery of the environment. Intelligence here interprets and applies information. This is the realm of the concrete linear modality.

The fourth, fifth and sixth dimensions likewise reflect this linear modality, but at more mental levels than the third.

Since this first range of dimensions (the third to the sixth) provide common territory and shared human identity, they allow for communication with people on different evolutionary and spiritual levels. This communication is made using the same language, even if people's

> Certain beats, like those of the drum and other ritualistic, tribal instruments, emit pulsations that alter the frequency of brainwaves, allowing humans to tune into biological and geological consciousness.

awareness of the subtleties of reality and inner needs are different. In this way, the third dimension is the realm of diplomatic tactics and the development of faculties that train the individual in the management of detail and the formation of concepts. Here you learn to harvest and direct personal power on the one hand, and on the other learn to influence, teach by example and raise the level of planetary consciousness.

Relationships are the training ground in the third dimension. Here, people communicate with one another and all living things, sending physical, mental and emotional messages that are often in conflict, and reveal a frenetic global entanglement of waves and wires that thread through humanity and its creations. People imbibe impressions from the media, their families and even the stranger crossing the street. Shutting off the mind or distracting yourself has little effect, as the bodies, levels of mind and emotional fields are constantly absorbing environmental and human pollution.

At the third dimension, the body provides stability; the emotions, flexibility; and the mind offers concrete tools to handle ideas. Attention functions in parts; each part builds a more complex unit. At this dimensional stage, insights acquire meaning.

Humanity is already well-advanced in the mental skills of the fourth dimension. Individuals who live, breathe and give life to technological advances reveal growing complexity in the fifth and sixth dimensions. Perception within these adjacent dimensions unfolds as intellectual, academic, informational, strategic and abstract reasoning. Information is handled and worked out in the fourth through to the sixth dimensions.

The third dimension serves as training in energy management for embodied Consciousness. Everything you do, feel or think involves the sum of parts. Things are put into a separated, linear perspective; stages must be mastered. You learn to walk a step at a time, until you can run or sprint, but you cannot fly. You are limited by the laws of matter, by weight and density. Each fraction of a part requires care, attention, appreciation and involvement, something only possible in the third dimension. Once this stage is mastered, you may grow in awareness and master energies in yet higher and higher dimensions.

The third dimension covers all aspects of physical reality and its interpretation. It also activates two major faculties linked to mastery over matter: setting limits and ownership. When you develop these, you may

> Humanity is already well-advanced in the mental skills of the fourth dimension. Individuals who live, breathe and give life to technological advances reveal growing complexity in the fifth and sixth dimensions.

develop emotional and mental equilibrium. However, when you have not set boundaries, when you do not find equilibrium and emotional or mental development supersedes physical integrity, you find that two shadow realities emerge. These I call astral and technological shadow realities and I define them below.

ASTRAL AND TECHNOLOGICAL SHADOW REALITIES

There are two 'shadow' realities that belong to the astral plane. These worlds are two sides of the same coin, but are made up of constructs and thoughtforms that pertain either to the emotional body – the astral realm– or the concrete mind – virtual reality.

The astral realm

The shadow world of the astral realm is one constructed by emotional desires. This lower astral dimension mirrors the third dimension. Your enthusiasm in your emotional faculties makes you grow in eagerness and desire. Desire accesses your vital force directly. It is the motor power for creativity, but desire is also the root of suffering.

Generally, the term 'astral' is restricted to the lower variety of frequencies that are still attached to the physical senses. This is a psychic reality, which is ruled by the emotional body, and it is generated in third-dimensional life. The astral realm is the world of desire in all its forms, glued together by need and attachment, and seeded by dependence and sexual (i.e. vital) force. Here, the physical body is entirely at the mercy of the whims and appetites of instinct and the emotional drives, and the mind is wholly coloured by the justifications provided by the emotional body. None of the three personal energy bodies function purely or appropriately within this level.

In most esoteric schools the astral realm is considered part and parcel of the third dimension; it reflects human problems and desires, exacerbating emotions and fostering superstition and belief. A great deal of spiritual work consists in breaking through its density and conquering the pull of accumulated collective energies. Accomplishing this step constitutes the first and perhaps greatest test of passage into higher Intelligence.

Consciousness at this level is especially prevalent today. There is no end to the relay of catalysts that leads to perpetually unresolved desires and senseless drives. Nothing is ever enough. Boredom prevails and stalkers abound. Heaviness and violence mark the tempo. Desire rules as an elusive possibility, forecasting the future as a culture of terrifying, robotic fantasy.

This is the world of 'hunger' that characterises addictions of all sorts, especially surrounding relationships, sex, possessiveness and raw ambition. Commonly, when people talk about 'extrasensory perception', such as auric readings and other parapsychological phenomena, they are usually speaking about impressions of a psychological nature that appear and influence psychophysical reality. Many psychics and mediums are only reading telepathic musings from the lower astral dimension, returning to people a picture of their own wishful (or fearful) thinking.

Furthermore, most dreams of unfulfilled or haunting desires are revealed here as primary triggers of baseline survival. They limit, condition and prime the physical senses to keep people earthbound. Further examples of astral phenomena include romantic attachment, dependent beliefs, addiction, ghosts, witchcraft, horror, thrillers and the macabre.[13]

The astral realm also includes the low-frequency thoughtforms of the personalities of disembodied human beings who are strongly 'bound' to their idea of existence solely in the physical world. When a human being does not have sufficient knowledge or trust in a higher form of life, holding expedient belief that they actually are the personality means that the thoughtforms constituting the personality gradually congeal into a shell. Whenever such a person who still clings to material reality passes on, they become trapped in their own creation and remain for a while in the lower astral realms of reality. These 'shells' created by their life impressions – hopes, dreams, anger, resentment, suffering, etc. – retain the vitality that the person gave them while embodied, sustained by the personal willpower to remain upon an earthly existence. Once disconnected from its Spirit-source, this shell roams the Earth in search

---

13 Some may be surprised to see that shamanic practices pertain to lower dimensions. All shamanic practices access the lower dimensions of natural life: those that dictate the formation of third-dimensional manifestation and also those that influence or alter their frequency as in some forms of herbal healing and other remedies. They are frequently misused by individuals seeking power over natural forces. Remember always that a 'lower' dimension does not imply that it is 'worse' than a higher dimension. All dimensions are essential for existence.

of human beings with kindred thoughts and feelings to feed from. These discarnate shells create great problems for embodied humans who are susceptible to suggestion. These are the astral entities that haunt places and obsess human beings, causing mental illness and disorder, and often persuading people to commit crime.

At this level, the personal focus of Consciousness manages strong physical pulsation at the physical level as well as in this astral range, through the linear aspect of the mind as obsessive or repetitive thinking. Only awareness of their Self, and a deliberate disciplined reformulation of their life's purpose according to higher principles can bring the subject out of this massive global delusion. The way back home is the recognition that they are not the personality but the Spirit or soul within, diminishing the pull of temporary physical identity.

There is a higher astral range of frequencies consisting of well-intentioned thoughts and desires, which lead to genuine devotion and inspiration, often selfless incentives for service, but are still linked to our third-dimensional physical reality and the idea of separation. They constitute the higher range of emotions and devotional ideas linked to the belief in a remote god. They appear as clearer colourations in the aura, where before, lower astral phenomena (thoughtforms) appear as darker, muddier discolourations of lower astral densification.

Virtual shadow reality

Conversely, on the mental level, humanity develops its imagination and projects desire in the form of endless creativity. With creativity, the intellect is developed and extends to the construction of machines and structures that respond to the growing hunger for information and variety. The virtual world of technology and mechanical devices, for instance, is bent on simulating life energies. In this shadow world, the individual learns to handle more and more complex forms, frequencies and meanings. Technological dimensions are simulations of the concrete mind, devoid of feeling or sensation. It is the world of projection, enabled by the intellect and its fascination with control and artificial gadgets. This ambition leads to excess and daring but can also cause a disconnection from natural life and drain their mental force.

Technology handles thinking in patterns that convey meaning. This type of thinking is logical, useful and interesting; it involves global

---

Conversely, on the mental level, humanity develops its imagination and projects desire in the form of endless creativity.

management of data and works through collective assessments reached through research, that may cut through the limitations of time and space. Examples of virtual shadow reality include the world of digital technology, scientific advancement, artificial intelligence and many forms of abstract reasoning.

The virtual shadow reality is not devoid of attachment; only emotionality here is of a different sort than at the astral range or at the physical third-dimensional level. Rather than human feeling, the range of virtual feeling extends from excitement and ambition to power craving and domination. The mind, with all its mechanical extensions, becomes all-powerful. Meanwhile, body vitality is kept at a minimum; it remains under-stimulated or becomes overstimulated to highly athletic proportions but lacks integrated body awareness and Self-consciousness.

This range of activity is so absorbing that the perception of and sensitivity to the subtleties of everyday life are completely overshadowed. Given the exaggerated emphasis placed on mental activity at this moment of history, a marked gap between the intellect and the physical body, especially muddled at the emotional level, is evident. The stereotypical 'geeks' who live in this dimension notoriously avoid emotions and personal involvement. This constitutes an obstacle to accessing subtle and higher life, which are foremost sentient and respond to physical, emotional and spiritual engagement.

Both astral and technological shadow worlds are self-motivated and self-interested, led by instinct and subliminal impulse. Inseparable from the personal ego-self, subconscious desires and ambitions mark a life of separation that builds and supports individuality and an identity with little or no connection to Self as Consciousness. We must be aware of our unconscious action and awareness at these levels, as it is in the uncovering of our subconscious and unconsciousness that we reach higher and finer subtleties of perception, raise our consciousness and become increasingly aware of Self.

HOLISTIC DIMENSIONS OF TRUTH:
THE SEVENTH, EIGHTH AND NINTH DIMENSIONS

The most important consideration for a seeker of truth is the way in which they resonate in the world: in other words, the quality emitted.

This next level of dimensions in the table (see pages 200–1) – the seventh, eighth and ninth – constitute holistic dimensions of truth. They demand the absence of personal preoccupation and open the way for wisdom.

You are meant to 'know'.

Your knowing could be tuning into your bloodstream and becoming aware when something is not right. Equally, you could acquire a wholly different perspective from the one habitually held. You could read impressions or images in collective memory, for instance, from remote antiquity without technological aid or scientific reasoning and bring back liberating information, free from the calculating, negotiating mind of the lower dimensions.

Just as you have learnt how to handle detail physically and mentally, how to project ideas and colour creations with emotionally charged nuances, by using Higher Mental faculties at these levels, you are able to attract, intuit, infer, induce and connect through space and time with all of life.

Consciousness at this second range of dimensions begins as holistic cognition and spreads into a conceptual experience of pure dynamics. This range of the seventh through to the ninth dimensions imply a consciousness that employs the sentient intelligence of the heart as Higher Mind.

Only a discriminating mind can distinguish truth from imitation. This range of dimensions is not reached by desire, thinking or simple integration. It requires a qualitative leap of intelligence, possible only when the Self that is centralised on personal and immediate reality has been set aside in favour of global perception and sensitivity.

The seventh dimension became popular with the surge of the New Age and is currently commonly referred to as the fifth dimension, or 5D, in other systems. This is the arena of Jungian archetypes and historical perspectives, the seat of holistic neutrality and humanity. Rather than arising out of emotional excess, the sentiment that colours this level responds to the clear insight that perfection, justice and a divine plan do in fact exist, and you form an integral part of this plan. At this level, the mystic and the scientist meet. They know what it is like to persevere through the ordinary obstacle course of everyday life for the sake of an ideal. At this stage, high levels of emotion and pure Mind are synonymous.

The seventh dimension is the place where time and space converge. The combination of past-present-future is embraced as an energetic experience of wholeness. Higher Mind perceives globally and coherently beyond divisions.

The eighth dimension is a potent nexus of dynamic vortices of energetic potential. When you tap into this range of frequencies, you experience the impulse that allows contact with new possibilities and configurations at the next dimension: the ninth. Whenever you wish to know something but lack the logical tools necessary, your mind involuntarily invokes the frequencies within the eighth dimension. Its arrowed purposefulness induces a search, and you find yourself vibrating with an impulse that stretches across time and space and will not stop until you reach the condition that will elicit an answer. This is pure dynamism and triggers the moment of 'eureka' or illumination that has to do with discovery and prophecy.

In a way, the eighth and ninth dimensions resemble a fantasy world containing spaceships and strange, ethereal winged creatures. Forms appear as luminous movement, and you experience transportation instantaneously. The frequencies of these dimensions catalyse knowledge and precipitate insight that you may bring back to the concrete, third-dimensional world.

The ninth dimension corresponds to the state of reverie of a musician, a mathematician or a scientist. It induces a subtle state of Being that lives, breathes and embodies the unique world of musical scores, numbers and formulas that lie as causal factors behind physical creation. This dimension holds concepts of form and measure, communication and transportation harmoniously.

Images, sensations and energetic qualifications serve as guides to the ninth dimension. The 'subtle senses' awaken to perceive emanation and energy rather than form and matter. Your senses perceive more finely and merge with one another. You perceive 'outward' impressions that resonate with body impressions. You perceive with your hearing and see through smell, touch and tone. You feel in colours and taste the right or wrongness of conditions. You understand through analogy and poetic association.

The range of frequencies of the ninth dimension is the natural realm of evolved men and women who have been graced with intuitive genius. It is also a spectrum that, although active in various ways in all of humanity, is not recognised or acknowledged sufficiently, largely because it is confused with sentimental illusion or pipe dreams.

Whenever the intelligent person wishes to understand a person, an event, a tendency or an evolutionary process, they intuitively connect with a cognitive faculty that is no longer linear, no longer dual or even multiple, because it addresses a unitary principle beyond diversity. This is the frequency of knowing at the seventh, eighth and ninth dimensions. These are the realms of the diplomat and the quantum physicist, of anyone who may conceive of past-present-future as a unit that arouses possibilities.

Peace is a holistic concept at this level, a concept that is anathema to the idea of peace which, in the realm of linear thought, is mere tolerance among disparate parts. Visions of processes of global scope that ignite brotherhood do not emerge from the brain. This type of peace is a result of the sentient intelligence of the heart that awakens through deeply humane concerns and our feeling–understanding capabilities. It is from here that the idea of justice emerges.

These finer frequencies define states of Being that are intensely dynamic. The influence of these dimensions, particularly the seventh, is very strong at the moment. They offer an important key to the transformation and eventual transmutation of our world as it starts resonating with Higher Mind. A great number of human beings who are integrating the past and the possibilities of the future are already poised here.

Imagine you were able to halt the movement of time and experience it in compacted space: in this way, you may understand the tremendous pressure of the higher dimensional range of experiences. The experience of these dimensions is an unbearable, unstoppable yearning at the heart of every human being towards the pursuit of truth, beauty, love and harmony that will manifest fully in the finest range of dimensional frequencies – this is what the truly spiritual experience is made of.

—
Whenever the intelligent person wishes to understand a person, an event, a tendency or an evolutionary process, they intuitively connect with a cognitive faculty that is no longer linear, no longer dual or even multiple, because it addresses a unitary principle beyond diversity.
—

TRANSCENDENT DIMENSIONS: THE TENTH, ELEVENTH AND TWELFTH DIMENSIONS

The tenth, eleventh and twelfth dimensions constitute the transcendent dimensions – the Spirit world. This range of dimensions requires the least amount of effort to focus and access the essence of Intelligence as Mind. These dimensions are the most difficult to explain and to attain, since there is no process, as such, to do so.

The human being is not used to accomplishing something without focus, deliberate intention and the stress and strain that comes with linear expression. It is easier said than done to stop the monopoly of thought in order to be able to appreciate and flow with the wholeness of manifest and non-manifest life. It may take years of practice, or only seconds of surrender, to yield the experience of illumination.

Conscious contact with finer dimensions instils in the individual the urge to bring their quality into the physical world tangibly, as they begin to access and decode truth at this level. A person who has contact with these dimensions becomes a bridge towards the construction of a better world: a world server.

When you conceive of perfect action, when you envision beauty and the sacred, when you search for truth or employ philosophical ideas of pure reason, you are tuning into these broader dimensional fields. This last range of dimensional frequencies employs the faculty of consciousness as no-mind. To 'know' at this level is to experience the reflection of your own Presence as it contains the whole. Only silence is able to transmit this Presence.

The higher the vibratory frequency of Consciousness, the more diaphanous and spacious its texture, and the finer its sentience. At this exalted state, perception is experienced as spherical and concentric, rather than linear and horizontal, spreading into an unlimited number of horizons. At this frequency, the human being is a fragrance, rather than a form, and life stands revealed as an ocean of infinite becoming. Experience here resembles feeling indescribably blessed and loved when in deep prayer and meditation.

At this level the spiritual, or inner, senses are triggered by participation in the resonance or irradiation that emerges from within. These senses unfold in an extremely intimate experience of Self without the imposition of purpose, personal power or utility. Here one may embrace all

---

When you conceive of perfect action, when you envision beauty and the sacred, when you search for truth or employ philosophical ideas of pure reason, you are tuning into these broader dimensional fields.

---

dimensions of Being equally, parting from the highest pre-conceptual and pre-substantial levels of Being. In the human being, this level of perception marks a life lived deeply and intensely, without judgement, anchored in the ever-present now-ness of existence.

The line of demarcation between the material (the first to sixth dimensions) and holistic (seventh to ninth) dimensions is one of breadth; the line of demarcation between the holistic and spiritual (tenth to twelfth) dimensions is one of depth. In the holistic dimensions the notion of time does not exist. In the spiritual dimensions, neither time nor physical space exist. Everything is now, here, eternal and infinite. There is nowhere to go. There is no need for technological machines or esoteric devices, rituals or special procedures, focus or calculation, gurus or outer authority figures.

At the highest levels, Consciousness, not matter, is supreme; there is only an insinuation of substance. Spirituality is the exaltation of matter into pure space. Higher dimensional forms are so vast that they appear transparent. Imagine a human body stretched out to the size of a galaxy, and you might understand structure at these levels. There is very little 'substance' in the spiritual dimensions. By contrast, pressure is more intense than substance. Should you tap into these dimensions physically, the atomic pressure would be impossible to sustain. Light vibrations would shatter physical matter. If you are having trouble understanding how this might be so, you only have to think of what would happen to an astronaut sent into outer space without their suit. If the individual is unprepared physically and mentally to sustain the voltages activated at these levels, they are bound to hallucinate, fantasise or speak of experiences that would easily be classified as insane.

In our interdimensional system, the first of the spiritual dimensions is the tenth dimension. This dimension is attained through prayer and meditation. Words like 'Heaven', *nirvana* or *samadhi* are used to describe it. These words describe a receptive, mindless state that taps into the frequency of Light as comfort and beauty. This Light is also present in the centre of the atomic structure.

Contact with the Elohim and Archangelic power is possible at this level and translates into angelic bliss and the intuition of perfection. This is a place you return to as often as you make space for it, a niche accessible to everyone in times of need, when the soul calls to itself. The simplest heart is the closest to this state of bliss. To become aware of this state and

---

At the highest levels, Consciousness, not matter, is supreme; there is only an insinuation of substance.

---

be able to sustain it, a person reverts to their own unique quality of Spirit, without personal importance.

The state of Being at this stage now magnifies inner perception to include emotional height as pure feeling, beyond the qualifying of this pure sentiment into emotions. From the perspective of the third-dimensional range, this state of Being appears as formlessness, yet, in reality, it is space as pure, essential Intelligence. From this height you contemplate generative, transcendental activity. You find refuge and rest, inspiration and the kind of security and confidence that issues from knowing that you are seen and loved by Self. It is the plane of divinity, filled with joy and vitality. On our human ladder of frequencies this plane works to instil hope by stilling the mind and raising emotion to a plane of perfection, beauty and luminosity. It is a realm of union and individuation that transports you from the limitations of matter to the sublime state of Perfection.

Experiences of the eleventh dimension are infrequent. The reason for this is that these frequencies are so shatteringly intense that we must relinquish, even if momentarily, the tenuous hold over our physical form, its faculties and all the attachments that this implies. A near-death experience can access this dimension. Mystics and illuminated individuals who have attained this state do not live life as we do. They have no need for words; their mere Presence conveys divinity.

This is the plane of Bodhisattvas and guardians of the great religions. It is the place of the I AM Presence. Each time you aspire to serve humanity, asking how you can do this, you contact the Source issuing from this plane. Occasionally, some dream experiences reflect this dimensional level. In these states, you contact teachers on the path of initiation and bring back electrifying memories.

As a last accessible outpost for planetary experience, this dimension responds to the soul-need of humankind as it searches for new paradigms. Humans spontaneously raise themselves to the eleventh dimension to receive the flash of inspiration that is subsequently decoded as 'revelation'. The experience of consciousness at the eleventh dimension provides a focal point of oscillation that constitutes our eternal energetic identity, a key to the Self that is also called the secret name. It is a combination of frequencies of Spirit that is unique to each individual in the long journey through the dimensions.

The highest dimension of all in our evolutionary system is an undifferentiated state of pure radiance, or Source. This is referred to as the twelfth dimension, but understand that this is a theoretical point of reference. This dimension represents Absolute Being, a state of pure irradiation at the threshold of a greater unknowable system of Consciousness.

You long for this ultimate height of divinity, to satiate yourself with that spiritual quality that guides and sustains you. By your participation in the dimensions below, you are constantly receiving the overflow of the twelfth, but you cannot tangibly touch it; you sense it, but do not see it. This state surrounds you, but it is constantly eluding you. It is within you, but you do not understand it.

THE RETURN JOURNEY

The dimensions constitute a perfect relay system of energetic transmission that responds to your every need. Descent consists of Spirit gradually concentrating and condensing Consciousness and matter into human faculties. Ascent through the dimensions, the so-called 'return' journey, consists in reclaiming the forms and faculties in all dimensions of Being. Your own potential resonates in tune at all stations and aspects of Creation. On the return journey, at every level of your consciousness, you recapture and employ the kind of force that allows you to access wisdom and responses from Creation.

As you bring these forces back to physical reality, the level of mental development you now possess enables you to unravel impressions and translate them in useful ways. This is why both mental discipline and sensitivity are so necessary in order to accompany neutral empathic resonance in depth.

It does not matter if you are not aware of the precise stages of dimensional activity and their meaning. Knowing the roadmap is not the key: surrender and acceptance of the Now and the fullness of your Being are. Fulfilment, joy, truth, revelation and knowledge: all these higher-dimensional qualities are accessible to those who attune themselves spontaneously to those frequencies.

The following two tables outline the dimensions once again in their ascending and descending order and outline the step-by-step stages of Consciousness in its journey up and down the dimensions, with the qualities and faculties available to it at each stage.

Sublimation and Transcendence

Dimension	How it manifests in human consciousness; Its structure; Its purpose
First and Second	**Quality of consciousness: rhythm and pulsation** *Structure, makeup:* • Subatomic world • Biological subconsciousness *Purpose and details:* • Gestation and elemental building blocks of physical world • Ruled by nature spirits or Devas (see page 231)
Third	**Quality of consciousness: senses and concrete mind** *Structure, makeup:* • Atomic structure • Dynamic of relativity, field of interaction *Purpose and uses of this dimension in human consciousness:* • Maintaining health and natural functions • Affecting material balance, harmonisation, polarity, allopathic methods of healing, manipulation, physiotherapy, massage • Synchronisation and management of physical nature (the healthy activity of the elements and their equilibrium)
Astral tier of the third dimension	*The world of astral phenomenology, such as lower, instinctual thoughtforms of humanity; or even the realm of wandering, earth-bound souls who have not 'passed on'*
Fourth	**Quality of consciousness: reflection, restructuring** *Structure, makeup:* • Mould or blueprint for the third dimension *Purpose and uses of this dimension in human consciousness:* • Attraction, reflection, dissolution, construction and projection of forms • Effecting qualitative changes in matter through dematerialisation or purification • Attracting a physical manifestation • Projecting ideas • Preparation of vibrational medicines • Healing the physical and the personality through the etheric mould of matter
Fifth	**Quality of consciousness: planning, probabilities** *Structure, makeup:* • Terrain of mental exploration *Purpose and uses of this dimension in human consciousness:* • Strategy – from the military to shopping lists • Calculation, mathematical abstraction • Relating and integrating data (e.g. architecture, engineering, chemistry) • Technical clarity • Resolving problems of strategy or calculation

Quality of consciousness: discernment, creativity

Structure, makeup:
• This dimension is formed of the energy of real and practical possibilities and potentialities

Purpose and uses of this dimension in human consciousness:
• Strengthening technical creativity
• Exploring possibilities
• Executing cybernetic technology
• Creating abstract art
• Finishing with the old, when a given direction has been exhausted and we turn towards the higher dimensions in search of 'the new'

Sixth

Concept of time
• From this dimension on, the experience of linear, sequential time no longer exists

Quality of consciousness: integration, intuition

Structure, makeup:
• Central station of the soul and its connection with the current personality
• Totality of simultaneous past-present-future, as situated in holographic space (the eternal present theory of physics)
• Point of integration of the concrete/abstract mind with holistic vision

Seventh
Purpose and uses of this dimension in human consciousness:
• Understanding, comprehension, inspiration and meaning
• Integrating the personality with soul
• Understanding incarnation and the 'lessons' of life
• Perfect and harmonious action with the Divine Plan and with the Law of the One
• Philosophical comprehension and complex order
• Finding an answer to any question
• Historical vision

Quality of consciousness: focused intention, searching – the 'eureka' dimension

Structure, makeup:
• This dimension is formed of the energy of pure dynamism and intentionality. Where we go to induce and obtain insight into concepts, which then need to be decoded in the sixth. It is here that we have the sensation that there is 'something' we need to know, but we do not know what it is.
• Here is a vast qualitative change: the experience of stopping time. From here on, the mental faculties, such as we know them, no longer function; rather, another state of understanding comes about which is accessed as a state of Being.

Eighth

Purpose and uses of this dimension in human consciousness:
• Activating the mental fields to grasp concepts that will be translated into ideas, activity or a practical form in the lower dimensions
• Mental incentive and motivation for new options
• Demonstrating an idea and/or its application

Quality of consciousness: state of knowing, seeing

Structure, makeup:
- The energy of formulas that underly the Universe forms this dimension
- Planetary movement

Ninth   *Purpose and uses of this dimension in human consciousness:*
- To leap to the state of no-mind, achieving mental serenity without intentionality
- Perception of movement and the projection of energies
- Holistic comprehension of forms and measures, e.g. the initial decoding of a symphony that has been intuited in the tenth dimension
- Perception of the inner dynamic of systems

Quality of consciousness: contemplation, silence, peace

Structure, makeup:
- Generative space of pure feeling: realm of ecstasy, the beatific experience of Love – what we might call Heaven or *nirvana*

Tenth   *Purpose and details:*
- Fusion with Beings who rule the kingdom of nature
- Finding peace; feeling 'at home'
- Essential inspiration
- Connecting with the driving force, or matrix, which determines the activity and expression of every manifestation in the lower worlds

---

Quality of consciousness: ardent aspiration, devotion, unconditional dedication

Structure, makeup:
- This is the central Station of Being in incarnation, or the realm of Intelligence (*élan vital* of the soul), representing the limit of the capacities of individual planetary intelligence, the sentience possessed by a whole planet. It is the space of every possibility for a 'new' life or human expression.

Eleventh   *Purpose and details:*
- Accessing new possibilities that require a new combination of ideas or new parameters and untried paradigms
- The dimension our Intelligence reaches when we no longer want more of the same, and we seek for a Master or a new path through meditation

---

Quality of consciousness: fusion, total quietude, plenitude, emptiness

Structure, makeup:
- The place of unity and Oneness, where all knowledge, all possibility, and the path reside. Even though we have no form for decoding what we experience in this dimension, it is to here that our Spirit leaps in yearning for fusion with the Absolute. All prayer or entreaty that arises in the third dimension leads here, whence the entreaty descends directly to the eleventh dimension in order to initiate its descent with the 'answer'.

Twelfth   *Purpose and details:*
- This is the dimension we access for pure spiritual nourishment

The following table outlines the dimensions from the perspective of the descent of Consciousness from the Oneness of the twelfth dimension to its third-dimensional embodiment. Our essence resides in the eleventh dimension, nourished by Source in the twelfth. In its descending movement through the lower dimensions, it proceeds to embody the forms of expression, together with the faculties we employ in manifestation, as body and mind.

THE HUMAN EXPERIENCE OF THE DIMENSIONS IN DESCENDING ORDER: THE DECODING PROCESS

Creation and Materialisation

Dimension	Quality; Location in Consciousness; Use in the descent of Consciousness
Twelfth	*Pure Consciousness, the Monad* Radiation or emanation, containing all; Essence without form; pure Light Point of departure into manifestation through a dynamic of gradual deceleration
Eleventh	*Essential Intelligence* Prism-like station; station of ascended beings evolutionary process This is the starting point for acquiring every conceivable expression and order for the journey into form. It is the first stage of the agglutination or densification of Consciousness, between the Infinite and the not-as-yet-defined finite state. It represents the newly emerged focal point, or 'I-ness'. From this point a rainbow of Consciousness issues as essential Intelligence, or the Divine Presence.
Tenth	*Supramental Intelligence*[14] The matrix, primary grid or network The rainbow of Consciousness passes this point and initiates a deceleration, leading to densification and resonance, as sound. At this point, the possibilities of Consciousness gain definition. Here a network, or hierarchy, is created out of which arises the range of concepts and ideas used for and by all of humanity. It is the realm of supramental Intelligence or the Intelligence of the super-mind, which is that upper plane of perfect knowledge, and it is the first bridge between essential Intelligence, pure Consciousness and the lower world of manifestation. Principles at this level include: • The laws of Matter and the One • Truth • The cycles of nature

---

14 The supramental level means 'above' linear cognition and embraces conceptual cognition, reaching 'idea-based cognition'. The level of the supramental is pure vibration, before it becomes form.

INNER ALCHEMY

218

	Higher Mind
	Systems
	Global systems, ideas and philosophical concepts form the ninth dimension, within which the seeds of planetary forms and measure are found. Here Intelligence adapts itself into the frequency of Higher Mind. Conceptual formulas, such as Einstein's mass-energy equivalence, exist here as reality, ready for exploration, development and application. It is here that the soul about to embody obtains the 'mould' or life-plan for its incarnation, in line with planetary or astral influences (as is taught in astrology).
Ninth	This is the wellspring of principles such as:
	• The dynamics and cycles of natural activity
	• Karma as the dynamic of the Law
	• The mineral and vegetable kingdoms
	• Systems for arriving at Truth
	Pure dynamism
	This is where the organising force of the concepts above propels manifestation. The first 'forms' emerge at the eighth dimension as luminous and highly abstract images, still without concrete definition or substance.
Eighth	The eighth dimension is the common station for grasping original concepts and ideas applicable for incarnated humanity. This is fertile ground and where the 'eureka' happens on the upwards journey, which when reached, launches us back into the sixth dimension for decoding.
	Intuition
	Central planetary station or meeting-place of human forces and energies. This is the level of the Akashic records, the dimension of symbols or the archetype.
	The seventh dimension is the place of integration and adaptation to the approaching physical reality. Concepts descend from the Higher Mental level and become more concrete, clothing themselves with the astral substance of the planet and adjusting to the concept of time. This is the historical plane, which puts relations between forms, events and evolutionary cycles. All the wisdom of the past and/or the possible future can be revealed at this point. On the upwards journey, this is the plane of human perfection.
Seventh	Principles at this level include:
	• The ecological or evolutionary vision of nature and its parts
	• God as humanity
	• All philosophies and their theories of Truth
	Reason, Higher logic
	Here we have mathematical abstraction. The transition to the concrete, lower mental state that comes about here eventually culminates in sequential thought as reason and higher logic, capable of formulating and reformulating ideas in technical and practical idioms.
Sixth	Here the principle is the logic we use to arrive at Truth.

Fifth	*Associative logic*
	Here Mind expresses itself through associating and constructing images, or creations, with a view to determining probabilities. Here is the emergence of concrete formulas, and the coordination of the possibility of manifestation.
	Principles at this level include:
	• Natural sciences
	• Concepts such as liberty, equality and fraternity
	• Associated values: Truth-justice

Fourth	*Synaesthesia*
	This is the mirror plane; it is the 'rehearsal' for the third dimension.
	This is the level of immediate projection, application and management of forms at the mental level used in the third dimension. At this point, images now acquire pre-material substance, creating etheric patterns. This is the plane or mould of everything created in the third dimension. The ideas conceived in the eighth and individuated in the six are structured here, acquiring direct applicability for the planet. These creations now appear in their totality. This level bears the results of introspection, such as discovering your basic delusions, which you then have the opportunity to correct in the third dimension.

Third	*The physical dynamic*
	We now arrive at the terrain that enables physical form and the rise of the sequential concrete mind with its cohesion with matter in a capacity to divide, analyse, explore and perfect parts. The 'mirror' of the fourth dimension is fragmented, giving way to the game of multiple combinations and forms, what in the East is called *maya*.
	All concrete patterns here are manifested and expressed physically, mentally and emotionally.

The knowledge provided in these tables provides a conceptual basis of the stages of Consciousness, and the frequencies, faculties, abilities and insights available for the individual who chooses to make the journey up and down the elevator of Consciousness. The following section provides a more detailed theoretical basis for understanding this 'elevator' and how we, as human beings, travel up and down it.

THE DYNAMICS OF INTELLIGENCE: SUMMARY OF THE DIMENSIONAL STAGES AND YOUR USE OF THEM

Dimensions are mere frequencies in which we vibrate life.

The implicit purpose of the interdimensional journey has always been to bring back information, energy, insight and possibility, and apply it in the construction of a better world. Whether the trip is on the ascending or on the descending scale, the purpose of linking Heaven and Earth, Spirit and matter is served, and the application of the Master Practice enables you to do this.

The descending journey of Consciousness culminates in embodiment. The ascendant drive towards transcendence allows you to reach beyond apparent limitations, reminding you that you are one with divinity.

Everyone rides the elevator.

THE DESCENT: DECODING AND MANIFESTING

View from the penthouse

In order to apply or translate dimensional experience coherently, one's personal focus of Consciousness pauses at specific stations to make the energy adjustments necessary for application in third-dimensional reality. The receptivity that occurs at the higher range is spontaneously interpreted at the eighth dimension as impulse and then translated for meaning at the seventh. These intuited impressions become tangible concepts, which start to acquire form and relevance at the sixth dimension, realising form fully at the third dimension through the moulding process of the fifth and fourth energy fields. This revelation transforms into a message to be fully and physically manifested in the third dimension.

View from the ground floor

To experience Creation, humanity necessarily experiences dimensional activity from the perspective of the body and everyday references. Even when an individual may make and have made the journey 'up' the dimensions, their primary commitment remains with matter, the body and daily life. They must remain rooted and understand the here and now in their life in order to manage Creation more adeptly.

Yet, while rooted in the third dimension, an individual's consciousness accesses other dimensions in order to reactivate, accelerate or contact faculties required for dealing with certain experiences in the third dimension. While living in the here and now, they also travel up the 'elevator' and become more adept at doing so the more they consciously live an interdimensional life concomitant with physical experience. In doing so they develop both inner and outer power.

In this process one develops faculties for abstraction. Often, through the good and also the sad times, yearning states are triggered that touch higher dimensional grace and determine a person's relationship with Source. Without knowing just how to do this, they access higher dimensions from the third-dimensional base and constantly attempts to translate and apply the inspirations or revelations gained through study, dreaming and artistic or meditative reverie.

The human being actively participates, consciously or unconsciously, in three basic stations: the third, seventh and the tenth. Active participation in the third dimension is obvious. It is here that we receive information, explore and implement data from all dimensions. We roam in the seventh, when we dream of probabilities based on present-day conditions. It is here where much of today's science fiction originates, blending past-present-future into a holistic vision of possibilities. The tenth dimension is known as Heaven or *nirvana*. This is the human ideal of peace and love. One need not know which dimension is which in order to access and experience all three.

In the end, the journey towards the top and the return to the ground floor requires awakened effort, discipline and persistence in modulating and adapting the sentient faculties of the third dimension to match their correlates in the higher frequencies of the upper dimensions.

To experience Creation, humanity necessarily experiences dimensional activity from the perspective of the body and everyday references.

INNER ALCHEMY

222

Remember, though, that all the time, you are *here*, in your body, living in the third dimension. This is where you remain, ultimately enjoining your multidimensional selves into a cohesive unit of endless apprenticeship and flexibility.

For some people, their inner search is very specific, so they halt the elevator in one or another of the stations along the way, specialising in that particular type of performance and energy field and realising their own incarnational purpose.

Ultimately, all the dimensions are yours. All you need to do is press the button and step off.

INTEGRATION STATIONS – FIFTH, SEVENTH, NINTH AND ELEVENTH DIMENSIONS

Integration stations allow for the exploration and integration of insights and experiences. They are the sites of exploration and decoding of the insights that have been received or intuited from higher dimensions. All integration stations are negatively charged.

The fifth dimension is used almost daily. At this level we may integrate ideas into a functioning unit, understanding the utility of the whole. Technology serves this function well, but even without machines, the human mind performs the fifth-dimensional task of linking fourth- and sixth-dimensional associated skills.

The kind of integration that happens at the seventh dimension is one of perspective. When we seek to understand within a historical reference how an idea or construction fits into the needs of humanity, for instance, we invariably turn to the past and also imagine it in a probable future. It is at this point that we access the full insight possible in the seventh dimension, accessing imprints or records engraved in the textures of this dimension. It is here that the coordination and integration of time in human evolution can occur.

The ninth dimension offers content and context. Those with a mathematical or musical bent find meaning in this frequency range, which ignites motivation and aspiration in Higher Mind, while soaked in aspirations of creative ardour. This station not only serves to integrate what has been contacted at these higher levels, it is also the realm where formulas exist as truth in mathematical language. The essence of formulas that trigger new perspectives in the lower dimension springs from this

The kind of integration that happens at the seventh dimension is one of perspective.

station of consciousness, such as Einstein's equivalence of energy and matter ($E=mc^2$), which represents an eternal law and has inspired so many people since he intuited and formulated it. This is where Beethoven 'heard' music and then transcribed it, and where Tesla 'saw' the formulas he lowered through his awareness into the fourth dimension, where he was able to explore them and then implement them in the third dimension. It is also where the soul about to embody obtains the 'mould' or life-plan of its incarnation, as is also taught in astrology.

The eleventh dimension brings nuances of probability. Having reached the pinnacle of Intelligence as Consciousness here, Consciousness now has nowhere else to go but into itself. A new world order is initiated. Innovators and futurists, world leaders and humanists find hidden energies here that spark unforeseen possibilities.

RESTING STATIONS – SEVENTH AND TENTH DIMENSIONS

The seventh and tenth dimensions constitute types of resting stations.

The seventh dimension is an intermediary station between higher and lower dimensions. The fourth to the sixth dimensions provide technical dynamics for the third dimension and relate to the needs of the third dimension. For human consciousness to arrive at the seventh dimension a leap of consciousness must occur (not a continuation). At the seventh dimension our human consciousness must deal with and integrate other forms of life and consciousness. In this sense, the seventh dimension is a resting station, where 'resting' is the word used to denote a *state* of quiet integration, rather than dynamic exploration.

Something similar happens at the tenth dimension. At the tenth dimension the human being recognises themselves as Spirit in coherence with both Angelic and Elohim evolutions. The tenth dimension provides a feeling of peace and at-one-ment. This dimension can be thought of as the ultimate resting place.

The seventh dimension is an idyllic panorama, where time in motion, like a magnificent oriental fan, stands revealed in a breathtaking layout of futuristic possibility enacted in the present. Humanity's wellbeing is prized here above all. This is a level where cosmic and planetary information is stored (the Akashic records). It is here we may tap into the combined wisdom of the souls of all humanity throughout incarnations to gain insights. Many perceive the Akashic records as archives or great libraries, all connected to the human purpose. All great moments of history, even remote achievements, are engraved upon the ether of this streaming energy.

The tenth dimension is your innermost secret place. People visit it through nature, in love, through religious practice, in deep passionate study, as dance and in the throes of ardent creativity. It is here that people seek silence within the shelter of a consecrated space. You fuse as a force of Love with another life or form of life. You imbibe and grow within the vast compassionate quality of this dimension. Here, you feel whole and at peace.

SUBLIMATION AND TRANSMUTATION – THIRD, SEVENTH AND TENTH DIMENSIONS

The third, seventh and tenth dimensions are most useful to humanity when it comes to the alchemical processes of transmutation and sublimation. They are the main stations of the Alchemical Alignment.

Sublimation is not merely substitution. Instead, it is an alchemical practice that demands the direct experience of energies, releasing the forces of transmutation that are brought about by awakened Consciousness in the form of intention and discipline. Sublimation is the purpose of the human journey and it is the effect of evolution and the expansion of consciousness.

Life after life, the human being seeks improvement and transcendence through direct experience. After many accidents and persistence as ego-gratifying attempts in self-indulgence, the human being recognises, like Lord Buddha, that human desire as attachment is the cause of human suffering. This is where they begin to step aside from the self, and when the real spiritual work begins at the third dimension.

Eventually, at some point (or lifetime) they discover that the power contained by emotions is also the key to transcendence. Many turn to books or to psychology and are content with information that may explain the cause of their addictions. This may be enough. Others, however, need to turn within and enter into the dynamic process of transmutation, enjoining mind and heart with Consciousness and leaping beyond logic into holistic perception.

Sublimation is achieved when emotions are faced, causes have been recognised and willpower has been garnered to redirect an individual's own personal forces into unknown territory. At this point a rescue begins, fostering self-understanding that becomes compassion. At the seventh dimension, fear becomes courage, anger becomes leadership, envy becomes understanding and actions become spontaneously humanitarian. This is where true understanding is born.

Upon reaching the tenth dimension, the process of sublimation is complete. Now it is time for implementation: the gigantic task of manifestation within your individual personal world. This is the painful, tedious, detailed care of imprinting manifestation of higher frequencies into lower ground, and spreading your anchored experience into the physical, material world you share with others, who are not as fortunate as you have been in discovering the nature and extent of the Power that lies within you. You now know you have the power to transform the world.

FACULTIES DEVELOPED THROUGH THE DIMENSIONS

In this section I examine the faculties one may develop through interdimensional access. Certain dimensions correspond more with either mental, emotional or physical faculties and capacities.

MENTAL DEVELOPMENT: FOURTH, FIFTH, SIXTH AND EIGHTH DIMENSIONS

The Personal Focus of Consciousness (PFC) develops the concrete, linear mind of the third dimension into a more focused and expansive instrument through experience within the energy fields of the fourth, fifth and sixth dimensions. If it is able to leap over the abyss of the seventh, which is a move beyond the fixation on linear thought and concepts, the PFC gains access to the eighth-dimensional arena of powerful mental impulses that ignites further research.

Manifestation brings insights from the eighth dimension. Mental impulses and insights become more and more defined at the sixth-dimensional range, becoming ever more concrete through their descent in the fifth and fourth dimensions.

EMOTIONAL DEVELOPMENT: THIRD, SEVENTH AND TENTH DIMENSIONS

The PFC develops emotional control and flexibility through the intensity of its ordinary emotional life in the third dimension. In the absence of the mental training of the fourth, fifth and sixth dimensions, it is possible for an ordinary person to leap into the seventh-dimensional and even the tenth-dimensional state of Being. These people are the 'pure of heart', who honour human life because they honour sensitivity.

PHYSICAL DEVELOPMENT: THIRD, SEVENTH AND NINTH DIMENSIONS

The third dimension is the arena for physical experience of every sort, gathering and circulating vitality, and learning to care for surrounding physical life. Incipient natural flashes of seventh-dimensional life inspire beauty and harmony in the ordinary world of matter. Through immersion in the world of matter, a person may contact and learn to decode the laws of nature that transmit human love, such as the principles of form and measure at the ninth-dimensional levels.

READING NON-PHYSICAL PHENOMENA

In this section I look deeper into the ways in which one may access non-physical phenomena in the third-dimensional experience and the ways these phenomena may manifest.

Every part of the known Universe serves the Human Model of evolution, from the lowest life forms that build matter, to the highest archangelic frequencies that inspire humanity. For evolution, one must learn to discriminate, distinguish, decode and ultimately commune with Intelligence through a merging of heart and mind, in the same way one learns to manage the concrete mind of the body in the here and now. To grasp the wisdom available at finer dimensional ranges requires a quantum leap into another way of thinking through a non-personal ego state.

To perceive the different layers of reality, the personal focus of consciousness of the human being must not be fixed in one perspective: for instance, in one body. It must be flexibly active and in tune with the non-possessive, impermanent nature of Creation. Flexibility implies openness and yielding, the capacity to embrace and merge as a way of gathering and identifying impressions. This is the immeasurable way of wisdom.

You see, feel and know what you are prepared to see, feel, know and understand. When you align perception with Creation, body awareness stays as a constant background anchor, but it no longer calls the shots.

Every part of the known Universe serves the Human Model of evolution, from the lowest life forms that build matter, to the highest archangelic frequencies that inspire humanity.

You no longer feel with the body, but rather sense *through* it. You thus become more grounded, but also more open to higher frequencies. Perception expands: the senses are no longer separate faculties; they combine, and you are imbibed and moved by them. Perception becomes very delicate.

At this level, the PFC positions itself at the heart, which becomes a gateway to the upper and lower stations of consciousness where it remains, keeping its access to the faculties and talents of the personality. Heart intelligence, instead of the personality, becomes the central outpost. Impressions caught by the subtle senses translate into expanded awareness. There is no longer a wall of separation from Creation.

The PFC, when focused at the level of Higher Mind, recognises and handles the equivalent of physical, emotional and mental forces, but it does so through association and experience as Self. These physical, emotional and mental forces are therefore experienced at higher frequencies. Body is felt as motion, feeling translates into quality and mind shines forth as purpose.

To read impressions at this level requires extremely patient and gentle inner attunement. To be able to decode requires that you commune with what is being decoded and fuse with it. Form, feelings and intelligence blossom into foci of activity that simultaneously absorb and emit vibration. The seeker of truth learns to sustain depths and heights of exaltation without losing momentum, focus or clarity, ready and able to translate phenomena into three-dimensional terminology.

> The seeker of truth learns to sustain depths and heights of exaltation without losing momentum, focus or clarity, ready and able to translate phenomena into three-dimensional terminology.

DIMENSIONAL BEINGS

When Spirit–Source precipitated itself into manifestation, it gave birth to various distinct evolutionary modes: the Elohim, the Human Model of evolution and the Archangelic Realm. All three evolutionary chains respond to the imprint of the seven rays. The Human Model of evolution, however, is the only one that possesses a personal focus of consciousness, which allows it to shift and modulate attention and energy into innumerable states of Being, while recognising itself as a centre and creator.

Both archangels and Elohim translate and construct forms of themselves into lower dimensions in service. Archangels are beings responsible for the building and maintenance of our bodies. They direct the forces of the elements (fire, water, earth and air) within the human structure.

The Elohim have often been called God in its plurality, as they radiate the qualities of the Rays into the natural world, caring for and sustaining it. The Elohim are the highest consciousness and office held in the elemental kingdom. Like archangels, they reside at the tenth dimension. Both nourish life.

The following chart outlines the Elohim and the masculine or feminine qualities they emit. The names correspond to a particular sonic vibration and create thoughtforms that link us to the particular energies that pertain to a particular ray. Although we identify them through their polar resonance in matter, their nature is androgynous.

ELOHIM MALE/FEMALE QUALITIES CHART

Ray	Elohim (male/female polar resonance)
First	Hercules/Amazon
Second	Cassiopeia/Minerva
Third	Orion/Angelica
Fourth	Clair/ Astrea
Fifth	Vista/Crystal
Sixth	Tranquillity/Pacifica
Seventh	Arcturus/Diana

As we outlined in the section on the rays, we may invoke the rays by visualising flames, inviting the activity of the Elohim within us.

The illustration on page 230 depicts the seven-leafed flame, which is the manifestation of the Elohim in a human being, located in the third eye. It can be invoked as a powerful protective visualisation. The picture displays the seven rays as seven leaves of flames in the order in which the rays appear within us.

Each of the flames in the forehead is the domain and activity of an Elohim. Historically, these rays, when embodied by the Elohim, were seen as emanations of Light surrounding the head and conveyed the power of the divine ruler in the form of a diadem or a crown.

1. Hercules | 2. Cassiopeia | 3. Orion | 4. Clair | 5. Vista | 6. Tranquillity | 7. Arcturus

The Seven-leafed Flame

Although the rays are depicted in block colours in this illustration, please note they act in combinations of colours. Each Elohim co-exists in wholeness with all the others.

The Human Model is in a unique position to invoke and collaborate with the archangels and the Elohim through our ability to coordinate energies and forces in our own energy fields, and through the power obtained by the management of attention, intention and the senses. Humans may collaborate and communicate at any dimensional level, from participating in the supreme voltages of archangelic radiation and the quasi-tangible emissions of its angels in the lower dimensions, to invoking the exalted state of the Elohim and supporting the work of nature spirits upon the Earth.

Angels and nature spirits

When you have tapped into interdimensional reality and experienced life at the different dimensions of Being, when you have intuited the Love, the teaching and the guidance that comes from higher realms through your own Higher Self, guides and masters, when you know that life exists in multiple and infinite forms, most invisible to ordinary sight, then you come to know that angels and nature spirits are real.

Angels are the emanations of archangels adapted to serve in the lower dimensions. They are sensed by humanity as Light forms, conveying qualities of purity, harmony and beauty, like wisps of fresh, clean air. Their wings are emissions of Light. If you can imagine a soap bubble, floating under a solid blue sky on a sunny day, you have an idea of the colouring and substance of angels.

Nature spirits (or Devas) are emanations of the Elohim into the lower dimensions (first and second dimensions). They vary in form and size, and are constructed of the substance of the Earth itself, varying according to the element they handle: earth, water, air or fire.

The evolution of both angels and nature spirits is different from the Human Model of evolution. They possess collective Consciousness. They obey the mandates of their creators, with the mission of absorbing and releasing energies and forces from their Light bodies.

The angelic ministry is as complex as the human. To keep a balance over Creation, they heal and clear etheric substance, and guard and protect humanity and the Earth. Each embodied person has a guardian angel whose sole activity is to guard and protect them.

Nature spirits are much more difficult to see and sense. They love to play and are simple creatures that, as form, evolve in the same way as humanity does – that is, through gaining experience. They become master builders in their own right, graduating someday into builders and sustainers of worlds.

Guides and masters

The soul is always the principal fountain of learning for the individual. When the Higher Self reaches the vibrational level of the soul, it becomes infused with it.

The soul is that aspect of yourself that has existed since the beginning of the long journey into embodiment. It has no body; instead, it is a field of Intelligence, and interface between Spirit and the personal self in embodiment. The soul constitutes the repository of your experiences as skills and lessons learned and applied through lifetimes. Its life and voice are your own integrated past-life experiences, available to you as teaching and guidance. It whispers within you as 'inner knowing', the highest state of intuition.

The Higher Self is a sheath-like energy field, which is a tool of the embodied self. It harbours holistic intelligence and allows you to function interdimensionally. It represents the texture of your own consciousness when it has reached personal maturity and awakens to higher Intelligence. Your purpose as a human being is to reach and sustain this level, whereby you may then become Soul-infused.

You also have guides, or friends, from the Spirit world, or the spiritual dimensions (tenth to twelfth dimensions). These guides are the spiritual correlate of humans, often souls between embodiments, who are in service to humanity. Their choice is to help those similar to themselves. They are many and fall into different categories, appearing in special moments, according to your need and openness.

Your 'special' guides are the masters and their students, who also serve your needs and guide you to fulfil the mission of your choice in your embodiment. They look after human beings living and working under them. Each person belongs to a certain ray type and, when they enter the spiritual path, they also belong to a developmental group working under a master. Although, according to our teachings, the soul ray never changes, the master you are connected to may change within your lifetime, depending on the task of your embodiment and your own spiritual growth.

There are also beings from other dimensions, particularly from the seventh, who reach out to you as helpers, radiating courage, support and inspiration. Our souls, guides, masters and friends communicate through impressions in dreams and in meditation. Together they are largely the medium through which you receive Light, Love, nourishment and teaching.

Communication with the inner worlds is different from the high intensity pitch needed for interdimensional perception. Communication with inner worlds implies surrender. The inner world corresponds to your higher emotional state, rather than to the mind. It also responds to your call for help and collaboration. It requires a yielding will.

The remainder of this chapter is dedicated to meditations to help you discover your multidimensional nature and to connect with the interdimensional guides, masters and friends.

MEDITATIONS ON INTERDIMENSIONAL SPACE

The following meditation invokes the frequencies of the twelfth dimension. The frequency of the twelfth dimension evokes the formlessness of your Spirit-self. Its sound corresponds to your life force as it was echoed at the moment of creation, when your essence projected itself from Source. This sound is not perceptible to the ordinary senses. Its particular sonic frequency resembles what you might hear in deep meditation as a white-sound blanket of absolute silence and stillness. The sonic imprint of your Spirit-self is triggered by the following exercise, in which you resonate different vowels in the cavities of your physical body, which culminates in a state of bliss.

 ## SONIC BREATHING

Vocally stimulate the indicated centres within your physical body as shown in the illustration on the right. Note that these areas are not always the chakras, although they may sometimes coincide. The focus of your attention should be on the cavities, and the effect that each series of vowels has on this space within you. Ultimately, the total inner resonance produced in the entire body should cause an inner opening, a dimensional doorway to the ultrasonic frequency of the God-self as it expresses itself in you.

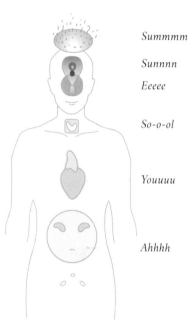

Summmm

Sunnnn

Eeee

So-o-ol

Youuuu

Ahhhh

Sonic Breathing

This exercise requires deep breathing, on the inhalation as on the exhalation. Inhale deeply, filling your lungs to full capacity, to have enough breath for a long exhalation that resonates the sounds called forth. Be sure to pronounce each letter, focusing on the last letter, prolonging its sound until you are emptied of air.

There are six sound combinations used in this exercise. The first is, '*ahhhh*', where the vowel is pronounced like the one in the word 'park'. The second is '*youuuu*', pronounced exactly as one would the pronoun, 'you', while drawing out the 'u' sound. The third is '*so-o-ol*', pronounced the same as in the Spanish word *sol* (sun) or in the English word 'module'. The fourth is '*eeeee*', like the Spanish vowel 'i', or the 'ee' in the word 'feet'. The fifth is '*sunnnn*', pronounced exactly like the word 'sun', while drawing out and vibrating the nasal 'n'. The final sound is '*summmm*', pronounced exactly like the word, 'sum', while drawing out and vibrating the nasal 'm'. The vowel in these last two words is pronounced the same, but with a small change in the acoustic property of the final nasal consonant.

The first place you address is the centre of your body, the solar plexus, where the adrenal glands are found. Vibrate this area by chanting *'ahhhh'* in one long outbreath. Do this three times.

The second place to address is the centre of the chest cavity. Same as before, resonate the sound *'youuuu'* in three long exhalations.

Next is the throat cavity. Fill and vibrate this to the sound *'so-o-ol'*, also in three long exhalations. To produce the necessary frequency of the *'o'*, you must make a hollow in your throat, as if you wanted to speak deeply. The *'l'* sound is pronounced inwardly.

The next sound is behind the nasal passages surrounding the sinuses. It should be especially shrill. Chant a very high pitched *'eeeee'*. Again, resonate this sound three times, fully expelling the air after each outbreath.

The next sound is in the centre of the forehead. Resonate the *'n'* in *'sunnnn'*. As before, do this for three outbreaths.

Finally, tune into the top of your head. Visualise the crown centre and imagine a balloon poised within it, extending upwards just above the head. In this spot chant the word *'summmm'* with accent on the *'m'*, becoming aware of the resonance of your entire cellular structure and the points of Light in your body. Do this three times, as above.

Then pause. Be still. Know your Self.

> Finally, tune into the
> top of your head.
> Visualise the crown
> centre and imagine a
> balloon poised within
> it, extending upwards
> just above the head.

⚱ CALIBRATION MEDITATION

This next meditation invokes the points of Light, referred to previously in Part Two (see page 46). The purpose of this meditation is to reach Consciousness at the highest dimensional range and to re-calibrate your energetic structure.

Recall that the Alchemical Alignment is the energetic connection with your Higher Self and it is the means to, as much as it is your connection with, the Source. By understanding it you will gain spiritual mastery – a mastery that is reflected in the very quality of your life, in your body, in your environment and in your relationships. This primary energetic alignment links your delicate receptors (your inner and outer senses) to the Earth and also to the heavens. You link yourself to the

Source of all power, all energy, all Light – to your Higher and to your Spirit-self.

As in the Master Practice, allow yourself to be fully aware and present in your body. Feel each and every part of your body from within. Become aware first of its parts and then the whole body as one unit. Feel its weight and also its fluidity, feel its fire and its space. Be sure that you are balanced and centred in your body and not weighted on one side or the other; that you are centred right inside your feet and not above your body.

Be aware of your body, its sensations and to the sense of space around you.

Sense the Earth beneath you, sense the presence of yourself in partnership with it. Close your eyes and feel your body perfectly aligned, relaxed and open. Become aware of your breathing. Feel the gentleness of that breath inside your body; that life within you. Conceive of the miracle of breath: we breathe in not only oxygen but Light and life force. There is a subtle combustion each time you breathe; the cells of your body are renewed.

Now direct yourself towards the heavens. Feel your Spirit reaching for infinity. Feel the longing and the joy that comes from that. You are both Earth and Heaven. You are the passage, and the circuit is within you.

Let go of your hold over the physical body now. Let it lie and rest deeply. Let go of the hold over the mind, as if there was nothing to do, nowhere to go. In this way you will transfer the focus from the material to the very subtle, but no less intense, aspects of life within and around you.

Within your body of matter, as you see it now, are billions of points of Light, which comprise your body of Light, your original blueprint, and that body, that substance, is absolutely perfect.

Sense the points of Light in your feet and make them brighter. Sense your feet alive with the tingling energy of these points of Light intensifying in brilliance.

Spread the sensation of tingling Light energy to your ankles, calves and knees, sensing the points of Light expanding, filling the inside of your legs with more and more Light particles.

Using the power of your attention – your visualisation and your feeling – bring your awareness to the inside of your thighs and up into your pelvic area, feeling the subtle currents flowing, glowing. Feel as though you now have legs made of bright, bright Light, and sense this

—

Become aware of your breathing. Feel the gentleness of that breath inside your body; that life within you.

—

Light igniting the points of Light beyond it, within the organs of your body, within your belly.

Feel that Light consume the density of your body, setting the matter of your body aglow with Light-substance.

Know that as the Light expands, it burns whatever is not perfection around it and thus heals and transmutes: it raises the level of vibration of your own vehicle, your body, and all that is housed within it your mind and your feelings.

Continue up through the stomach region; up your back and torso; your chest; into the lungs and heart; and up to your shoulders. You are now feeling, breathing, being Light!

Feel the Light coming down the shoulders, down the arms and setting your hands aglow. You now have arms of Light!

Feel yourself aglow now, your own body responding to your direction. Feel the movement up through the neck and into the base of the skull. Sense the Light bursting into crystal sounds at the base of the skull. Hear the sound of Light: crystal gold, which is the colour of these points of Light. Feel this crystal gold, expanding now.

Sense, feel and see the points of Light within your brain, illuminating it. See the grey matter of your brain become golden now. Feel that golden glow as your own brain seems to intensify in frequency, raising in vibration, that it may receive finer and finer impressions.

Expanding the points of Light to set your skin aglow, set the skull, the eyes, the nose aglow, so that your entire body now, from head to foot, is one glowing body of Light. You are ablaze with Light. As that Light is blazing, feel the burning, the consuming, of everything that is less than the perfection of your inner Self.

As the heavier, denser elements of your body seem to fall, like ash, to the ground, all disease, all fear, all limitation, all signs of age, excess flesh and tension seem to drop away, as you, once again, claim your body of Light and all its powers.

Feel yourself as this body of Light within matter and sense how your frequency has been raised. You are within a body that is capable of tuning into cosmic channels, a beautiful, wonderful, complex instrument.

Use the power of your own feeling, that positive aspect of your emotions, to ignite life and the joy of life into each and every atom of your body. Visualise and feel billions of little particles of Light glowing,

---

As the heavier, denser elements of your body seem to fall, like ash, to the ground, all disease, all fear, all limitation, all signs of age, excess flesh and tension seem to drop away, as you, once again, claim your body of Light and all its powers.

intensifying, as if you are electrically charged. Choose to identify yourself with the Light within you and with its perfection. Allow its reflection to recreate your body, your mind and your emotions in purity and love.

Now ground this body of Light into the body of the planet. Sense lines of force going right through earth, rock, water, mineral, through the gems and gases and fires of the Earth, reaching into the crystal core at the planet's centre, made of radiant golden Light, just like your body now. Feel the homecoming and rejoice.

Send your Love to this intelligent sphere, this being, this planet, for housing you and giving you of itself. Feel the solidity, the sense of form loaned to us by this great Mother. It is in this solidity that we may stand, firmly, in our divinity, in our spirituality and our cosmic Self. Anchor yourself within the deep roots of the planet and allow your branches to reach for the highest!

Now connect with that other dimension of your Being, the dimension of pure Intelligence, of cosmic space, in your dream body, your body of Light that you may grow and multiply the glory of Light in matter.

Very gently, come back.

MEDITATION ON MULTIDIMENSIONAL REALITY: INTRODUCTION TO ENERGY ACCELERATION

Elemental forces build atoms around lines of force, whether they are the atoms of your bodies or the atoms of anything in Creation. Substance spins, first in a horizontal spin and then in a vertical spin. The web of these spins creates the atomic structure and the substance around us.

In a very real way, we are like atoms in a body greater than any universe we can conceive of. The beam of Light that is anchored in the heart is our central lifeline and main connection to our Self as an interdimensional entity comprised of many aspects, bodies and consciousnesses.

Close your eyes. Sit comfortably. Occupy your body fully and set it to rest in deep relaxation. Follow the procedure as for previous practices.

Begin with the Master Practice. Make the following invocation:

'We call upon the brotherhood of Light beings everywhere for assistance, guidance and illumination and to our own Higher Self and angel friends to open the way and lead us.

We seek to know you all (the various aspects of our Self), so that we may work in partnership with you, in harmonious cooperation, for the enlightenment of all. We seek to embody the Light and to know the Creator at the highest levels of truth and love and with the deepest integrity.'

Visualise yourself in relation to your individualised God-self. See that Divine Spark anchored in your physical heart. See the beam of Light that connects it to your physical self. Establish yourself within your Tube of Light.

Ignite the flame in your heart. Now locate the beam of Light from your individualised Spirit-self that is anchored in your physical heart and follow it up to the centre of your head.

Allow this golden Light within the centre of your head to ignite now, and let it fill your entire brain. Feel this golden Light intensifying in brilliance through your entire head.

Make it as bright as you can. Keep intensifying it. Follow the golden beam of Light right upwards.

Project your awareness over your head to a focus about three feet (one metre) over your head.

Take notice of the vibration experienced in your physical body as you do this, and also of any images, sounds or sensations you may have.

Move up a little higher now, to another focus of Light about six feet (two metres) over your physical form.

Take notice of the changes within your physical body and in your perception.

Allow yourself to rise even higher, through the beam of Light of your consciousness anchored in your heart.

Go about ten feet (three metres) high now.

Allow your Consciousness to expand with a sense of Light and brilliance, with a sense of Love and space and peace.

Make the invocation:

'Beloved God-self, which I AM: I seek to know you. Who am I?'

Look around you. Ask yourself: *'Where am I? Who am I?'*

Allow yourself to go higher still now, igniting that flame of Love in your heart that takes you further and further upwards.

Project yourself further into that source of all life, going higher and higher, reaching each time greater intensities of Light-energy, which you sense in your own body.

Allow yourself to reach right out to about thirty feet (nine metres) over your head, which in consciousness is much further out, out through the farthest reaches of this planet.

Sustain these frequencies as you make the invocation:

'Beloved God-self, which I AM: reveal yourself to me.'

Continue to reach, reach, reach as high as you can and know: I AM!

Notice the atmosphere around you, wherever you may be. Notice the bodies, structures or forms of life and coloration. Take notice of your own existence at these levels.

Now, at the highest level of Being available to you in this moment, picture the focus of Light, that individualised presence of God, your God-self.

Embody luminous presence, which I AM; the I AM in each of us. Feel and know yourself. Identify that frequency.

As you look down at all the selves that you also are, pause at the level of the seventh plane, the level of where your Higher Self resides.

From there, project down to the third-dimensional self now. See your physical body and send your love to it. Embrace it with your heart's flame.

Now bring down with you the clarity and intelligence from the seventh plane, drawing with you all the parts of yourself above and below that into the physical body. Bring those consciousnesses down into the physical body and sense the feeling of fullness.

Open your eyes for just a moment and take notice of what and how you perceive through the body now. Allow all these parts of yourself to see through your eyes now; just for a moment, and then close your eyes again.

Next, you ascend once again; all the way up, to the farthest outermost rim of your being.

Pause there for the moment, within the electronic fields of your life source and again become aware of the frequency you are in.

Now, at the highest level of being available to you in this moment, picture the focus of Light, that individualised presence of God, your God-self.

Now begin your descent again, only now leave the different bodies of energy at the corresponding levels behind you.

Separate from each of them, as you slowly come back, identifying and leaving each of the energy bodies behind, bringing back only your third-dimensional self.

Open your eyes again and look around briefly. Notice your perception and the sense of yourself. Close your eyes again.

Now you shall invite your Higher Self to link with you through your Tube of Light.

Anchor yourself at the seventh plane. Feel yourself there and simultaneously feel yourself here in the third dimension. Feel both frequencies. Follow that feeling through the beam of Light anchored in your physical heart. Affirm:

'I AM here and I AM there. I AM the conscious Presence everywhere.'

Re-establish the energetic circuit between the dimensions through the Alchemical Alignment.

Project yourself back down to the three-dimensional physical self, having the vantage point of the seventh plane as well.

Be here, be there, simultaneously. Very, very gently come back here.

 SPIRAL MEDITATION

This meditation involves the use of music and visualisation. It takes you through the experience of interdimensional space into cosmic and spiritual reality.

You may find visualising this meditation quite complicated. The illustration, opposite, is provided to help you visualise the spiral of Light that you will weave in and around your body.

Select a piece of music that can carry you through concentric space. It should be an even piece, fairly repetitive and with a slow, deep, electronic resonance to it.

Follow the initial preparatory stages that generate the energy you require to mobilise your higher bodies, such as the Figure of Light grounding, meditation, breathing exercises and so on.

Spiral Meditation

When you are ready, lie down spread-eagled on the floor. Turn the volume of the music loud enough for it to surround you.

You are going to be moving your energy, through the power of your thought, in a spiral fashion. Counter-clockwise opens and clockwise closes or returns you to the third dimension.

Begin with the Master Practice (see pages 21–5).

Visualise a thread of silver Light, the consistency of finely spun metal, pliable but not liquid.

Locate your vital energy at the level of the solar plexus. This is the centre that provides the basic energy for all functions initiated at the level of physicality. Now, from the solar plexus, visualise a thread of silver Light spiralling anticlockwise into the heart chakra and curving around and over to the belly or second chakra; continuing in circular fashion up to the throat chakra; down and around to the base of the spine; around and up to the third eye (through the middle of the forehead); continuing to the minor chakras of the knees; circling back up to the crown chakra; back down to the soles of the feet; and continuing a spiralling journey over and around the head and body in widening circles.

Go around again, and again and again.

Allow the spiral to become wider and wider, larger and larger; it stretches beyond your city, beyond your country, beyond the planet.

Let it go around and around.

Allow yourself to go as far as you can, beyond the reaches of the mind, beyond your ordinary states of consciousness.

Return after the period of time you have allocated, or when the person you have entrusted with bringing you back calls you. Bring that energy back with you, returning step-by-step via the spiral in a clockwise direction, coming from the outermost periphery into your aura.

Bring this energy back through the spiral, looping from the top of your head to below your feet; from the third eye to your feet; back up to the base of the skull and the middle of your face; to your knees, your throat, your palms to your shoulders; from the sacrum to your heart and back within the recesses of your solar plexus.

Be still. Feel the Universe within you.

Be extra careful about grounding yourself before returning fully to waking consciousness. After this exercise, and all exercises that take you to interdimensional space, you would do well to outline the space that your physical body occupies – both its length and breadth. Sense the space within your body and feel its weight. Be sure your energy is within that space and distributed evenly throughout your body.

'E O LIHUM' EXERCISE

This is another of the Essenic Light practices.[15] This particular exercise is especially helpful in connecting you to your Higher Self. The initial Essenic practice suggests using the figure of Jesus Christ as the model of the Higher Self. You may do this if you wish or use the image of a master or a symbol with which you feel a close connection.

Perform the Master Practice (see pages 21–5) first.

Invoke your Higher Self at the level of the seventh dimension.

The master will mirror the truth, the beauty and the Love that your God-self is pouring through the medium of your own Higher selves.

This exercise is done sitting. Silence and still yourself.

Pronounce the phrase '*E O Lihum*': '*e*' as in 'seen', '*o*' as in 'oh', '*Li-hum*' as in 'lee-hoom'. Practise it a few times and feel the fluidity of the sound. The sound '*Li-hum*' should be especially mellow and wisp-like.

Practise saying it internally now, combining it with the breath. On the inbreath say '*E-O*' and on the outbreath '*Li-hum*'.

Visualise now a crystal-coloured stream of Light, the colour of clear water and with like consistency, only in Light.

See and feel this crystal-coloured Light stream entering into your left temple. See and feel it coursing right through the inside of your head and mind, cleaning, clearing, cooling it.

Now picture your Higher Self in front and above you.

You are going to thread your lower mind with your Higher Mind, using a crystal-coloured Light stream. As the crystal Light streams into your left temple and comes out your right temple, it curves in front and spirals upwards into the God-self.

You are ready to begin the exercise.

Breathe in, visualising the crystal-coloured Light entering your left temple to the inner sound '*e*'. To the inner sound '*o*' (still on the inbreath) the Light circles over to the Higher Self and loops through it. Then on the outbreath, to the inner sound '*Li-hum*' the crystal thread spirals up into infinity. The illustration on page 244 may serve as a visual guide.

Repeat as long as desired. Remain in that silence and that intimacy with your Self for as long as possible.

---

15 The Essenes were mainly desert-dwelling ascetics with great knowledge of nature and natural law, Light and energy.

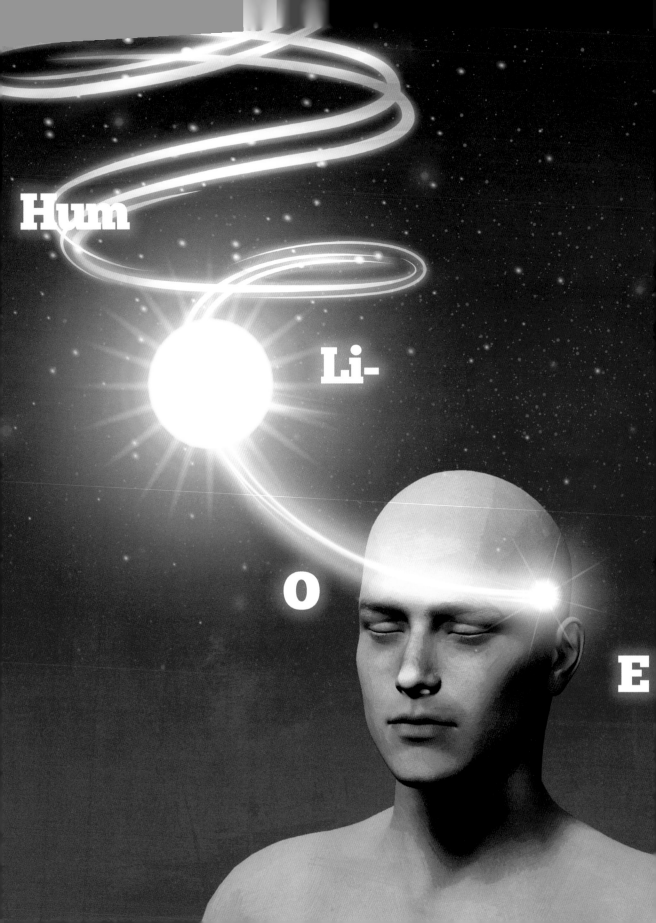

SPIRIT

There is little that can be said directly about the purely spiritual
experience, since it is so far removed from our reality and possibility.
Re-activate the feeling you have in your longing for the highest Love,
the greatest beauty, the greatest good, the ultimate Truth. In that longing
resides the echo, the memory of Spirit.

In your love and in your joys are the whisperings of Spirit. In your
prayer, in your dreams, in your gratitude and in your creativity are the
workings of Spirit. Look around you everywhere, particularly when you
are sad and down. Notice the beauty of the flower or of a sunny day, the
magnificence of life everywhere. Touch a kitten or a rabbit, remember the
innocence of children. Look into the eyes of a newborn. There you will
find Spirit, the force of the Creator.

The Creator is in the created and you; you, my dear friend, my
brother, my sister, are both the Creator and the created. Spirit is
everywhere around you and Spirit is in the innermost recesses of your
depths. In your ecstasy and in your sadness is the sound, the living
resonance of Spirit.

Jesus Christ bowed before the power and magnificence of Spirit.
'Your will be done!', he said. 'I AM the Way', Spirit then said within Him,
and 'I AM with you always'.

The following and final two meditations in this chapter are devoted
to exploring your nature as Spirit and the Love that is part of the
spiritual experience.

> Jesus Christ bowed
> before the power and
> magnificence of Spirit.
> 'Your will be done!',
> he said. 'I AM the
> Way', Spirit then said
> within Him, and 'I AM
> with you always'.

'E O Lihum' Exercise

DRAWING AND RADIATING LOVE MEDITATION

First perform the Master Practice (see pages 21–5).

Open your heart to the deepest innermost longing for the highest reality. Reach for the greatest Love. Fan the fire of that Love within your heart, the sacred fire heart. See its flames ignite and soar, enveloping you in wings of Light. Affirm:

'Beloved God-self, which I AM! I seek to know you!'

Direct your feeling upwards and visualise the beam of Light anchored in your heart. Follow it up through all the dimensions of Being to the God-self plane. Sense its vibration streaming down through that beam of Light into your own physical heart and flooding you with its love, its Light, its healing, nourishing, compassionate understanding. Be loved.

Feel yourself here, and there.

Now, drawing from the power of your own God-self into your physical heart, send out rings of love to all directions of the Earth; to people you know and to people you don't know; to the animals and plants of the Earth; to the lands and seas and waters of the Earth; to the minerals, gases and substances of the Earth.

Feel these rings expanding like concentric orbs of Light. Become a sun radiating Light, emanating, pulsating Light through your very own body.

Expand the power now to include the dimensions around the Earth. Fill the entire space with your love and your life force. Feel this as it spirals outwards to infinity; reaching, reaching, reaching, exploring and simultaneously emitting your love-Light to all that is.

Continue the process for as long as you can.

Gently reverse the process. Feel the Love of infinity pouring back into you, as concentric rings of Light falling into an infinity within you!

Continue as needed. Be blessed.

Come back gently, reverently, gratefully.

Bow before the Creator and the creation. Bow before the magnificence of yourself. Affirm:

'Beloved God-presence, which I AM!'

ILLUMINATION IS YOUR NATURE: THE THREEFOLD
FLAME MEDITATION

First perform the Master Practice (see pages 21–5). Invoke:

*'I AM Light... I AM all Light... I AM the Light of God within, bringing
peace and joy and power regained. Illumination is my nature.'*

You are Light. The endless creative flow, the ebb and flow of life,
continuous life. You are a projection of Light into matter. Your home
is Light.

Feel yourself as Light now; a beam of Light projected onto Earth. Your
body is a function of that Light. Each atom of your physical body contains
a tiny sun of cosmic Light. You are a scintillating galaxy of shining stars,
right here within this flesh form. You are this Light right now.

Within this body of scintillating suns is a focus, just around the heart
area; a Central Sun to your million suns. Look within it now. It is so
brilliant that it is a white beyond any white that you have ever seen. All
colours vibrate around its orb in magnetic rings of throbbing splendour,
but within its centre, within this infinity of crystalline white, is a flame,
your flame, the source of your life and energy consciousness; the seed of
your God-self.

Allow yourself to be within the flame in the centre of your heart.
You will see that the flame has three main tongues. The centre portion
is golden, with rich flickering tones of warm golden hues. To the right is
an exquisite blue flame; deep electric blue with swirls of the palest blues.
To the left is a soft pink flame with specks of a deeper pink and magenta.
Together these flames form one magnificent flame, which is the centre
of your power. Once this flame was so large that it enveloped and went
beyond your entire physical body.

Allow the tiny flame in your heart to grow again into its full size, to
glow brighter and brighter and expand larger and larger. Feel as though
your heart has ignited and expanded. Affirm:

*'I AM Light... I AM all Light... I AM the Light of God within, bringing
peace and joy and power regained. Illumination is my nature.'*

Keep the awareness of your physical body as a form of Light, encased within matter, but allow that Light to shine through. You are a body of Light within matter. Within your heart is a magnificent sun. Within that sun is a flame, now expanded to contain all of you. Feel the power regained by this Light. Feel the joy and beauty that you now are, that you have always been, only you had forgotten.

Remember now. Allow yourself to remember.

Illumination is your birthright.

Let yourself move and sway as Light. You can do this physically or through your imagination. Experience the freedom of Light in matter. The release! The joy!

You will notice that wherever you go there is a violet glow around you and around others. This is the ultraviolet fire of transmutation.

The ultraviolet fire of transmutation around you is a manifestation of your Light and is the healing flame. Feel yourself as a centre of healing, transmuting love, reaching out in tongues of violet to purify and set the world alight. Be healed and be a source of healing.

Illumination is your gift to life!

You are a sun of Light within a greater sun. You are a child of the Light. Light is your nature. Illumination is your birthright and your gift to life. Let your thoughts wander now and picture the people and the places you'd like to bless with your Love-light. Let it travel the world over, over space and time. There is no limit to where you can reach with your Love-light. Affirm:

'I AM Light... I AM all Light... I AM the Light of God within, bringing peace and joy and power regained. Illumination is my nature!'

Let yourself move and sway as Light. You can do this physically or through your imagination. Experience the freedom of Light in matter. The release! The joy!

REVIEW

Matter evolves and Consciousness expands through our direct, intimate and somewhat formidable experience in multiple dimensions of Being. I have repeated this maxim several times. By now, you should have an insight into what it may mean to you.

You are now on the third stage of the alchemical path. Your conscious contact with higher dimensions instils the urge to bring their quality into the world tangibly, accessing and decoding truth at every level. You become a bridge towards the construction of a better world. You become a World Server.

Familiarity with higher planes should never be a cause to abandon third-dimensional concerns: awareness and mastery of the third dimension constitute the first initiation in any esoteric tradition. The purpose of third-dimensional consciousness is to build a bridge between self-consciousness and Self-consciousness.

On our journey through the human experience, no dimension is better or greater than another. It does not matter if we are not aware of the precise stages of dimensional activity. Fulfilment, joy, truth, revelation and knowledge are accessible to those who attune themselves honestly to those frequencies. Only here, at the third dimension, souls of varied levels of dimensional specialisation meet and interact to challenge and inspire one another. Some people are more attuned to the attributes of one or several dimensions, but we exist and function within all of them, even if we are not aware of this… yet.

——

On our journey through the human experience, no dimension is better or greater than another.

——

ALCHEMY IN OUR LIVES

As a departure from theory, Part Six furnishes the reader with practical advice, exercises and meditations for individual self-mastery. Especial attention is paid to the release of personal habits ingrained into the subtle layers of the lower self, karma and to sleep/dreaming practices. This chapter concludes with a suggested schedule for incorporating Inner Alchemy practices daily and into routines.

THE WAY OF
INNER ALCHEMY

This part of the book addresses ways in which you may manage your energetic anatomy so that it can offer you the best possibilities for overall management and performance in your life, providing you with increasingly subtle practice and accelerated experience on the dimensional journey of Consciousness.

HOW YOU LIVE

Start with looking at how you live, think and perceive now: consider the foods you eat, the exercise you do and your social and sexual behaviour.

See how much sleep you get and examine the pattern.

Question yourself: how important are your surroundings for you? How important is the care of your home and your property?

Reflect on your appearance. How do you picture and treat yourself? How often, if ever, do you look into the mirror and see your *whole* body, your face; how often do you look deeply into your eyes? How do you feel about what you practise and who you see?

How do people perceive you? How does that compare to the way you feel about yourself? Are you living under any pretences?

No one can tell you what to do or how to go about cleaning up the way you live. Simply begin by acting consciously. Let your every act be an expression and a reflection of your authenticity. Where you observe a need for change, begin gently and consistently.

Pour your love into everything. Do not censor but do not indulge in excess either.

The way you look, the way you live, the way you eat and sleep; these all reflect your state of mind and your level of consciousness. A messy or cluttered home mirrors a messy, cluttered mind. Ragged underwear and socks with holes in them say a lot about the way you feel and treat yourself. Simplicity, cleanliness, orderliness and purity do not have a price-tag. They require only awareness and care: the two basic ingredients for consciousness. Everything you do is connected to everything else within you and within the Universe of form. Spiritual mastery begins with clean linen.

You are constantly giving off and absorbing energy through your body and senses, both on subtle and dense levels. Energies constantly circulate through you. You are responsible for what you put into yourself and for what you give out. You put food in your body in the way of sound, colour and nourishment. You give out colour and sound vibrations through your behaviour.

Once you have organised yourself and have made certain choices about your lifestyle, you are ready to use protection methods consciously. Psychic self-defence practices and spiritual methods of protection will

> The way you look, the way you live, the way you eat and sleep; these all reflect your state of mind and your level of consciousness.

produce results proportionate to the quality of your intent. It is *what you are* that protects you.

Spiritual life calls for strength, individuality and tremendous personal integrity. It is not blind surrender.

Spirituality calls for discernment, requiring decisiveness and the ability to act. Once you embark on the path of spiritual development, everything becomes heightened. You become aware of all that you have ignored, misused or miscreated. Your own thoughtforms return to you.

You begin to notice your own and others' projections. Your emotional body undergoes tremendous fluctuations in energy. Everything seems to rise up against you. Often you become impatient with yourself.

Keeping control over yourself is not easy, as each aspect of you calls to be mastered. The more aware you become, the more automatic habits come up for review. You begin questioning how much of what is happening is your reflection.

You know now that there is no escape from a world that you create. As the ascended Master St Germain has said, you now need to 'stand, face and conquer'.

When you practise energy mastery, people will be attracted to you for reasons you don't always understand. Your emotional history will reflect you. According to each response (or lack of it), you create other responses. Karma, the law of cause and effect, shows up. There is no escape from this mechanism. Even in non-doing you are 'doing', as evasion is also a choice.

The highest moral principle in the East is a universal principle. It is the Buddhist notion of harmlessness or *ahimsa*. Harmlessness means purity, steadiness, equilibrium: the middle way. When you are in the middle, you can 'stand, face and conquer'.

Beware of righteousness. Hold others, even discordant people, in the image of divine reflection. Get into the habit of visualising their I AM Selves above them, connected to their hearts. As you view people like this, they respond in kind. You begin to live change from within. This is the real revolution. The miracles are possible.

People may be reached inwardly, invisibly, neutrally, when we stop viewing the world personally. Part of why the world is the way it is, is because of personal investment in being right. Re-examine this.

Your attitudes about yourself, and through yourself about others, are fundamental to the quality of spiritual protection you can induce.

When using spiritual protection techniques, become increasingly aware of being an instrument of the Light. You recognise this Light as the source of life and activity and acknowledge everything that comes to you, comes from Spirit. You accept your participation in an intelligent Universe of beings of Light working in harmony and in brotherhood.

This recognition in itself is all that you need to be shielded by the Light. The visualisation and feeling that accompanies this acknowledgement, sustains a wall of Light around you. Then, move in an ocean of influences, subject to them at all levels, but nothing may harm you.

Awakening to the Light of Consciousness goes hand in hand with practical change in the physical world. In making the journey from self to Self, it is imperative that you consider the voice of the little self, the personality, so that it may grow and expand together with your level of consciousness. The next section contains a list of suggestions that are by no means exhaustive. They will aid you in this expansion.

REVIEW OF PRACTICAL SUGGESTIONS FOR A PERSONALITY 'CLEAN-UP'

FOR THE PHYSICAL BODY

- Bathe frequently and wear clean clothing. Clothing holds energy from the surrounding environment for hours.
- When possible, have alternate hot and cold showers, to strengthen your nervous system and resistance to disease, as well as your physical-etheric balance.
- Treat yourself to a massage occasionally, addressing the whole energetic system and your joy with it.
- Love your body from the inside and from the outside. Look at it with appreciation and with a view to wholeness.
- Become aware of the physical company that you keep. Remember that other people's thoughtforms, especially in close relationships, are likely to adhere to yours in affinity. Keep 'holy' company.

FOR THE EMOTIONAL BODY

- Use the visualisation of Light, particularly the golden Light that soothes the nerves and brings peace, around the solar plexus in the form of a disc or sphere.
- Visualise surrounding your waist with a wide belt of electric blue Light, shielding your solar plexus from the front and back.
- Visualise a suit of dark blue Light covering the entire body. This is a tonic for the physical level as well as for the emotional.
- Visualise a mirrored shield around yourself, which acts to reflect all energies that are not of the Light to sender.
- Picture crosses of blue flame (or white or golden flame) before you at the level of the solar plexus and belly. They can be as large as your physical body. This is a general protective and stabilising visualisation, good for all levels of your being.
- Imagine a stream of golden liquid Light pouring from Spirit into you in the Alchemical Alignment, pouring over your spine and streaming out into the nervous system, especially covering the brain. This visualisation is good for the nervous system and for the mind.
- Picture yourself within a golden sun-sphere, which is the presence of your God-self, or of any being or Master that you may invoke.
- Imagine wielding a sword of blue flame and cutting yourself (or another) free from any lines of force or influence that may be impinging upon the freedom and sustenance of Light in your being. Accompany it with the command: 'You have no power!'. Charge it with the fuel force of your feelings.
- Call upon the angelic host. The names of archangels Michael, Raphael, Gabriel and Uriel hold special power. Invite them and their legions of angels to dissolve negative impingement. You may also address the angels of any quality you require: victory, freedom, purity, peace, healing.

FOR THE MENTAL BODY

- Hold the presence of Light within the physical brain, particularly golden Light. See it transmuting the grey matter of your brain into light golden substance, raising the level of vibration in your brain so that you may receive higher impressions.
- Visualise a cap of bright white or crystal Light, shielding your skull, or wear a band of golden Light around the head (see illustration on page 161).
- Invite the luminous presence of beings of Light, beginning with your own divine Presence, to overshadow you, to clear your mind, to help you think better or to remember something. Connect with the Presence behind you.
- Visualise the flames of the seven rays inside your head behind the forehead, which relate directly to the activity of the Elohim. Use the illustration of the Elohim, or the Seven-leafed Flame, on page 230 as an aid.

The world of colour and Light is magnificently beautiful, nourishing and uplifting. There is no greater power than the power of Light.

These visualisations are offered by the Brotherhood of Light, a group of Lightworkers at a higher level of evolution, who have free access within all dimensions. We may avail ourselves of them as the brothers and sisters that they are to humanity.

As your practices intensify and you are able to attune yourself directly to Source, more formations of Light will be revealed to you. The world of colour and Light is magnificently beautiful, nourishing and uplifting. There is no greater power than the power of Light. Remember that, and allow yourself to live in this way.

Establish times and rhythms for your practices. No matter how brief, be sure to begin and end your day with a practice of Light as acknowledgement and gratitude. Do this before you leave your home; protect your house, yourself and your vehicle. Visualise yourself shielded in an armour of Light. Alternatively, picture around yourself, or around the area you want to protect, the old tried-and-tested visualisation of the magical ring pass-not, the protective circle of Light around an object or person, used by magicians, sorcerers and alchemists throughout the ages.

Remember the power of the spoken word. Pay attention to your speech and what and who you empower. Whatever you think and say will come to pass in some way, at some time.

Know that the Light is growing in radiance within and through you and shines on everyone you meet. In this way as you purify, perfect and protect yourself, you are purifying, perfecting and protecting others through the sacred fire of Spirit. Be this instrument of Light in the world, always beginning with your own protection inside your Tube of Light in Alchemical Alignment.

SLEEP AWARENESS PROGRAMME

The following section contains practical suggestions for sleeping better and with greater awareness.

Understand the nature of sleep and prepare accordingly. Sleep is a time for attunement, purification and illumination, even service. Prepare physically and mentally for it, as if you were entering a temple to visit God Himself.

Sleep in fresh, clean bedding. Clear your bedroom and your surroundings of psychic clutter by using a purification technique such as the Violet Flame Activation (see pages 25–6), crosses of blue flame, rays and so on. Allow your quarters to be filled by light and re-dedicate yourself to the service of the Light daily. Erect and sustain a wall of Light (visualised by you) around your home, and more particularly, when you are ready to enter sleep, around your bed.

Let your last thoughts of the day be of Light and your identification with yourself as Light. Such are thoughts of joy, gratitude and beauty.

Let your last thoughts of the day be of Light and your identification with yourself as Light. Such are thoughts of joy, gratitude and beauty.

RECOMMENDED PROCEDURES IN PREPARATION FOR SLEEP

- Review the events of the day. If there are any actions that were automatic or offensive to others, or if you were hurt by another, take note of how you might have responded differently. Change your automatic emotional response to the events of the day.
- Forgive yourself for unconscious behaviour and decide how you may right it through direct action later. Release others who may have wronged you by not harbouring a grudge. See them surrounded by Light and yourself healed in your lower bodies, as well as understanding the event deeply, i.e. how you attracted it to begin with. Release it. The releasing process allows you to enter sleep awareness with more sensitivity to finer frequencies.

- Understand and bless those persons with whom you have lessons to complete. Speak to their Higher Self and ask for greater clarity and healing. Call for the dissolution of any destructive etheric records between you.
- Sustain your protective shield, including the Tube of Light, that prevents you from activating or hooking into the psychic or lower astral dimensions.
- State your intent, if you have any; i.e. if there is anything you seek in the way of guidance and illumination, healing or verification. Define it, picture it, ask out loud and specifically for its revelation. Ask to remember your dreams, should they provide any revelation at a later date.
- Fill your heart with gratitude for this knowledge of the Law of Light that you have learned and let go into sleep with the certainty that your calls will be answered by your very own God-self, with the help and protection of beings of Light everywhere.

These steps will help impress everything that you invoke or picture before you go to sleep into positive thoughtforms, as mental and emotional substance, which can act much more deeply, constructively and expediently while you sleep.

Understand that doubt and fear come from body consciousness and are always connected to cellular memory and survival: they cannot touch your essence. All the training programmes in Inner Alchemy aim at facilitating the transfer from identification with matter to identification with Light; from identification with your personality as a self to your soul as a Being.

When you know that you and Spirit are one, how can you fear?

Begin your day in praise of the Light you are and hold within you. Live as fully as you can within the principles of Inner Alchemy, freeing yourself from debilitating doubt and fear.

KARMA: A NEW WAY

Karma is the Sanskrit term for the feedback circle of energy created by an individual through their interaction with others and with life. Although the term is usually employed to denote negative effects, there is also 'good' karma, the return from self-refinement and the accumulation of deeds performed through applied consciousness.

The negative cycles stop the closer you live according to the Law of Light from the perspective of cause, and no longer at the mercy of haphazard effects. You become a master over the effects in your life. You enter the realm of Inner Alchemy, into the domain of the soul and of Spirit. Instead of moving horizontally, at the level of personality, your energy rises vertically. You begin to relate in terms of the Higher Self.

The teachings presented in this book are part of a great transformation as you accept Love, Light and greater life, allowing you to step out of the wheel of cause and effect. At this point, vital life behaviours must change: defensive and aggressive patterns prove ineffectual and unnecessary. You begin to use higher powers in alignment with higher law, and you attract that which you have come to embody: Light. You stop putting out energy that limits and binds you to other things or people.

Completion and release happen in deep love. If only people who divorce, parents who watch their children leave home or lovers who become separated from their loved one through death, would liberate the other in the fullness of Love, with gratitude for lessons learned, saying 'goodbye' and 'thank you', or 'we are now richer for having known one another'. In this way we free our own and other people's energies, enabling growth and greater capacity for service. Would this not lead to a better world for everyone?

It is difficult, in our third-dimensional existence, to conceive of love without possessiveness. Dignity and greatness lie in that freedom and in the fullness of each moment lived intensely.

Love is not a set of rules, or an excuse to manipulate and possess. Love is a Consciousness-awakening process, a way of learning cooperation and respect. Love is a validating experience based on the equality of difference and higher purpose. Love aligns with higher law: blessing, sharing and expanding. Love reflects true commitment to life and to others, through an awakened, illumined commitment to the Self. Love sets a pragmatic psycho-spiritual stage.

Karma is the Sanskrit term for the feedback circle of energy created by an individual through their interaction with others and with life.

In true friendship, which is the highest or purest form of human love, there is always equality. Giving is unconditional. There is acceptance of the other, not a demand that they be different and fill your ego needs.

Each moment should be lived to its fullest, as if it were the last. Each meeting should be as the first, never taking another for granted. Learn to surrender, with dignity, to Love itself – not to another person. Each party leads in wholeness and autonomy, coming together in honesty without seeking completion.

It is said that deep relationships are like a little death, and when it comes to death, the death of the little self, the transformation of your personal self is the ultimate alchemy. Close, intimate relationships are a dress rehearsal for life eternal.

Moving through every moment with the awareness of embodying the Alchemical Alignment leads to mastery. Physical recalibration is a direct result of proximity to Light.

In order to come together with someone, first you need to embrace the experience of being alone: all-one, whole in yourself. Know that all resides within you and that the Universe, existence, is ready to give you what you ask for. With this realisation comes the dissolution of neediness. Then you come together out of abundance rather than lack.

Each kind of relationship throws light upon the blanket of experiences that constitute our lives, enriching, embellishing and strengthening the varieties of interpersonal exchange. We are forged by the fire of emotional involvement. In the depth of experience is transcendence. Everything that you do to yourself, you do to everyone. You actually bless the world and everyone in it by refining yourself. Alchemy in relationships is living the God in you with the God in the other, so that all of creation is enhanced.

Forgiveness implies liberation from an attitude or a belief. This may concern anything you 'relate' to, from the way you envision and therefore treat yourself – in other words, the quality of energy you impress upon your body and psyche – to the events that unfold between people, groups and circumstances that trigger discomfort.

Forgiveness sets you free from limiting beliefs and attachments.

Forgiveness is the energetic upliftment that sets parties free from the momentum of cause and effect. It is the application of the fire of pure Love onto the subtle, astrally engendered chains that bind us karmically.

KARMIC RELEASE PRACTICES

The following are three ways in which you can affect the release and ultimate dissolution of the lines of force that bind you to another.

KARMIC RELEASE THROUGH AFFIRMATION

Visualise yourself and the person(s) to be released, sitting within the Alchemical Alignment (see pages 142–7). Emphasise not only their connection to their own Higher Self, but the connection between your Higher Self and theirs. Talk to their Higher Self through yours:

'Through the power of my God-self and with your permission, I address you as a Being of Light. I ask for your help in freeing [name] and me from the entanglements of the lower bodies. Transmute the energies between us into their highest form in the fulfilment of the divine plan for each of our lifestreams in this embodiment.'

Pause and then affirm:

'I release you, [name (say name three times)] and I release myself, [name (say three times)]. With your greater clarity, courage, direction and protection, which is eternal, you, [name (say three times)], are free! Receive my love, gratitude and praise!'

Then you say:

'I AM free! I AM free! I AM free!'

Allow yourself to feel the release. See the lines of force dissolving, and the purified energies returning to each of you.

KARMIC RELEASE WITH A PARTNER

This practice is especially good for group or family release. The technique is drawn from a practice followed by the *Kahuuna* priestesses of Hawaii.

A basin of water is placed between the partners, which serves to symbolically wash away their karmic debris. At the appropriate moment of release, the person speaking sprinkles the water around themselves and the person they are releasing.

It is essential that, during each invocation, the voice of the speaker represents both parties involved. When one partner speaks, their speech represents the speech and will of the other partner, and vice versa.

STEP ONE

Begin with an invocation. You may choose your own, or you may use the *Kahuuna* version:

'Divine Creator: Father-Mother-Son as One!'

Now, addressing the person you want to forgive and be forgiven by, you say:

'If we [say name/s], my/our families, relatives and ancestors have ever offended you [say name], your families, relatives and ancestors, in thoughts, words, deeds and actions, from the beginning of our Creation to the present, humbly, humbly, we ask you all for forgiveness for all efforts, resentments, guilts, offences, blocks and attachments we have created and accumulated.'

Then ask, looking directly into their eyes, connecting at an emotional level:

'Will you forgive us?'

STEP TWO

The partner answers:

'Yes, we forgive you. Let this water release us all from spiritual, mental, physical, material and karmic bondage!'

Next, addressing the God-self:

'Pull out from our memory bank and computer, sever and cut [said emphatically] all the unwanted, negative memories and blocks that tie, bind and attach us together. Cleanse, purify and transmute all these unwanted energies into pure Light. Fill the spaces left by cleansing these unwanted energies with divine Light. Let divine order, Light,

Love, peace, balance, wisdom, understanding and abundance be made manifest for us all and our affairs through the divine Power of the divine Creator: Father–Mother–Son as One, in whom we rest, abide and have our Being, now and forever more. Amen.'

It is important that eye contact be maintained and that the person receiving the release (if present) takes time to experience the release and to accept it.

There should be a meaningful pause for integration and then the entire process is repeated for the other partner.

 ## RHYTHM OF FORGIVENESS VISUALISATION

Do not look upon forgiving people with any sense of virtue. Instead, see it as an imminent necessity.

Forgiveness brings us freedom from the illusion of conditionality and separation. It is a forgetting. Normally, you are unable to forget, because you hold onto memories as impressions. The heart, however, has no memory, it is always in the present.

Vibrations are held by the Earth, which is sensitive to all impressions. Our bodies hold onto imprints and memories until a greater force, such as Love, dissolves them.

This next exercise is the last Essenic practice we are including in this book. It consists of a flash of Light that permanently carries away all memory of the past, unless we choose to keep recreating it.

THE EXERCISE

For the rhythm of forgiveness exercise, Light is flashed in the body in a zigzag rhythm of eight, described below.

To prepare begin by performing the Alchemical Alignment (see pages 142–7). Strengthen the personal heart-connection to your Higher Self and make the call for forgiveness.

An especially powerful colour to use in connection with forgiveness is deep pink. Wash yourself in it. Absorb it from your own Divine essence.

You are now ready to return the gift of energy back to the Creator. You are ready to offer up all the imperfections that prevent you from loving Self, and, by extension, others. The rhythm of forgiveness starts the moment you intend to release the hold over substance in the way of thoughts and feelings in the aura and return it to Source.

On the inbreath, visualise a light flashing from the left side of the back to the following points:

- To a point on the right side under your right arm
- To the top of your left shoulder
- To the same point on the top of your right shoulder
- To your left ear
- Through the head to your right ear
- To a point on the left side of your head, halfway between your left ear and the top of your head
- To a similar point on the right side of your head
- Out of the top of your head, on an outbreath.

Use the illustration, opposite, as a guide, should you need a visual aid for this exercise.

Do this exercise for as long as you need. When assisting another person, you may physically draw the zigzagging line over the back of the person with your hand, evoking sensation.

 GOD I AM/RAINBOW SELF MEDITATION

Begin with the Master Practice (see pages 21–5). Refer to the illustration of the Master Practice at the beginning of the book (see page 20), paying particular attention to the orbs of colour around the Sun Presence.

Fill your body now with the presence of your Self. Ignite the centre of each atom within your body, visualising a tiny sun of pale golden Light that becomes brighter and brighter. Pause long enough to allow this activity to set off a tingling sensation in your body.

Allow each cell to be filled with the joy of life and see the cells expand and become brighter and brighter. Feel your entire body aglow with the presence of your Self, the millions and millions of tiny suns within your body, a body of Light within your physical body.

Rhythm of Forgiveness Visualisation

Now direct your attention for a moment to the body of the planet and go directly through into the centre of the Earth. There, in the centre, is a crystalline structure of pink and golden Light-substance, just like those little suns in your body. Your body is part of the body of the planet.

Connect with this heart centre of the planet. Feel yourself held there. Anchor your own form into it. Feel safe, held within the solidity of Mother Earth and your own body.

Now, direct your attention to the centre of your chest. Go within and locate the heart centre. This is a globe of iridescent Light, within which is the threefold flame of intense radiance and power. Here is where your divinity is anchored, that is, your Spirit, the Light which you are as Intelligence, Consciousness, life and vitality.

Leave your body within the safety of the Mother Earth and follow the beam of Light that is anchored in your heart up into the greater Source above you. Follow the Light beam right up through your throat and head and continue upwards.

Become aware of the changes in vibration, or the inner sounds and sensations, until you reach a space of infinite peace and intensity, an immensely brilliant luminosity, which you are.

Know that you are in a body of matter and you are also a source of Light. Affirm:

'I AM here. I AM there. I AM THAT I AM.

Beyond millions of suns, I AM crystal Light with rainbow hues, a great Central Sun within suns of glorious Light, concentric spheres of colour expanding.

I AM an infinite brilliant white as of a thousand suns, blinding pearl of unlimited creative force... expanding.

I AM a shimmering golden sun-sphere suspended in space, infinite peace and knowingness... expanding.

I AM a glowing effervescent globe of scintillating pink, healing, nourishing love... expanding.

> Connect with this heart centre of the planet. Feel yourself held there. Anchor your own form into it. Feel safe, held within the solidity of Mother Earth and your own body.

I AM a jewel of ruby love, sheltering depth, a protective shield...
expanding.

I AM a violet flaming heart with orbs that reach into infinity;
transmuting, purifying grace... expanding.

I AM the verdant embers of apple-green suns; abundant life and
wealth... expanding.

I AM the glorious cosmic blue of cosmic purity; the matrix of all
Creation, the backdrop for all my forms... expanding.

The sacred fire breath of God I AM, pulsating Life, pulsating Love.
God I AM. God I AM. God I AM.'

GRATITUDE

Love is the projected Consciousness of Spirit as it expresses Itself
through levels, aspects and dimensions. It is the most powerful cohesive
force in existence.

First you experience love in relation to others, conditions and things
that reflect back to you. Upon embarking on the spiritual path, through
continued refinement and awakening, you soon discover that it is not the
other person or situation that elicits the feeling of love. The more you
embody spiritual practice, the more you discover that Love is possible
only if you are awake and aware. On higher levels of consciousness, you
realise that you *are* Love, it is your nature. By the power of the Source
within, you attract and interact with other parts of life.

It is your own Spirit-self that makes the experience of Love tangible,
spontaneously emitting the Light-substance of Love that inspires, uplifts
and refines all life, when linked to a conscious individual.

You now begin to feel spontaneous gratitude. This is not the result of
reflection or good manners; it is the force of Love that issues from your
state of fullness.

You come to appreciate all that life brings into your sphere of
influence. You learn from everything and become grateful for the

—
Love is the projected
Consciousness of Spirit
as it expresses Itself
through levels, aspects
and dimensions. It is the
most powerful cohesive
force in existence.
—

possibility of seeing 'behind-the-scenes' into the truth of people and circumstances. You will always find traces of Love.

Gratitude expands the joy and fullness that Love engenders, while at the same time blessing and releasing a tide of loving force into the environment.

Human evolution is unique in that it builds individuality and awareness of Self. The alchemical path is designed for the purpose of learning mastery and co-creation with the Godhead. Each human is a Godseed. Each human soul in embodiment is the individualised Consciousness of the Godhead, with all its powers and unlimited, although perhaps not yet integrated, possibility.

The next two topics deal with dreaming and dying, two inevitable human experiences where you interact subliminally with interdimensional life. It is useful to understand what happens in dreaming states and death, and how these experiences serve human evolution and the expansion of Consciousness.

—

Human evolution is unique in that it builds individuality and awareness of Self.

—

DREAMS, DREAMING AND LEVELS OF DREAMLIFE

Whether asleep or awake, the dynamic of dreaming is the very stuff upon which Creation revolves. Every time you look, think, remember, plan or deliberately imagine, a visual image is created, filed away and impressed upon your memory bank, and too often released into the environment without your conscious intent. Many psychological studies have documented the essential role that images bear upon memory, experience and thinking itself.

Mind is a faculty of Intelligence that creates forms, but also a warehouse of images: from current life and beliefs, from past, present and future possibility, from interdimensional insight, from cosmic sources and from every conceivable area of activity in the Universe. You construct and gain access to images corresponding to each level of life, through the lens of personal history. You dream dreams within dreams with every breath, consciously and subconsciously.

When you fall asleep, your mind does not stop functioning. Unresolved daily issues surface in the dream state, seeking resolution. This represents the first level of dreaming concerning your immediate third-dimensional reality: your body, your relationships, and daily affairs.

Conclusions reached at this level are expedient, turning out as positive or negative, according to the emotions involved.

If you are clear in daily life, conscious of your hopes and actions and perhaps have found a satisfying creative outlet, the levels of dreaming you reach will likely lead you to interdimensional life or rest and silence where dreaming is not necessary. Problems posed by the Higher Mind find solutions in interdimensional life. The level of your dreaming corresponds to the degree of self-awareness and consciousness you have developed.

There is another stage of dreaming that consists in higher dimensional activity. These dreams might include participation in the circle of a Master's disciples, imprints from an out-of-body initiation or transmitted messages from your own soul. These impressions might come through symbols, from the collective to the highly abstract colour formations that are typical of higher dimensional life. They may convey the hint of transfiguring encounters or vivid experience of past lives that unfold neutrally as if in a movie and bring light to similar issues in your current life. Prophetic dreams fall into this category, as well as meetings with wise figures, your own Soul, or archetypical figureheads of myth and fantasy that transmit energetic resonances. Ordinary emotional response is replaced by expansive and heightened awareness of Light.

All of these levels of dreaming relate to experience within the world of images from the lower, higher and Spirit-self and can apply equally to waking and sleeping states. They include fantasising, daydreaming, meditating and intuiting flashes of inexplicable recall.

CLEARING PRACTICES BEFORE SLEEP

I recommend you perform these visualisations before retiring at night. This first set of practices are to be used for clearing the 'junk' that may surface in your dreams and for grounding yourself (although they are useful exercises to perform at any time).

The first exercise is presented in two parts: Gold Spirals and Blue Circles.

The section on night-time and dream procedures refers explicitly to dealing with dreamlife and the need for 'protection' from harmful astral energies and other influences before you are able to rise into a higher state of consciousness.

You must remember that when your consciousness separates from the body, its nature takes it up towards the Light, unless there is an astral substitute to weigh it down.

The following exercise is in two parts and is taken from Olive Pixley's Essenic Light exercise repertoire and is best done in the evening, before going to bed. The first part clears away the thoughtforms, feelings and impressions accumulated during the day and from the past. The second clears your unconscious resistance to a new quality of life and protects you by sealing you in a blue aura.

In both instances, stand relaxed. Be sure that your body is aligned – knees should be loose (not locked), the pelvis tucked in a bit to permit the flow of energy up and down the spine, shoulders relaxed, chin down, allowing the energy from the spine to rise up and also descend from the brain.

Feel yourself held within the stream of Light that is anchored in your heart and which also arises from the Earth.

Sense your feet firmly planted on the ground, the weight distributed evenly between the heel and the ball of the foot.

 PART ONE: GOLD SPIRALS

Now visualise a long gold thread, like a flexible golden wire, with which you are going to thread yourself through the spine nine times. Each subsequent spiral intersects a portion of your body.

You will see in the illustration opposite that the thread originates at the nape of the neck and is drawn over the head from back to front in the form of spirals.

Pierce the exact spot over your body with the thread, each time on an inbreath, and draw it out of your body on the outbreath.

Pull it over the head and through the throat on the first breath.

Next, on the outbreath, take the thread through the throat, and out the back of the neck, up and over, piercing your body at the level of the breastbone on the second inbreath.

Gold Spirals and Blue Circles Visualisations

Continue in this way until the thread has pierced the body down the spinal column nine times.

Understand that this golden Light is an actual substance that cuts through other substances without effort. It is not an easy exercise to do; often Light will not cut straight through you. It may dart away to the side. The more this happens, or the more difficult it is to feel and see the Light piercing through you, the more important it is to insist on it.

PART TWO: BLUE CIRCLES

This next part is a form of protective blessing.

Visualise a circle of glorious blue, like the glow of a living sapphire, just above your head, wide enough to encircle your head but not to touch you. Below and around your body eight more circles appear, with the last one, as depicted in the illustration on page 273, floating right by the soles of your feet.

On an outbreath, pull the blue ring above your head down to the second ring. Hold the picture for a moment, and then allow the two rings to coalesce. As you draw each ring down, the feeling is one of being coated by blue purifying light.

Next, pull the rings down to the level of your heart, and see the three rings becoming a unit as well.

Continue pulling the rings down through each ring like above. Repeat the process until you have encircled yourself nine times, descending from the uppermost rings to the lower rings. When the rings, now nine-in-one, reach your feet, they vanish and you start anew.

It helps to do this exercise three times.

When you get into bed, you can visualise yourself as a cross of Light, extending from your head to feet and across the shoulders.

'SAH VAY' VISUALISATION

This visualisation is also done while standing and includes the entire energy circuitry of your bodies.

Visualise a golden half-moon above the head on the right side, and another of deep blue between the feet, containing them.

To the inner sound 'sah' (i.e. pronounced inwardly), on a deep exhale, draw the golden half-moon down to the ground through your body.

Simultaneously, draw the blue half-moon up through the centre of the body, all the way up to the top of the head, where it, as a sort of chalice or cup, is filled with Light.

Now, on an inhale to the inner sound '*vay*', visualise the golden half-moon rising and the blue half-moon descending.

Again, on the outbreath (to the inner sound '*sah*'), repeat the first movement. Visualise the Light that has poured into the blue half-moon being distributed down the body and into every cell.

Do this exercise three times.

Use the illustration on the right for guidance, if necessary.

NIGHT-TIME AND DREAM PROCEDURES

Once you begin the practices of Light, your sleep patterns may change as your awareness in altered consciousness states increases. This is due to intensified intentionality. As this activity happens, you attract greater energies. The more you embody Light, the more darkness is also attracted. Light is what attracts your past (dark) miscreations to you so that they can be transmuted, requalified and reintegrated.

Your physical body is especially vulnerable when you sleep. If left unprotected, atmospheric energies impinge upon your physical and emotional bodies, stimulating them, depleting or altering them in other ways. These atmospheric energies include astral influence from disembodied entities or emotional thought projections from living people. If you remember that 'like attracts like', and that you are working through much of your old unconscious habits and desires, you can see why it is important to shield yourself and to invoke the help that is offered to you by Intelligence from the realms of Light to clear the thoughtforms that you yourself created.

When you retire at night, leave the physical body within the Tube of Light as per the Master Practice (see pages 21–5). You may add any of the following visualisations:

· Call on Violet Flame activity to promote purification and transmutation of substance (see pages 151–3).

· Visualise a spiral blue flame (see pages 63–5) surrounding your body to create a powerful vortex of first ray activity that severs impure substance at the etheric level and is protective.

· The Seven-leafed Flame (see pages 229–30) joins together the activity of the seven primary rays of creation. Expand your visualisation of

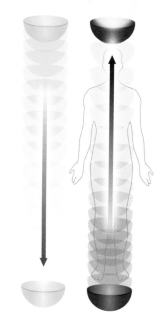

Sah (Exhalation)

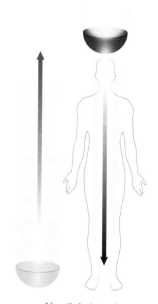

Vay (Inhalation)

'Sah Vay' Visualisation

this phenomenon over your aura to create a terrific force that serves as a shield.

- Call upon your God-self to clothe your physical and etheric bodies with an armour of Light (see page 161). This looks somewhat like a suit of armour and includes a crystal-like skull cap and a brilliant crystal cross. If you remember, the symbol of the cross, particularly in Light, cuts across all lines of force and represents the most complete and immediate protection possible.
- Finally, visualise the threefold flame within the heart (see pages 247–8) to bring equilibrium at every level. With these visualisations you enter into partnership with Spirit forces.

If you should awaken in the middle of the night, always endeavour to remember where you have been and, as suggested earlier, record whatever you bring back with you. Should you awaken in any way that is disturbing, such as during a nightmare, take courage, pull yourself together and go after the cause of the disturbance. Once you have located this cause, flood it with the Violet Flame (see pages 151–3) and, if you wish, call upon the beings of Light to dissolve that cause. Reaffirm your circle of protection from page 274 and go back to sleep, knowing that is so.

If this is not enough, repeat out loud whatever affirmation is appropriate to cut through the hold of the imprint over you. You might like to visualise yourself holding the sword of blue flame and physically cutting the lines of etheric energy around you, while declaring again and again:

'Through the power and authority of my God-self, I command that you be consumed by the fires of Light and Love! You have no power!'

These affirmations, although pronounced energetically with great power, must be done without fear or anger. Allow the decrees to come through the voice of the Spirit-self within you and remember:

'The Light of God never fails!'

The following are a set of procedures to enhance your dreamlife.

PERMISSION TO REMEMBER DREAMS EXERCISE

You may want to record the text below in your own voice, spoken softly and then listen.

Begin with the Master Practice (see pages 21–5). Then listen to or read the following:

In a few moments, you will begin entering into another, less ordinary, level of reality. You may begin to feel more awake or alert than usual, and yet your body will start to rest deeply. You will feel more present and yet you will sense your body in a state of deep relaxation.

Just allow your body to relax now, to sink softly into the mattress. You can let go of your hold over the body now.

You can let go of your hold over the mind, too. There is no need to go anywhere; no need to do anything; no need to direct or control anything. Your body and your mind deserve a rest. Anything unresolved can be finished tomorrow, if you still want to. For now, just allow yourself to relax. Allow yourself to trust the Now.

You can give yourself permission to begin to remember your dreams and your activities in other levels of reality now. As time goes by, you will remember more and more of your dreams and activities at other levels of reality. As time goes by, you will be able to follow the thread of consciousness during sleep and wakefulness more and more easily. Soon, you will begin remembering more and more of your participation in other states of reality and you will remember more and more of your dreams, so that you may record them and bring that information back with you, gaining clearer insight into your essence, your flowering, and also that of others. This is a process that will happen as quickly as you want it to happen, so take courage.

Remember your dreams. Remember your Self.

Keep Love in your heart. Surround yourself in Light and allow this Light to lead you where you need to go.

Rest now. Trust in your God-self. Trust.

Move towards truth and Love. Remember your Self.

Remember that you can tune in to your own God-presence, which is Light and Consciousness, at any time.

Remember your Self!

In the morning, you will awaken refreshed and alert, remembering your dreams more and more accurately, remembering your nature and

> You can give yourself permission to begin to remember your dreams and your activities in other levels of reality now. As time goes by, you will remember more and more of your dreams and activities at other levels of reality.

understanding the nature of reality more and more clearly. You will awaken rested, and eager to welcome life and the new day.

You are loved. You are Love.

Remember your dreams. Remember your Self!

FINE-TUNING FOR DREAMING: THE GOLDEN RING MEDITATION

As you prepare for sleep, know that you will journey through other realities and other dimensions of Being, where you also have aspects of your being.

Begin with the Master Practice (see pages 21–5).

Lie down. Let go of your body weight completely and become aware of your body from the inside. Wherever you direct your awareness, know that you are directing Light. Fill your body with Light and know that all tension, all darkness, all density will be dissolved by the Light.

Become aware now of any tensions in the mind, any worries, fears and expectations – any busy-ness – and allow your thoughts, memories and emotions to slide away from the mind. Feel your mind as liquid now. See it as a clear-flowing brook, cool, flowing without obstacles.

Remind yourself now of your intent to become more and more aware, more and more conscious, more and more of a witness: a witness to your body, to your mind and to your Spirit.

Notice your breathing. Allow it to become more and more relaxed as you let go of your hold over the body and the mind. Your body and your mind are not needed now where you are going. Sense the energy field within and around your body now. Within you is an ocean of energy. Around you is an ocean of energy. The ocean is inside of you, and outside of you. Allow the inside and the outside to merge into the totality of yourself at this moment. Become pure energy: a vibrant energy field.

Note the pulsing and throbbing vibrations that make up your body and your energy field. Notice them and enjoy them. Allow them to be pleasurable. Let them lift you into peace, into bliss.

Surround yourself in the colours of Love, in the feeling of Love.

Sense a field of deep, deep blue, or violet or pink.

Now, imagine a golden ring that is wide enough for your body and your energy field to go through. See it loom right over your head and sense it coming towards you. Pull it towards you and allow it to slide right over your body: over, under and around it. See, sense and feel this glittering, electric, golden substance surrounding you now. Hear its sizzling sound. Feel it as it gently slides over, under and around your body, slowly lighting up and quickening your entire energy field. You become intensely finer.

Next, this golden ring slides gently and steadily down, down to your feet and three feet (one metre) beyond your feet. Hold it there; then release it. See it disappear into infinity below you. Sense another ring, like a wave, coming to you. See and feel it gently rising from below, over and under you, as if pulling you higher and higher. See it gently and steadily rising to your head, and then three feet beyond it. Hold the feeling of this golden energy ring at this point three feet over your head. Then release it. Follow it as it dissolves into infinity above you.

Allow another ring to descend now, just like the first one, right through and around you into infinity below. Let another ring ascend now, extending upwards, gently, steadily rising through you and around you into infinity above.

Stretching downwards and upwards, a continual flow of energy rings pulsates through and beyond you into infinity below, above and around.

Continue feeling golden rings of Light-substance, like waves rising and falling, up and down your body. Allow your body to dissolve within the rings, endlessly streaming with all that is!

Feel your consciousness rising higher and higher, wider and wider, into and through the rings, in and through the tunnel of Light into pure Spirit, where dreams are real and reality is but a dream!

Awaken to the endlessness that you are.

DEATH AND DYING

Embodiment lends Consciousness the texture of matter as clothing, which, since it is subject to the laws of nature, decays and eventually disintegrates. Physical death is like changing clothing, unveiling and living the transparency of Spirit-self as the indwelling Consciousness. For someone who is unfamiliar with the nature of Consciousness, death appears to be a disappointment and a loss.

As physical substance disintegrates in death, its counterpart at the level of the lower mind (that which held onto personal identity) lasts for a while, before the physical, emotional and mental bodies eventually dissolve. This is not the case with the higher bodies. When the individual is soul-infused, these casements assume their luminous nature and guide the being 'back home' to Spirit.

The truth is that you are constantly dying. Every outbreath is a spontaneous release of energies, residues of thought and feeling; every inbreath offers a new possibility for expression, bringing in new air (or Light). Such is physical life.

The real you as Spiritual-self never dies. It simply disconnects from its temporary facade and changes form.

EGO DEATH

It is possible to experience death emotionally and mentally while still in embodiment. This is intrinsic to spiritual development. Apply yourself to the transformation of the egoism of personality, fostering modalities that are in tune with your emerging soul. Inner Alchemy deliberately provokes disidentification with both body and personality from the beginning of the teaching, while simultaneously cultivating authenticity and individuation at the level of Consciousness, transferring the point of reference from a separate self to a broad inclusive spiritual awareness. There is no room for fear or bewilderment.

The third-dimensional experience provides the arena needed for the development of skill in the higher dimensional worlds, and therefore beyond physical death. When you no longer project distractions, obstacles, fears and limitations that cause loss of control and yearning for physical restrictions, then transmutation or advanced cellular recalibration is possible. This amplifies the frequency of the points of Light permanently, allowing you to sustain higher vibrations and perspectives.

Now you are able to give birth to yourself or, in other words, remould your energy bodies in accordance with the original patterns of perfection dictated by Spirit, transforming or restructuring the personality – influencing the physical, the emotional and the lower mental structures.

There is infinity beyond physical life. The journey through the afterlife, as revealed throughout the ages, exposes you to trials that at this level are much stranger than those presented in daily life. Each aspect of

It is possible to experience death emotionally and mentally while still in embodiment. This is intrinsic to spiritual development.

the journey calls for a certain skill. Each of these skills has been taught in mystery schools from the Vedic to the shamanic. The elements of the journey are the same for everyone. The Tibetan map of the afterlife only superficially varies from that of the Egyptian, the Hopi or the Australian Aborigine. Every school of thought throughout history has endeavoured to exercise the individual human being in the use of the skills he needs to have in order to attain mastery over matter and energy. This endeavour is never limited to the physical-material realm.

Each spiritual path will require that you learn discernment, surrender, appropriate resistance and an ability to sustain heightened levels of intensity and focus. You are asked to develop the ability to resist illusion and those thoughtforms that make up our baggage. You are shown how to embody power in its different expressions. You are encouraged to silence the chatter of the mind in order to perceive the real behind the illusory, and you are taught how to still the whirlpools of emotions through developing purpose and integrity.

You are launched into practices that put you in touch with the transience of form and its permutations; that is, the entire universe of energy as expressed through sound, colour and Light. You are instructed how to channel feeling into form. Lastly, you are coaxed into alignment with the Godhead and into claiming your legacy: existence becomes your playground.

Whether your journey through the afterlife resembles a Tibetan tapestry or a Christian cavalry, the essential experience is the same. To succeed in such a journey is to attain levels of mastery; to fail is to be thrust into a lower level of life, to which your habits attract you. Either way, you are confronted with life, with your creations and with yourself.

Death provides you with the opportunity for supreme alchemy.

But you do not need to wait for the moment of physical death to initiate this transformation. The process begins with you, now.

Each spiritual path will require that you learn discernment, surrender, appropriate resistance and an ability to sustain heightened levels of intensity and focus.

A TO-DO LIST THAT IS NOT REALLY A TO-DO LIST

The following section serves as a sort of addendum to Part Six. Its purpose is to illustrate how you may incorporate the knowledge and practices outlined so far in the book into your daily life. As you should be aware by now, I have written this book for your practical application, and the practices and techniques I have provided will mean nothing if they are not performed regularly and often. As such, I have drawn up a few tables of suggestions. They are by no means prescriptive, and you should alter your practice as you wish. You may be surprised by the transformation that they offer.

The most important element for transformation is the way you perceive. This means your mind, the way you think about yourself, the world around you, and lastly, your notion of and relationship with reality. No amount of technique will change anything about you or your world unless you change your way of thinking and perceiving. Change will not occur by itself; it is a deliberate and sustained choice. As has been extensively outlined in this book, Inner Alchemy work is based on the development of sensibility. The new alchemical posture will invariably lead you to recognise the filters in your personal psychology that determine the feelings clouding the mind. This part of the work on yourself should emerge from understanding, rather than imposition.

Implant constructive thoughtforms in your psyche to neutralise the automatic ones. I suggest you compose a personal affirmation and say it aloud every morning upon awakening, and repeat it again, silently, when you are in bed at night. Let this be a high-frequency statement similar to those suggested by the Lucis Trust in 'The Affirmation of the Disciple', or by the Saint Germain Foundation. The affirmation suggested by the latter is as follows:

'I AM a Child of the Light. I love the Light. I live in the Light. I serve the Light. I bless the Light. I AM eternally supplied by the Light, protected by the Light, healed by the Light and forever sustained by the Light. And "I AM" the limitless outpouring of all Light.'

The following seven basic constructive thought-patterns may replace automatic ones. Should you wish, repeat and incorporate one, several or all of these high-frequency statements to yourself morning and night:

- 'I am never alone.'
- 'Love is the primary substance of the Universe.'
- 'I exist on simultaneous multidimensional levels of activity.'
- 'The real "I" is a Presence; my personality is an instrument.'
- 'The world I see is not all there is; there are always several perspectives interacting.'
- 'The way I think determines my perception at all levels.'
- 'I influence all life around me.'

I have selected a few exercises below to be practised daily (or as often as possible), while others are optional and respond to need or interest. Some create deeper opening of sensibility and accelerate your ability to sustain and manage greater levels of Light. Always remember that this work is about the coherence between inner and outer practices aimed at communion with Light.

DAILY PRACTICES

The following tables are organised according to time of day, with appropriate practices indicated in each of them.

MORNING
The first three practices are strongly recommended.

Become aware of your first thoughts upon waking, as these thoughtforms will qualify your whole day.   You might find it useful to write them down and keep tabs on them.
Perform your personal affirmation. You may use one of those outlined above or select your own.
Create the Alchemical Alignment (i.e. perform the Master Practice on pages 21–5), followed by the Tube of Light (see pages 146–9), before leaving your home or engaging in work – even quickly in the shower will help. Both processes should be repeated, briefly, several times a day, creating the habit of sensing yourself from the standpoint of your ordinary body but also from Source.
The Violet Flame Activation practice (see pages 25–6).
For physical centring, grounding and stability for the rest of your day, perform the Horse Posture (see pages 91–2).

DAYTIME

All of the following suggestions are optional but develop useful habits that will accelerate your learning.

Notice how you occupy your body and use it. Notice which emotions are stirred. Notice principally the nature of the thoughts that evoke sensations, opinions and feelings. If possible, list them in order to work on them.

Reinforce the Alchemical Alignment and reinforce the Tube of Light as protection (see pages 142–9).

Avail yourself of any of the clearing practices for the mind, or energising practices, as outlined in the book, such as the 'E O Lihum' Exercise (see pages 243–4) or the Exercise to Clear the Mind (see pages 138–9) to expel any negativity that might arise.

Practise stilling the mind, even for a few moments at a time, finding intervals during the day and in the middle of activities to disconnect from old habitual reactions.

NIGHT-TIME

Before sleep, take a bath or a shower to cleanse your aura, as well as your body from the dust and thoughtforms of the day.

As the last thing you do before getting into bed, perform the clearing practice of the Gold Spirals and Blue Circles visualisations (see pages 272–4).

While in bed, reinforce your Alignment and your Tube of Light (see pages 142–9), extending the Tube to encircle your sleeping space.

Go to sleep with a conscious, joyful feeling, no matter what has transpired in your day, setting aside your problems and incomplete experiences for later resolution. Evoke gratitude and joy.

While preparing to sleep, become aware of your inner silence. Listen to the inner sounds. You may hear the resonance of life within you through the pulsation of your body.

WEEKLY PRACTICES

This table outlines some practices that are worth performing weekly. Choose one day a week when you can set aside a regular time for yourself and make sure you are removed from any disturbance.

Practise the more complex Violet Flame exercise, such as the shaking activation outlined (see pages 25–6) or the Master Practice (see pages 21–5) in more detail. This will integrate the three lower bodies (physical, emotional, mental bodies) and give you greater flexibility in each one.

For mental cleansing or to combat tiredness and worry, practice the Exercise to Unite Heart and Mind (see pages 134–5). This can be performed any time you feel necessary.

For balancing your energies, try the Re-balancing the Body with the Three Primary Rays (see pages 121–3). This can also be done any day, when necessary.

Bless someone or all humanity. You may do this by visualising the subject/s under their own Alchemical Alignment, connecting and reinforcing the contact with the soul and the Spirit-self.

REVIEW

My dear reader, you have now come to the end of your journey through this book, but this is only a beginning stage of your alchemical journey of transmutation.

The alchemical path is never linear, it is concentric. You will find that you circle around many issues again and again, each time at deeper levels.

I remind you not to put away this manual of Inner Alchemy for good. Come back to it. See what greater insights may be revealed to you at different stages of your own journey.

Develop your sensing-feeling ability. Look to establish communication with your Spirit-self and its voice within, which will gradually enable you to be able to identify it and contact it at will.

Know that you are your own best teacher. Always remember that your every thought, feeling and act influences the world around you and reflects back upon your own structure. The tone you use with yourself and this work is important. Allow yourself to feel loved, because you are, you know it, you have experienced it! You, at the level of your Presence, are your best ally, lover and friend. Establish an intimate relationship with your Self. This relationship is the most important element at the very core of Inner Alchemy.

POSTSCRIPT

Spiritual development and material progress go hand in hand. Success is built upon a foundation of underlying spiritualisation or focus of Light-power. We are now experiencing a collective urgency towards qualitative change. As we head into the future, we need to look at ourselves with a fresh perspective, separate from the influences set by previous cycles.

The need today is for the formation of a certain individualised will of Spirit. The Consciousness required is one of action – action from the level of activated higher chakras and faculties. Persons responding to this call show a special kind of *identity* adapted to third-dimensional situations, but fully conscious of its union with the whole. Within that identity there lies a mastery, a determined will-activity. Leadership.

Life is the process. Living is the alchemy. You are the instrument that turns experience into alchemy and living into Love. Every breath you take in consciousness lights the heavens which shed light upon the world as if through a shower of stars.

When we become aware of what we truly are, we have touched the heavens and stand before the Creator, both as creation and as the Creator Itself. It is a most difficult realisation to acknowledge that all we have sought outside and beyond is right here. That all the prayers and magic you invoked are answered by a simple state of awareness.

Ah! But this awareness extinguishes all that you set up in your search for answers and truth outside. All that work! For nothing? Not exactly. Every search is for the One, only we do not know this yet, not until we have looked everywhere. Not until we stand naked, helpless, empty-handed and innocent, do we realize the grandeur of life and that this life is within us, accessible if we would only stop to look, to feel, to witness and to behold.

Your life is the scenario for Inner Alchemy. The Light of Consciousness within you is the key to mastery and full realisation. Each action, each feeling, each thought brings you closer to the empty backdrop, wherein all treasures are found.

Welcome to your Self.

INDEX